P9-CPZ-663

Experience, Explanation and Faith

Experience, Explanation and Faith

An Introduction to the Philosophy of Religion

Anthony O'Hear
Department of Philosophy
University of Surrey

Routledge & Kegan Paul
London, Boston, Melbourne and Henley

First published in 1984
by Routledge & Kegan Paul plc
39 Store Street, London WC1E 7DD, England
9 Park Street, Boston, Mass. 02108, USA
464 St Kilda Road, Melbourne,
Victoria 3004, Australia and
Broadway House, Newtown Roau,
Henley-on-Thames, Oxon RG9 1EN, England
Set in Bembo; 10 on 12pt
by Columns of Reading
and printed in Great Britain by
Billing & Sons Ltd, Worcester

Library of Congress Cataloging in Publication Data

O'Hear, Anthony.

Experience, explanation and faith.
Includes index.
1. Religion — Philosophy. I. Title.
BL51.O35   1983   200'.1   83-15957

ISBN 0-7100-9768-9

For Natasha, my daughter

Contents

Preface

Some theologians maintain that the subject matter of religion is the subject matter of one's ultimate concern. There is indeed a sense in which the possibility or impossibility of religious belief for each one of us forms the ultimate horizon of our thought and action. In this wide sense of the term, I must have discussed religion with vast numbers of people in all sorts of circumstances. However, in the narrower sense of the term, as relating to specific sets of beliefs about God or gods, I have also discussed religion with a great many people. To all of them, friends, colleagues and students, I am grateful for the ways in which they have helped me, consciously or unconsciously, in my thinking about the matters I deal with in this book. I am also grateful in a more direct and conscious way to those colleagues who have read and commented on this manuscript, or on parts of it. I am therefore very happy to be able to thank Mark Platts, Mark Sainsbury, Richard Swinburne and Shivesh Thakur for the help they have given me. I should also like to thank Lindsay Carew for typing and retyping the manuscript, despite the many other demands on her time.

December 1982

Introduction

Religious people characteristically believe that underlying the phenomena of everyday experience there is a power (or collection of powers) whose scope and influence transcends the limits normally predicated of material beings, such as ourselves, who are confined to specific positions in space and time. In this book, I consider the reasons that might be offered for such a belief, where these reasons go beyond a merely superstitious faith in the automatic efficacy of religious words and practices in bringing about particular results in the material world. The reasonableness of such superstitious faith would need to be examined empirically, if it is felt to be worth examining at all. The types of reasons I am concerned with are reasons which point to a supposed need for ultimate explanations of a religious sort. My general approach, then, is firmly within the classical tradition of natural theology.

At the same time, I do not confine myself to considering the justifications that might be offered for belief in the personal God of the Christian Bible. In looking at religion and religious experience, one quickly becomes aware of the importance of rather different conceptions of the divine. Indeed, one of the underlying themes of the book will be to stress the tension there is between a conception of God as an active, personal creator, clearly distinct from his creation, and a conception of the divine as pure being, beyond all attributes, the indeterminate ground of everything determinate, but not clearly separable from it. I shall attempt to show how both conceptions are necessary to answer different aspects of the religious search for an ultimate explanation of reality, and to show that this is why both conceptions are present to a greater or lesser extent in many religious traditions. (If this seems a surprising thing to say about mainstream Christianity, it could be pointed out straightaway that it is Aquinas himself who says that God is subsistent being itself, indeterminate in all ways.) But I do not believe that the conceptions of God as pure being and as a personal creator are mutually consistent, and that this inconsistency points to a fundamental flaw in the religious search itself.

After a preliminary chapter on the role religion plays in people's lives, and a dismissal of the suggestion that we can justify religious belief primarily as if it were a way of life rather than a matter of accepting certain controversial propositions, I examine efforts to base religious belief on religious experience. Powerful and impressive as accounts of religious experience can be, I argue that religious experience lacks the consistency and predictability needed to form the basis of any factual belief at all. I conclude that some basis other than religious experience is necessary, if religious belief is to be rational. In the third chapter, in the face of theological claims to the contrary, I argue that human knowledge, talk of truth and our apprehension of value do not need to be based in appeals to anything transcendent, and suggest ways in which they can be naturalistically explained and non-theistically justified. Ch. 4 is the central chapter of the book, for there, after criticizing claims to the effect that religion is no less rational than other fundamental beliefs we have about ourselves and the world, I consider and criticize several arguments to the effect that it is actually more rational than agnosticism or atheism. It is here that the traditional philosophical arguments for God's existence – cosmological, teleological and ontological – are discussed; at the same time, I attempt to relate the ontological argument to some specifically religious conceptions of God as pure being, and I close the chapter with some remarks on process thought. In Ch. 5, I deal with the problem of evil, and conclude that, while evil and suffering need in themselves be no bar to a belief in a God, because we have no grounds for deciding whether a world such as ours, with its amount of evil and suffering, would be worse in any absolute sense than a necessarily very different world in which there was neither suffering nor beings inclined to evil, the approaches to the question of evil found in two main religious traditions are unconvincing. In these chapters, my methods is to assess the claims of religious thinkers, both on their own grounds, and in the light of the way they fit into our corpus of rationally justified knowledge. There is, of course, no way of examining religious claims (or any other claims to knowledge, for

that matter) by a direct comparison between the claims and reality,
if only because the idea of a direct inspection of reality is a myth.
All that can be done, and all that can be asked for, is to see how one
set of claims in a given area relates or fails to relate to the rest of
what we know, and how it compares with the rest of what we have
come to regard as rationally acceptable.

My conclusion is that religious beliefs, at least in the forms in
which I have examined them, are not rationally acceptable. In the
sixth and final chapter, I return to the subject of religious faith, and
try to show how such faith derives its undeniable strength and
value, both for individuals and for groups, largely from its inbuilt
tendency to uncritical dogmatism. This, combined with the lack of
rational justification for religious beliefs is, I argue, just the reason
why rational men should look beyond religion for the fulfilment of
their spiritual needs.

I'm a mystic at bottom and I believe in nothing.
                                    Gustave Flaubert

1

Faith and Religious Life

Anyone who studies religion, or who has been religious at one time and then has ceased to be, cannot fail to be struck by the fact that for the religious believer religious belief is a personal commitment, something nearer to a love for one's family or loyalty to one's country, than to that calm and provisional acceptance of some abstract theory which is sometimes taken to characterize the attitude of the ideal scientist towards his currently favoured scientific propositions. Although I think that most religious believers would accept what I said in my opening sentence, there is, of course, a world of difference between the attitude to what it states of the uncommitted student of religion and the person who has ceased to be religious, on the one hand, and that of the convinced religious believer on the other. For the religious believer, seeing religious belief as loyalty or commitment, or as *faith*, will present no problem. Yet, for the non–believer it is just the phenomenon of religious faith which is the first and insuperable hurdle. For how can you make an open-ended commitment of belief to a set of propositions, particularly to a set which is essentially contested in the way religious propositions are? Religious apologists are fond of drawing analogies between their faith and the trust a mother might have in her son, or an underground resistance group might continue to have in a leader whose overt behaviour is more like collaboration with the enemy than resistance. It is not entirely clear that such analogies help to clarify the concept of religious faith. Faced with overwhelming counter-evidence a mother would just be mad to go on believing that her son was honest. Family love and loyalty surely should not entail that one is blind to evidence or that one deceives oneself about the faults of one's family. Indeed love and loyalty in themselves carry

1

no commitment to any specific beliefs about the objects of one's love or loyalty. Yet religious believers often appear to non-believers to invoke faith to fill the gap between evidence and belief at just the point where family loyalty would fail to carry us to a rational belief in the honesty of a son.

Religious people would not, of course, see faith in this way. They do not see that there is such a tremendous gap to be bridged between evidence and religious belief. They are not convinced of what non-believers see as the enormity of what they believe. In *On Certainty* (1969, p. 32), Wittgenstein remarks that one thing of which *he* is indubitably certain is that every human being on this earth had two parents, but he adds that Catholics do not believe this. Yet, when I was a Catholic, I do not remember that the Virgin Birth of Christ posed any particular problems for me or even that it seemed especially strange. God could surely do such a thing, if He wished. Part of my faith consisted just in not seeing any contradictions or radical tension between this and other things I believed. In discussing religion, we should not under-estimate the relativities in perception of strangeness that exist between believers and non-believers. Faith does not come in to fill a perceived gap between evidence and belief; it acts rather to convince the believer that there is no such gap to be filled. The phenomenon of religious conversion is not a matter of solving a problem, but rather of seeing the problem dissolve before one's eyes in a sudden access of emotion. Faith is a gift, we are told, or, more neutrally, it involves a change of world view.

Faith, indeed, for the religious believer is not a belief or a set of beliefs alongside scientific beliefs, historical beliefs, psychological beliefs and the rest. It is something much more like an all-encompassing set of attitudes to human life and the world, a context in which one's whole life, including one's cognitive life is set. Faith, says Tolstoy, is that which men live by. A satisfactory philosophical account of religion must acknowledge this fundamental fact about religion, that for believers faith is overwhelmingly a matter of living and of acting.

Although it is probably fruitless to search for any definition of religion in terms of necessary and sufficient conditions relating to either beliefs or practice, all religions can in one way or another be seen as providing a framework of meaningfulness for the lives and thought of their adherents and as making personal demands on

2

them. It is surely significant that in cases where religions have become too public and impersonal for the faithful and too much bound up with state ritual, the people have gone elsewhere for personal inspiration. One can think in this context of the Panathenaia being balanced by the cults at Eleusis, of John Wesley's impact on eighteenth-century Anglicanism, of Christianity itself in the Roman Empire. There is indeed a sense in which people do have certain wants which can, it seems, be satisfied only by a personal religious involvement. Religions, in providing frameworks for life which are at once all-encompassing and deeply personal, give to many people both security and significance. They make people feel that their lives are not purely biological events; that despite the apparent hostility and vastness of the environment and the inescapable fact of death, there is in each person's life something of ultimate significance, which, in many cases, will survive death. At all events, religions characteristically assure individual people that what they do, even in the outwardly insignificant moments of their lives, matters, and matters more in the overall scheme of things than many events whose repercussions are superficially more widespread and noticeable. Whether we think here of a Buddhist working out his karma, or of a Christian thinking of his eternal salvation, or even of an African village priest striving by his rites to ensure the rising of the new moon, the effect is always to endow individual human actions with cosmic significance – at least from the point of view of the individuals involved. Whether or not the fall of a sparrow is noticed by our heavenly Father, religions assure us that through religious activity we can transcend the insigificance of the merely natural.

In saying that religions give transcendent significance to people's lives and efforts, I am not suggesting that this can be done out of the blue, as it were. It is not as if religions are superimposed on life in an arbitrary or haphazard fashion. Rather, they build on those aspects of life which for the participants are naturally charged with emotion. Birth, copulation and death are never treated by us as purely mechanical happenings, nor are those aspects of life associated with them, such as the upbringing of children. Whether this tendency to see such things as deeply significant is based in some genetic endowment, or whether it is due more to social and environmental factors (including, of course, religious ones) is not

3

something we need explore further here. What is important for our purposes is the way religions build on and accentuate the universal human tendency to find a deep significance in certain specific aspects of life, particularly those closely related to the creation, preservation and destruction of human life.

Religions do not only characteristically promise a living explanation of life and an overcoming of death or at least a means towards the calm acceptance of death, they also make sense of many critical moments and feelings within life. Thus they may help a person to overcome his or her sense of inadequacy in life, or a sense of self-repudiation or of guilt, or a sense of fear. Notions like the forgiveness of sin, the divine care for men, or the Indian idea of maya are in their different ways powerful means enabling people to come to terms with their shortcomings. Equally, the more positive feelings of oneness with the world, of joy at existence and of ecstasy are given a place in and made sense of in many religions. So too are many family and social ties. Religion is never a purely individual affair: the religious community is always of paramount importance. Religions often sanctify and celebrate and thereby tighten the bonds which unite individuals to their families and families to the larger units of which they are a part. On other occasions, when there is alienation of individuals as groups from the society they belong to, we often see religion itself acting as a larger family with which the alienated individuals can identify, or sometimes even itself being the group which pulls individuals away from other groups.

Both the social integration and the social alienation wrought by religions derive from the communal aspect of religion itself. No one who looks at religion can fail to be impressed by the domination in religious practice of the religious community, by the importance of its traditions and hierarchies and by the sense of loyalty the community elicits from its members. The individual in return derives from the community a sense of belonging, and from its authority a certainty, purpose and direction to his life. The community supports him when he is weak in faith and observance, and reinforces him when he is strong. Within the community, ideally, he finds a type of compassion and caring that is rarely met elsewhere, and which often contrasts very favourably with that provided by professional welfare agencies. And, of course, finally, the community is seen as deriving from and bearing witness to the

4

higher reality from which both the individual and the community itself derive their meaning and ultimate redemption.

Religions, then, through their promise of the conquest of evil and of death, through their communities and, above all, through their integration within and raising up of the lives of their adherents can and ideally do perform a unique service for those who are part of some faith and who live by it. The way in which religion can seem so attractive and even so plausible to an erstwhile doubter, when it is genuinely and unselfconsciously part of the lives of a people has been well illustrated by Tolstoy in his *Confession*:

> I turned from the life of our circle, acknowledging that ours is not life but a simulation of life – that the conditions of superfluity in which we live deprive us of the possibility of understanding life, and that in order to understand life I must understand not an exceptional life such as ours who are parasites on life, but the life of the simple labouring folk – those who make life – and the meaning they attribute to it. The simplest labouring people around me were the Russian people, and I turned to them and to the meaning of life which they give. That meaning, if one can put it into words, was as follows: Every man has come into this world by the will of God. And God has so made man that every man can destroy his soul or save it. The aim of man in life is to save his soul, and to save his soul he must live 'godly' and to live 'godly' he must renounce all the pleasures of life, must labour, must humble himself, suffer and be merciful. That meaning the people obtain from the whole teaching of faith transmitted to them by their pastors and by the traditions that live among the people. This meaning was clear to me and near to my heart. But together with this meaning of the popular faith of our non-sectarian folk, among whom I live, much was inseparably bound up that revolted me and seemed to me inexplicable: sacraments, Church services, fasts, and the adoration of relics and icons. The people cannot separate one from the other, nor could I. And strange as much of what entered in to the faith of these people was to me, I accepted everything, and attended the services, knelt morning and evening in prayer, fasted, and prepared to receive the Eucharist: and at first my reason did not resist anything. The very things that had formerly seemed to me impossible did not now evoke

in me any opposition.

My relations to faith before and after were quite different. Formerly life itself seemed to me full of meaning and faith presented itself as the arbitrary assertion of propositions to me quite unnecessary, unreasonable and disconnected from life. I then asked myself what meaning those propositions had and, convinced that they had none, I rejected them. Now on the contrary I knew firmly that my life otherwise has, and can have, no meaning and the articles of faith were far from presenting themselves to me as unnecessary – on the contrary I had been led by indubitable experience to the conviction that only these propositions presented by faith give life a meaning. Formerly I looked on them as on some quite unnecessary gibberish, but now, if I did not understand them, I yet knew that they had a meaning, and I said to myself that I must learn to understand them. (1882, pp. 67-8)

How can living the faith give 'quite unnecessary gibberish' a meaning, and a promise of understanding what is not otherwise intelligible? We can extract from some writings of Wittgenstein an account of religious faith very much in harmony with that of Tolstoy, which seeks to base the meaning and understanding of religious propositions in the religious life and practices of the believer.

Underlying any account of religious language which we may extract from the writings of Wittgenstein is Wittgenstein's view of language in general. (As is well known Wittgenstein held two opposed views on language during his lifetime. The writings on religion we shall be considering are all from the later part of his life, and so the view of language we shall consider here will also be the later one.) The key point of Wittgenstein's later theory of language is often summarized by the slogan that meaning is use. As it stands, this is not very helpful, but part of what is intended by the slogan is a demand that we should not think of the meaning of all utterances as deriving in a uniform and mechanical way from their grammatical structure and the dictionary entries associated with the words used in them. Such a view would encourage what Wittgenstein considers to be the erroneous assumption that all statements worked in the same way as, say, statements in the natural sciences (with the consequent tendency to belittle statements that did not apparently meet the criteria for testing and meaningfulness prevalent in the natural sciences). In *Philosophical Investigations* (1958, p. 102), Wittgenstein remarks that language does not always function to 'convey thoughts' indiscriminately about 'houses, pains, good and evil, or anything else you please'. The point here is that when one talks about one's pains, or about good and evil one may be doing something very different from what an architect is doing when he describes a house. One might be giving expression to a sensation, evincing an attitude, teaching a child to respect the feelings of others, or countless other things, all quite different from each other and from a technical or scientific description, and all significant and important within life as we live it.

Elsewhere in *Philosophical Investigations* (pp. 52-3), Wittgenstein questions the usefulness of making any general claim to the effect that all propositions state in some way or other 'This is how things are'. He himself had made such a claim in his earlier work, and it is still a widely held view among philosophers that the meaning of any sentence of a given language (the object language) can be given by stating its truth conditions. These will in turn be given by providing a translation of the original sentence in the meta-language, or language in which we are discussing the object language. Thus, if French is our object language, and English our meta-language, we can state the meaning of, say, 'La neige est blanche' by giving its truth conditions, thus:

'La neige est blanche' is true if and only if snow is white.

If English is both object and meta-language, we will get:

'Snow is white' is true if and only if snow is white.

Whatever the technical virtues of a theory of meaning which actually yields such an equivalence for every sentence of a given object language (and such a theory is not easy to construct for any language with a potential infinity of sentences, where we cannot simply list all the equivalences, but have to provide devices for generating them out of a finite stock of words and grammatical constructions), Wittgenstein would appear to regard any such theory as irrelevant to explaining our understanding of language. For it would tell us nothing informative about the circumstances in which we learn or regard ourselves as entitled to assert given sentences, or regard their truth conditions as satisfied. Wittgenstein says that truth and falsity *belong* to our concept of what a proposition is, and do not *fit* it. We do not learn what a proposition is, or what makes it true or what it means by placing the proposition alongside truth, as if truth were a pre-existing cog-wheel we had direct access to, and then seeing whether and how the proposition is engaged by the cog-wheel of truth. Wittgenstein would see us as learning the meaning of sentences not by comparing them directly with some non-linguistic reality, but rather by seeing how they fit in with our practices, including, of course, our linguistic practices. Calling things true or false is itself something that belongs to some of our practices, and grasped in and through grasping those practices. In order to see what the understanding of language consists in, what we should do, in Wittgenstein's view, is to describe the *use* within our lives of each particular form of sentence and the circumstances (if any) in which we call it true or false, rather than attempting a speciously general account of whole tracts of language divorced from the practices in which they are embedded. There is no a priori presumption that all forms of language, even all forms of statement making language, will function in the same way, and much of Wittgenstein's work in *Philosophical Investigations* and elsewhere is devoted to marking out the differences in function and mode of verification between, say, a statement that my foot is hurting and one that my house is painted green. We shall have to return to Wittgenstein's overall theory of language later in this chapter, but, before doing so, we will examine his account of religious language, beginning with his criticisms of Frazer's *Golden Bough*, which he sees as a particularly crude case of the assimilation of one form of activity to another.

Frazer's *Golden Bough* is a vast work, in twelve volumes. Even the abridged edition runs to almost a thousand pages. It takes the form of an extremely circuitous answer to a puzzle. The puzzle is why, around Diana's grove at Nemi, even in classical times a restless and sinister figure should lurk day and night, sword in hand, a figure whom Frazer describes as a priest, a king and a murderer, and who will himself eventually be murdered by his successor. Frazer's technique is to pile up a mass of evidence of religious and magical rites from various places and times, which in the cumulative effect he thinks throw light on the Nemi rite and on primitive ritual in general. Frazer's view, roughly put, is that all the primitive rites and customs that he describes are mistaken attempts to manipulate the course of nature. The Nemi rite is thus seen as a relic of an even older type of belief in which the success of a tribe and its crops was held to depend on the strength of the priest king, which therefore had to be tested by young challengers. It is true that Frazer does make a distinction (Ch. 4) between magical rites and religious rites, and there is a sense in which he is more sympathetic to magic than to religion. For, in his view, magic, like science, assumes the uniformity of nature and the regular association of cause and effect; the mistake made in magic is not in these underlying beliefs, but rather in belief in the particular associations picked on. It is just not the case that, say, harming a piece of a man's clothing harms the man, but it might have been, in the way that harming his food often does harm him. As Frazer puts it, it is,

> a truism, almost a tautology to say that all magic is necessarily false and barren: for were it ever to become true and fruitful, it would no longer be magic but science. (1922, p. 65)

Religion, on the other hand, believes in the power of gods to intervene in the course of nature, and in the power of priests to affect the gods. Frazer sees a great divide between magic and religions in their respective attitudes to causality and the uniformity of nature, although he admits that in practice, in actual primitive rites, there is often a mixture of magical and religious elements. However this distinction need not concern us now, nor need Frazer's evidently impoverished conception of natural science as a piecemeal picking out of elements constantly associated in our experience, for what Wittgenstein attacks are two other aspects of Frazer's analysis. These are, first, the assumption that the whole point of both religion and magic is technological or manipulative, and second, that both magic and religion are dependent logically and psychologically on false beliefs. As Frazer puts it, about religion:

> religion consists of two elements, a theoretical and a practical, namely a belief in powers higher than men and an attempt to propitiate or please them. Of the two, belief clearly comes first, since we must believe in the existence of a divine being before we can attempt to please him. (1922, pp. 65-6)

By contrast, Wittgenstein sees belief as secondary to practice in religion, and he sees religious practice in non-purposive terms.

The first point Wittgenstein draws our attention to in his criticisms of Frazer is that neither religious people nor those involved in the rites Frazer describes are involved in putting forward theories about nature or anything else. Because of this, it would be misleading to think of what they are doing as mistaken or erroneous in the way a scientific theory might be, and doubly mistaken to think that the practices would cease if the 'error' was pointed out to the participants. Frazer, who thinks of primitive ritual as simply mistaken technology suggests that the longevity of many of the rites was due to the fact that the desired effect, such as rain, always did occur sooner or later anyway. To this, Wittgenstein replies that it is queer that the people involved did not notice this for themselves and significant that rites connected with crops and the seasons take place at the appropriate times of year. He goes on to suggest that 'savages' in fact have a more than adequate understanding of the workings of nature and of the difference between technology and ritual:

> The same savage who, apparently in order to kill his enemy, sticks his knife through a picture of him, really does build his hut of wood and cuts his arrow with skill and not in effigy.
> (1967, p. 31)

Magic, according to Wittgenstein, rests on symbolism, and is in a deep sense ritual activity. Ritual itself is fundamentally action 'without purpose' (cf. *Remarks on the Foundations of Mathematics*, 1978, p. 95), symbolizing and expressing our feelings and attitudes, and not in the first instance aiming at any further effect, and this is as true of the practices Frazer describes, such as burning in effigy, as it is of our ceremonial, public and private, baptisms, coronations and the like. We understand the sorts of things Frazer describes because, even if public ceremonial disgusts us today precisely because it expresses nothing we really feel, we all privately engage in similarly 'pointless' actions, such as kissing pictures of loved ones, or tearing them up at the end of a relationship, and also because the things Frazer describes, unlike failed scientific experiments, are always highly charged with strange and terrible emotions. The story of the King of the Wood at Nemi *is* terrible, and to realize this is at the same time to realize what might drive people to engage in it. Any belief or view that goes along with the practice is not the mainspring of the practice, but both 'go together' (1967, p. 29).

In Wittgenstein's view, there is in human beings a deep need to symbolize and express what is important to them in their lives. We find this wherever we look in history and in culture:

> When we watch the life and behaviour of men all over the earth
> we see that apart from what we might call animal activities,
> taking food, etc., etc., men also carry out actions that bear a
> peculiar character and might be called ritualistic.

These rituals do not replace causally efficacious means of bringing about natural effects, but appear to co-exist with such means. Wittgenstein goes on to say that

> It is nonsense to say that the characteristic feature of these (i.e.
> 'ritualistic') actions is that they spring from wrong ideas about
> the physics of things. (This is what Frazer does when he says
> magic is really false physics, or as the case may be false medicine,
> technology, etc.)

> What makes the character of ritual action is not any view or
> opinion, either right or wrong, although an opinion – a belief –
> itself can be ritualistic, or belong to a rite. (1967, p. 33)

Although Wittgenstein remarks later that sometimes things are organized by a priest so as to prevent any obvious falsification of a ritualistic belief, his whole emphasis is to stress the expressive and symbolic aspects of primitive magic and religion, and to draw connections between these rites and aspects of our own behaviour, with a view to making it intelligible to us as symbolic behaviour and hence not requiring an explanation in Frazerian terms.

Frazer's own description of the Nemi rite, indeed, does not read like an account of Priestley isolating 'phlogiston' or of Michelson vainly searching for the ether. The description itself fills *us* with awe and horror, and, in a way, that is all the explanation we need if we are to understand it as a rite. Primitive rituals and their accompanying beliefs do for those who participate in them what the symbolic acts we have do for us, expressing and evoking deep needs and emotions. Wittgenstein writes that

> When I am angry about something I sometimes beat on the ground or against a tree with my stick. But I certainly do not believe that the earth is guilty or that beating it can help. 'I give vent to my anger.' And all rites are of this sort. Such actions can be called instinctive. A historical explanation e.g. that I or my ancestors at one time believed that beating the earth would help – is illusory . . . for it explains nothing. What is important is the similarity of the act with an act of punishment, and there is nothing further than this similarity to be noticed. (1967, p. 244)

So for Wittgenstein, an explanation of a rite in terms of an underlying belief fails to bring out the expressive and symbolic character of the act, and hence totally fails to explain how it is conceived by the participants and why they continue to engage in it.

While Wittgenstein certainly has pertinent criticisms of Frazer – rites are not technological devices and have quite a different function in the lives of people – one wonders whether he is right to play down the element of belief in ritual to the extent that he does. After all, if you were able to show those who engage in vegetation rites that what they do is quite irrelevant to harvests, would they not have to revise their attitude to the rites, however much the symbolism of the rite might permit a continuance of the rite in a 'demythologized', symbolic form, as a harvest festival, or something of the sort? To this, a follower of Wittgenstein might well reply that in asking this question in this way, I have very possibly misconstrued the belief, if any, involved in the rite, in the same way as someone two hundred years hence would be misconstruing what I do now in laying flowers on a grave if he were to say that what I do is because I believe that the spirits of the dead are appeased by my gifts of flowers. (Norman Malcolm did so reply to this question when I once put it to him.) The Wittgensteinian reply may well have force in connection with ritual *practices*, for they are not statements of belief and may well have no very clear or definite relations with any particular statements of belief or indeed with any beliefs at all. Once again, we can see the force of the criticisms of Frazer. Nevertheless, Wittgenstein does speak directly about uncontroversial cases of religious belief in a way that is very similar to what we have inferred about his view of religious belief from his remarks on Frazer, and which raises the same problems.

In his *Lectures on and Conversations on Aesthetics, Psychology and Religious Belief* (1972), Wittgenstein concentrates on the example of the Christian belief in the Last Judgment. He points out that though it is not well established from an empirical point of view, and though in his ordinary life he may use criteria for empirical judgments in the same way as the rest of us, the believer holds to his belief unshakeably, regulating his life by it in a way that he would use no ordinary empirical forecast, however soundly based. The believer appears to be basing 'enormous things' on 'extremely flimsy' evidence. In discussion with him, we feel that the ordinary criteria of reasonableness and unreasonableness are just not applicable to him, because what he is doing is too big even to be called a mistake. There is a sense in which in his belief he is stepping right outside our normal techniques of language, and in which the religious apologist, who tries to defend his beliefs rationally, is, because of the weakness of the defence, paradoxically less reasonable and more superstitious than the man who simply accepts that the religious way of life is necessarily going to appear folly to the non-religious. In the end, what we have is dogma or faith, rather than opinion, or belief in the ordinary sense, something that will show not by the believer 'reasoning or by appeal to ordinary grounds for belief, but rather by regulating for in all his life.' (1972, p. 54)

Some further understanding of what is meant by a religious belief regulating one's life and yet not being based on any appeal to reasoning can be gained from some of the remarks on religion in *Culture and Value* (1980). In 1937, Wittgenstein wrote that Christianity is not a theory about what has happened and what will happen to the human soul but 'a description of something that actually takes place in human life. For "consciousness of sin" is a real event and so are despair and salvation through faith' (p. 28). The idea seems to be that one experiences in one's own life certain things, particularly suffering, and you thereby see the truth in the religious interpretation:

Religion says: *Do this!* – *Think like that!* but it cannot justify this and once it even tries to, it becomes repellent; because for every

> reason it offers there is a valid counter-reason. It is more
> convincing to say: 'Think like this! however strangely it may
> strike you.' Or: 'Won't you do this? – however repugnant you
> find it.' (1980, p. 29)

Again, in harmony with the treatment of Frazer, the doctrine of
predestination for the man who suffers is not a theory, or even a
truth he utters. It is 'a sight or a cry'. People at different religious
levels may find different religious doctrines valid. The Gospels may
be historically false, as well as rationally unjustifiable, yet this need
not matter to belief, because 'the historical proof-game' is
irrelevant to belief. What matters is the message being seized on
'lovingly' (1980, p. 32), by my heart and soul, not by my
speculative intelligence.

> What combats doubt is, as it were, *redemption*. Holding fast to
> *this* must be holding fast to that belief. So what that means is:
> first you must be redeemed and hold on to your redemption:
> . . . then you will see that you are holding fast to this belief.
> (1980, p. 33)

How though can this come about? Wittgenstein goes on to insist
that what is required is a change of direction in one's life, and hence
of attitude:

> This (redemption) can come about only if you no longer rest
> your weight on the earth but suspend yourself from heaven.
> Then *everything* will be different and it will be 'no wonder' if you
> can do things that you cannot do now.

This wholesale change of aspect has similarities with the remarks in
Wittgenstein's 1914-18 Notebooks concerning the completely
different look and feel the same world has to a man who is happy
compared to the look and feel it has to an unhappy man. (Waxing
rather than waning.) But while faith no doubt does produce such a
change of aspect, in *Culture and Value* Wittgenstein is insistent on
the change of aspect being itself rooted in an active principle – a
change of life, a passion, something that moves you (1980, p. 53).
'Although it's belief, it's really a way of living'; instruction in faith
therefore requires an appeal to conscience as well as a system of

reference (1980, p. 64). 'Perhaps,' he writes in 1950, 'one could "convince someone that God exists" by means of a certain kind of upbringing, by shaping his life in such and such a way' (1980, p. 85); life, especially suffering can 'force' the concept of God on us, in a similar way to the way the concept 'object' is forced on us. The point Wittgenstein makes about our knowledge of objects (especially in *On Certainty*) is that we do not begin by theorizing about their existence or by inferring them from sense data or anything of that sort. We begin by reacting to them and acting on them, by obeying commands to move them this way and that, by seeing them as part of our life in the world. And so too it must be with religion and with God. Whereas *theology* 'gesticulates with words' trying to say something it cannot express (much like the philosopher 'constructing' the world out of sense data), in religion, as elsewhere, what gives the words their sense is *practice*: '*Die Praxis gibt den Worten ihren Sinn.*' (1980, p. 85)

The key to Wittgenstein's views on religion in the works we have been considering is, as we suggested earlier, his philosophy of language as use. As he puts it in *Culture and Value*, echoing both Goethe and the remark on practice just quoted:

> The origin and the primitive form of the language game is a reaction; only from this can more complicated forms develop.
> Language – I want to say – is a refinement, 'in the beginning was the deed'. (1980, p. 31)

What effect does the view that language is a refinement have on religion? The answer presumably depends in part on just how the relationship between the language and what it is a refinement of is conceived, and we seem to get different answers from Wittgenstein at different times. In *Culture and Value* (1980, p. 85), in accordance with the 'expressive' line put forward in the *Remarks* on Frazer, we find Wittgenstein speaking of the point of the religious man's asking of cosmological questions about the origin of things as being the expression of 'a certain craving', not a demand for causal explanation. The trouble, though, with treating religious rites and beliefs as expressive of instincts or cravings or feelings is not only that it is vague, but it is also unable to explain the complexity and intellectual sophistication commonly found in the linguistic aspects of religion, let alone giving an explanation of why the feelings have taken the intelligible forms they have. On the other hand, in other places, Wittgenstein shows himself quite aware of the limitations of a purely expressive account. In the *Lectures and Conversations on Aesthetics*, he denies that in religion one could arbitrarily substitute one statement or picture for another, even though both might be equally expressive of a certain attitude. In religion, as opposed to chess or geometry, say, it is as important as anything just what picture is used. 'The whole *weight* may be in the picture.' (1972, p. 72)

Once it is admitted that the specific picture is essential to religion in this way, it is clear that religion cannot be regarded as just the expression of a feeling which has already been formed and which exists independently of its expression. The picture is constitutive of religion in a way a cry is not constitutive of pain. Religious people quarrel and fight over the details of the picture in a way that would not be the case if the attitude existed on its own and the picture was merely one of several equally possible external expressions or representations of the attitude. The problem that remains, however, is to know how to read or interpret a religious picture. Religious similies, says Wittgenstein (in *Culture and Value*, 1980, p. 29), move on the edge of an abyss. We can only draw *some* of the conclusions that the pictures naturally suggest. If we think of Bunyan's road, we are not to add to our understanding of the picture the thought that the Lord of the Road put all the traps, quicksands and wrong turnings on the road, nor that he created all the monsters, thieves and robbers on it. Bunyan's picture is, of course, intended allegorically, but the suspension of inference we find in religious allegory and picture also figures in statements about God that are intended non-figuratively. Thus Newman, in *A Grammar of Assent* argues that mysteriousness is an unavoidable aspect of any statement expressing the doctrine of the Trinity, because our reason cannot but be mystified by it: 'if an educated man, to whom it is presented, does not perceive that mysteriousness at once, that is a sure token that he does not rightly apprehend the propositions which contain the doctrine.' (1870, p. 114) He suggests further that although the propositions expressing the doctrine may be apprehended satisfactorily when taken individually one by one, when combined together, there is nothing but contradiction and mystery. It is not that the doctrine itself is contradictory, but our minds are incapable of perceiving it except as contradictory. Devotion overcomes this, as Tolstoy suggests, by knowing that in the end the contradictions will be ironed out.

Newman is, of course, only one example among many possible ones from many different religious traditions, all of whom assert that religious pictures and religious statements are only pointers to *the* truth, and are not to be pressed beyond what they will bear by a spurious demand for intellectual consistency. The problem with this, though, is that if we do not know what conclusions can legitimately be derived from what we believe we can hardly be said to know what it is we believe, or the direction in which we are being pointed. The answer that Wittgenstein and the Tolstoy of the passage quoted earlier might be inclined to give here is that by entering into the life of religion and the religious community you will learn what use is made of religious statements, what conclusions are to be drawn from them, how they can help us to direct and make sense of our life and so on. While it is certainly true that religious statements have a practical import in this way, that they are embedded in the life of the believer and that their full existential significance can only be grasped through experience, we cannot help feeling that there is a certain disingenuousness in this approach. For nothing has been said so far that would allow us to assess the comparative merits of competing religious pictures. No doubt the Christian has certain things to say and do in a crisis in his life, but so also does the Muslim, the Buddhist and the Moonie. Very likely each could claim with equal validity that it was only his faith that enabled him to come through his trouble, and point in detail to the way that this was so.

What takes us to the crux of the matter, and ultimately back to a consideration of meaning, is the way in which the religious believer conceives his faith. While it certainly is what he lives by, he does not conceive it as a set of formulas to direct his life, nor does he conceive the significance of the formulas to be exhausted by the role they play in his life. His faith is a set of formulas to direct his life because he thinks that what it says is true. He does not conceive it as one of many alternative accounts of how the world is, or, if he does, he has to explain how it is that the obvious and fundamental contradictions between, say Christianity and Judaism or Islam and Hinduism are to be ironed out. There are indeed some religious people who, despairing of the literal truth of their faith, regard it all as in some broad sense symbolic. However, if there is not

ultimately a non-symbolic and literal statement that can be
unearthed from the layers of symbolism, in the absence of a theory
of language explaining how purely 'symbolic' religious utterances
are supposed to convey any sense at all, it is hard to regard attempts
at 'demythologization' of traditional beliefs as presenting us with
viable intellectual options. I say this despite the fact that such
demythologization may help sophisticated believers to live with
their doubts.

The point about the typical religious believer conceiving his
faith as a true account of the world and its role in his life depending
on his seeing it in this way will, if it is correct, allow us to criticize
Wittgenstein's account of religious belief from within a Wittgensteinian standpoint on the nature of language. For Wittgenstein
argues that meaning is based in use, but our criticism of his account
of religion is that he has misconstrued the use of religious language.
There is, indeed, some reason to think that this might be true. As
we saw, Wittgenstein criticizes religious apologetics as superstitious. In line with Wittgenstein's treatment of Frazer, D.Z. Phillips
(who admits being influenced by Wittgenstein) says that petitionary
prayer (i.e. prayer for specific empirical results) is superstitious
rather than religious (cf. Phillips, 1970, p. 83). Yet, in many religious
traditions, both apologetics and petitionary prayer play a large part,
and petitionary prayer need not be purely superstitious. Why
should God not intervene in the world as a free response to human
devotion? Even with Frazer, it is not so easy to be sure that
Wittgenstein does not exaggerate the symbolic at the expense of
genuinely manipulative aspects of the rites. Moreover, as we saw in
connection with various doctrines and religions Wittgenstein is
inclined to interpret them in terms of the significance they bring to
the lives of individual believers rather than in terms of their
objective truth or historical actuality. One has the feeling that
Wittgenstein has an ideal concept of religion, which is not the same
as that which is widely and generally held, and which he uses to
discriminate in actual cases between 'religious' and 'superstitious'
elements. However, I want to end this chapter by suggesting a
more fundamental line of criticism of Wittgenstein's approach to
religion, which will be based not simply on arguing that his
analysis of religious practice is incorrect in practice, but which
questions the approach to language and meaning on which the
analysis itself is based.

To speak of meaning in terms of use is, by itself, not particularly perspicuous. What needs to be done is to give more specifications of the aspects of use which are intended. It is clear, in his analysis of religious statements, that Wittgenstein is particularly interested in the expressive and life-directing uses they undoubtedly have. What I have just been suggesting, however, is that the particular power and character of the expressive and life-directing functions of religious utterances is due in large measure to their descriptive content. In other words, religious language is no mere refinement of feeling, but the feeling is the feeling it is because of the descriptive claims and pictures embodied in the statements in question. It is not so much a matter of practice giving the words their sense, as of the sense of the words giving a direction to feeling and practice. In these remarks, I am guided by Karl Popper's development of Bühler's ideas about the functions of language (cf. *Objective Knowledge*, 1979, pp. 235-7). Popper sees *all* behaviour, including language, as being in the first instance expressive of the state of the behaving organism. Second, *some* behaviour can be not only expressive of the behaving organism's state but also a signal for a second organism to react in some way. This signalling function is a feature of animal communication systems as well as of human language, and at the lower levels, it may be no more than a trigger to set off a response in another creature. It need have no inherent intelligibility in itself. That only comes with language proper, which allows us humans (and possibly some animals) to express and signal through descriptions of states of affairs. Popper's point is that although I can express and signal (even linguistically) without any description, when I use language to describe I am, at the same time, expressing myself and making signals to my hearers. Popper sees the descriptive function of language (and the argumentative function which he sees as superimposed on description) as being of great significance to us as a species, as they allow us to formulate hypotheses and pictures of how the world is, and to criticize them rationally and objectively. Wittgenstein is undoubtedly right as against Frazer, say, to emphasize the importance of expression and what is, in a broad sense, signalling in religious discourse, but open to criticism if, as appears to be the case, it leads him to minimize the descriptive function of religious language (and possibly even to rule out the argumentative function altogether). Where the descriptive function of language is at work, as it is in

statements of religious belief, the resulting expression and signalling will, in standard cases, derive their sense from that of the
description. However crude a thinker Frazer may be, he is surely
right to give belief some sort of logical primacy over practice in
religion. However much religious ritual might be *like* kissing a
loved one's picture or a coronation there is in religion an irreducible
core of belief, and hence of description.

It is at this point, however, that we are taken to the most
fundamental aspect of Wittgenstein's theory of language, for what
might now be said by a follower of Wittgenstein is that the criteria
for the application of a statement are constitutive of its meaning.
Religious statements can be descriptive, if you like, but do not
conclude from that that their logic or verification is like that of
descriptions of houses or clocks. Each type of statement is
introduced in its own way and involved its own context and type of
checking, and what it is to be construed as signifying is constituted
by the way it is standardly held to impinge on our life and
experience. If you change the way a type of statement is held to
impinge on experience you change its meaning. Thus if we start
speaking of pain where there is and could be no pain behaviour
(e.g. in the case of machines or plants), we are not talking of the
same thing as we are when we say that Wittgenstein is in pain.
Presumably, too, if we withdraw religious statements from their
embedding in the religious form of life and experience and start to
discuss their truth by applying criteria drawn from other fields to
them, we change the subject matter in the same way, and fail to
engage with the real meaning religious statements have.

What is controversial in the theory of meaning just sketched is
not so much the implicit claim that the checking procedures of
religion are different from those of physics, as the view that the
checking procedures of a type of statement are part of its meaning.
While one might want to say that for an individual to understand
some types of statement involves some idea on his part of how they
might be checked (an example would be those asserting the
presence in our environment of primary sensory data), to generalize
this to all statements, or, even more, to say that in general part of
the *meaning* of a statement is given by the criteria for its use, has
some highly implausible consequences. For one thing, there are
many statements, such as those asserting universal scientific laws,
or those about the remote past, whose use and criteria for checking

fall far short of supporting what they apparently assert. It is
difficult to see how, if meaning is use, the meaning can so outstrip
any possible means we have of determining their truth or falsity
and any actual use we can make of them. As far as anything we can
do or experience goes, universal scientific laws would appear to be
indistinguishable from far more restricted statements about comparatively small segments of space and time, and the same goes for
two conflicting statements about the number of hairs on Julius
Caesar's head the day he crossed the Rubicon. Are we then to say
that what they apparently say is really indeterminate, because
asserting them is no different in practice from asserting other,
apparently conflicting statements, or that what they really mean is
just the way they actually impinge on experience and are used in
our lives? Neither course is attractive in view of the role the literal
meaning of such statements plays in building up our picture of the
world; the idea of laws obtaining throughout space and time, and
that of things happening in the past beyond anything we could
possibly check are undoubtedly a central element in the way we
conceive ourselves and our world. If it is then said that giving us
such pictures *is* the role such statements play in our lives, it has to
be explained how this position differs from that which claims that
the descriptive meaning of a statement is constituted not by its
criteria – the way it impinges on our experience – but by its truth-
conditions, which may transcend anything we are ever in experiential contact with. Further, are we to say that statements about gold,
say, have changed in meaning because the old criteria for the
presence of gold have been superseded by advances in chemistry?
Finally, making the criteria for the application of statements part of
their meaning makes it difficult to explain how a notion such as
magic could be criticized using concepts from science, given that
the criteria and hence the concepts in each system are different.

I do not want to say here that an account of meaning in which
the notion of meaning is dependent on criteria is in the end either
incoherent or indefensible, but rather to point to the way it accords
badly both with the view of the world and language which we
normally work with and with the status of the claims which
religions characteristically put forward. The view of the world we
do work with sees the world as independent of our knowledge, and
our language as making statements about that world whose sense
and whose truth and falsity are not determined solely by the criteria

we might use to decide on their truth and the way we use them. That is to say, a statement about the world, about the remote past, say, has the same sense now as the corresponding present tense statement had when the event described was present, and correspondingly, the same truth value, whereas this would not be the case on the criterial view if, in view of the remoteness of the event, we lost all means of deciding on the truth-value of the statement. In the same way, a statement about some sub-atomic particle does not change its sense or its truth value when a means of verifying the existence of the particle first becomes available. Such a means of verification will normally be held to lead to a discovery concerning what had earlier been conjectured and not known, not to a change in the concept. Particularly relevant to the relationship between religion and other areas of human experience, we think of our statements about the world from different areas of knowledge as being descriptions of the same world and needing to be brought into some sort of harmony with each other, although, to be sure, such a process of harmonization need not (indeed, should not) involve a reduction of all knowledge and all versions of the world into One True Theory, nor need it entail that we have any access to the one world except through our activities and language games. But we do not see there being separate worlds of magic, of religion, of science, of history and so on; we see one world, facets of which we may or may not regard as revealed by magic, religion, science and history. We do not see sets of new and possibly conflicting worlds springing into being from nothing as a result of our various cognitive activities and language games, which is the picture given by the view that a statement may change in sense and even in truth value when new criteria for the terms involved in it are adopted. Rather, we see our language games as a whole as being valid or invalid in accordance with the way they relate and inter-relate to the one world of our experience, and the particular statements in them as being true or false independently of the criteria used in a particular language game at a given time to decide their truth. Thus, even though some of our well-corroborated theories about gravity, say, fulfil all the criteria we have for inductive statements and continue to fulfil them until the human race becomes extinct, we do not take their truth thereby to be established, nor their meaning to be equivalent to what human beings experience of gravity and are disposed to say about it even to the end of time. We take such theories to have implications beyond what anyone could experience, beyond, in other words, any possible satisfaction of the criteria for their use. If the reply is then that meaning is not restricted to what criteria can establish, we will have to ask the difference between a criterial account of meaning and one which asserts that the meaning of a sentence, in the end, just is its truth conditions, whether or not we can in practice ever establish the satisfaction of those conditions.

The view that meaning is use is, of course, a descendent of the verificationist theory of meaning according to which the meaning of a statement is the way in which it is verified. (Wittgenstein flirted with verificationism in the early 1930s.) Although more sophisticated than verificationism particularly in its stress on the role a form of words plays in our life, it shares with verificationism the central thesis that the meaning of a statement is to be analysed in terms of dispositions to act and respond to it on the part of speakers. Against this, I have been sketching what is often nowadays known as the realist theory of meaning, which envisages meaning as reaching out to the world, on occasion beyond any possible experience on the part of speakers of the language and, above all, independently of the way in which they might seek to establish the truth of sentences. As I mentioned earlier, although the realistic view of language accords better with our intuitions and practice than the non-realistic view, this is not enough to settle the matter as between realism and non-realism. (As Dummett has suggested, this might do no more than reflect a prejudice on our part.) However, as far as religion goes, we may be more confident in the direction of realism about meaning, for religion is above all the realm in which a reality beyond human experience is postulated. Moreover, it is worth considering whether a religious person could be as easy-going epistemologically as the previous paragraph. Wouldn't God's knowledge constitute just that One True Theory, which I implied we could not grasp? If so, it is yet further evidence of the perversity of analysing religious statements non-literally, for they are nothing if not attempts to point at the existence of The Truth.

My conclusion at this point, then, is that although faith is something lived rather than reasoned about and although living the life of faith may deepen one's personal understanding of religious language and even bring someone to accept as true something that previously meant nothing to him (in the same way as one might be said to know more about love at the age of forty than one did at the age of ten), it would be quite wrong to say that religious practice gives religious language and the statements believed in by the faithful their meaning if one intended by this an account of the semantics of religious language, for this would be to stress the expressive and signalling aspects of that language at the expense of its descriptive aspect, and to rob the descriptive element of just that appeal to the transcendent from which much of the practice surely gets its sense. This is not, of course, to deny the problems involved in interpreting religious statements, some of which we have touched on already, but the problems are not to be dissolved by a theory of meaning which, by stressing the lived aspects of faith, falsifies the extent to which religious statements are understood realistically by believers. Such an approach both diminishes the seriousness of the beliefs of believers and prevents any reasonable comparisons of religious systems between themselves and between non-religious accounts of the world. What we now have to do, and what will occupy us in Chs 2 to 5 is to see how far we can find any basis in reason or experience for thinking that the characteristic religious assertion that there is such a transcendent being of some sort might be true. If we find that, however such a being might be described, there is no reason to think that there is such a thing, and that the claim that there is receives no support from or even conflicts with the rest of what we know and believe, then we shall have to return to the notion of religious faith, to see how faith might then be evaluated, and this we will do in Ch. 6.

2

Religious Experience and Religious Knowledge

What I want to explore in this chapter is the connection between experience and knowledge in the religious context. Of course, one can say in general that outside the sphere of purely abstract reasoning at least, all knowledge involves some sort of relationship to experience, and that part of what is meant by knowing something is that what is known impinges on experience in some way. The very general empiricism of the previous sentence is not a purely arbitrary dogma. Since Kant, at least, the epistemological status of the unexperienceable thing-in-itself has been rightly regarded as highly problematic, precisely because of the way it fails to impinge at all on our experience. Strawson has summed up the difficulty well in what he calls Kant's principle of significance: 'the principle that we can make no significant use of concepts in propositions claiming to express knowledge unless we have empirical criteria for the application of those concepts' (1966, p. 241), and certainly the onus is on the metaphysician to meet Kant's demand 'that he should at least give a satisfactory account of how, and by what kind of inner illumination, he believes himself capable of soaring so far above all possible experience, on the wings of mere ideas.' (1787, p. 529)

Whatever might be said about metaphysical speculation, religious knowledge is usually thought of as essentially personal and individual – certainly more a matter of personal acquaintance than of remote description. This is hardly surprising, given the role of religion in people's lives, central to them and to how they see themselves to be. Something that is known merely in the way a distant scientific or historical fact is known could hardly fill the centre of anyone's affective and moral concern, even if that fact were something apparently remarkable or miraculous. Thus, if

Christians are moved at all by the 'historical evidence' for the Resurrection, this is surely not because of its historical cogency, for equally cogent 'proofs' could no doubt be found for other miracles of other faiths, and Christians are not generally moved by them, but because of the way the Resurrection is part of their religious faith and connected to their experience of religion. William James writes with some plausibility that

> what religion reports . . . always purports to be fact of experience: the divine is actually present, religion says, and between it and ourselves relations of give and take are actual. If definite perceptions of fact like this cannot stand upon their own feet, surely abstract reasoning cannot give them the support they are in need of. . . . There is always a *plus*; a *thisness*, which feeling alone can answer for. Philosophy in this sphere is thus a secondary function, unable to warrant faith's veracity. . . . (1902, p. 436)

From a specifically Christian standpoint, we can find the noted theologian John Baillie saying

> it is not as the result of an inference of any kind, whether explicit or implicit, whether laboriously excogitated or swiftly intuited, that the knowledge of God's reality comes to us. It comes rather through our direct, personal encounter with Him in the Person of Jesus Christ, His Son, our Lord. (1949, p. 143)

Statements such as these, which could be easily multiplied from within Christianity and from other religions, are claiming in effect that the fundamental source of religious knowledge is the religious experience of the believer.

Religious experience is an extremely wide, not to say vague term. This is unavoidable if what is being claimed by James and Baillie about the fundamental source of religious knowledge is not to be obviously false, because there is no reason to suppose that every religious person's experiences are the same. Religious experience ranges from intense and possibly ecstatic and mystical states to the feeling of warmth and security many people frequently feel at religious services. What they have in common is that they are not cases of perception through the five senses, but of some other sort of sensitivity altogether. What we will be primarily examining here is the extent that parallels can be drawn between religious experience and sensory perception.

The variety and extent of religious experience has been examined at great length by William James in his classic work on the subject, but even this is open to criticism for an over-concentration on privately generated experiences at the expense of experiences which arise in the context of public religious services. Nevertheless, James's description (1902, pp. 73 and 87) of religious experiences as revelations or perceptions of a kind of reality, more deep and general than anything perceptible by the particular senses, does get to the essential point about religious experiences of all kinds, namely that in them the believer feels himself to be in personal contact with some non-sensory reality. A similar point is made by Ninian Smart when he speaks of religious experience as involving 'some kind of "perception" of the invisible world, or involves a perception that some visible person or thing is a manifestation of the invisible world' (1971, p. 28). Although I do not want to place any arbitrary limits on the types of religious experience there might be, for the purposes of this chapter, by 'religious experience' I intend to speak of experiences of a non-sensory sort, and so to exclude apparently miraculous events which are perceptible in normal ways. (I shall have something to say about such events in Ch. 6.) What is of interest to us here is the claim that men have a means of directly and non-sensorily contacting a transcendent reality.

It is the idea of direct personal contact with a non-sensory reality that non-believers will find hard to grasp. In order to bring out the nature of the difficulty, I will consider the extent to which religious experiences can provide evidence for the existence of a reality beyond the experience itself. In doing this, I do not want to suggest that religious people actually argue in this way. Presumably people who are convinced that they are in personal contact with some super-reality will not often attempt to argue or prove their conviction at all, nor will their conviction be arrived at inferentially, any more than we normally infer from statements about our sensations to statements about physical objects. Nevertheless the question of the extent to which the conviction can be justified by the experience naturally arises, just as much as it does in the case of other judgments and other experiences. Indeed, part of the point of

27

this chapter will be to compare the relationships between religious experience and religious belief, on the one hand, with the relationships between empirical beliefs and sensory experience on the other. This comparison is not gratuitous. For not only is it the case that empirical beliefs based on ordinary sensory experience form the foundation of a common human language, as well as affording the least problematic cases of justified true belief, but an analogy between sensory perception and religious experience is one that is frequently exploited by religious writers. If nothing else, the analogy deserves examination both because of its apologetic power, and because of the way it has been carefully developed by James at the end of his chapter on Mysticism (1902, pp. 407-13).

James is somewhat equivocal in his explicit claims for mystical states. He says that while they are justifiably authoritative over those who have them, they are not such as to force others to accept their revelations uncritically. At the same time, they do overthrow 'the pretension of non-mystical states to be the sole and ultimate dictates of what we believe' and they open out the possibility of 'other orders of truth'. They could well be 'superior points of view, windows through which the mind looks out upon a more extensive and inclusive world'.

If mystical states really do overthrow the pretension of non-mystical states to be the sole and ultimate dictates of what we believe, one wonders if their existence should not be more compelling, even on those who do not experience them. After all, research into psychic phenomena, for example, and testing of psychic claims could in principle demonstrate to the non-psychic that there is something in the claims of psychics to gain knowledge non-sensorily, in which case it would be just perverse for anyone, psychic or not, to hold that there was no such thing as extra-sensory perception. Equally, the sighted man in the kingdom of the blind would have every reason to object to dogmatic refusals of the blind to consider his claims to a primary mode of knowledge which they lack. So why does the subject of religious experience, which is claimed by Baillie to be also a primary mode of knowledge (1949, p. 217) have to be as reticent as James initially suggests he should be in demanding general recognition of his claims?

Indeed, James's reticence on this point appears especially surprising in the light of his further claim that from an absolute point of view, mystical experience and ordinary sensory experience are on the same epistemological footing:

> Our own more 'rational' beliefs are based on evidence exactly
> similar in nature to that which the mystics quote for theirs. Our
> senses, namely, have assured us of certain states of fact; but
> mystical experiences are as direct perceptions of fact for those
> who have them as any sensations ever were for us. The records
> show that even though the five senses be in abeyance in them,
> they are absolutely sensational in their epistemological quality, if
> I may be pardoned the barbarous expression – that is, they are
> face to face presentations of what seems immediately to exist.
> (p. 408)

The implication of what James says here[1] is clearly that many of
our factual judgments are justified by the directness, clarity and
immediacy of certain sensations we have. If this *were* how they are
justified, given that we have no reason to doubt the sincerity or the
rationality of many of the mystics, we non-mystics should surely
take very seriously the claims of the mystics to mystical perception
based as they are on equally vivid experiences. While it is true that
if the epistemological justification of two types of claim were
relevantly similar – as would appear to be the case here if James
were correct – then we should accept the one as much as we accept
the other. What I now want to suggest is that James misconstrues
the logic of epistemological justification in the quoted passage, and
that what is really the case is that the mystic himself, far from being
in a position safely to ignore the sceptical attitude of non-believers,
as James asserts, should rather begin to wonder about his own
interpretation of his mystical states.

The first point to notice is that, despite what James says, our
senses on their own assure us of nothing. On their own, they are, in
a sense, dumb. From the indefinite barrage of sensory stimulation
we are subjected to at any given moment, nothing coherent can
emerge without the use of some organizing principles. Even to
begin to perceive patterns within our experience, we have to group
stimulations in specific ways, and this implies that we mark some
as more similar to each other than to the rest. This perception of
similarity itself presupposes some predisposition to focus on certain
specific types of similarity, for any two objects or sensations have
an indefinite number of ways of being seen as both similar to and

different from each other. Thus a red pencil and a blue pencil and a red bus can be seen to have multifarious possible inter-relationships of similarity and dissimilarity and so do the sensations which go to make up the perceptions of pencils and buses. So to organize and sort our sensory input in any way at all certain frameworks of classification, inborn or acquired, must be present to enable us to fix on features of certain types as a basis of the organization. Thus in colour sorting, we tend to group objects according to their closeness in colour hue, as on the spectrum, rather than according to their closeness in colour intensity, say. It is clear that the two ways of sorting will often yield different groupings, for you might have a bright and dull red and a bright and a dull blue. Thus to notice and be assured that we are having such and such a sensation at a given time requires not only a sensory input, but also the interest or classificatory scheme which allows us to focus on and register the particular type of quality in question to the exclusion of all the other potentially noticeable qualities in our current sensory input.

Having adopted or been born with predispositions to react to data of certain sorts, we will be disposed to perceive regularities of specific sorts within our experience, and hence to notice that some types of stimulation are regularly followed by others, or fall into more complicated patterns and relationships. From the point of view of our sensory input, it is obviously the existence and persistence of such patterns in our experience that permits us to think of our world as being populated with enduring physical objects. I have argued elsewhere (1980, pp. 80–5) that without a coincidence between actual reproducible regularities in our experience and our schemes of classification, we would not be able successfully to develop any empirical concepts at all, even those referring to qualities such as colours, whose postulation at any single moment does not itself require more than a momentary perception. This is because of the need to assure ourselves that on future occasions of application of a given sensory concept, we are using it in the same way as in the past. The most basic way of being able to check our memory of the original learning is to assume that a certain quality will be re-experienceable when we put ourselves again in circumstances similar to those in which its application was originally learned. An example of what is intended here would be the use of a certain object as a sample of a certain colour, say red; so we can check our present understanding of red by remembering where the red sample is located and returning to it. But this sort of check would work only assuming that the red colour sample had not in the meantime changed so much as to be unrecognizable or so as to take on a different colour, and this is what led me to argue that even our scheme of purely sensory concepts required the assumption of a world populated with stable, enduring objects. The present argument does not depend on this account of the possession of concepts referring to sensory qualities, but the stability of objects is relevant to our present concerns, for when we perceive something, as, say, a table, we thereby have all sorts of expectations as to its future behaviour including its behaviour when it is being observed by no-one. Even less than seeing something as blue or red can such a judgment be assured simply and solely by our senses, which is where James's epistemology is at fault from the start.

It is not sensation alone that assures us of states of fact, whether these states of fact are that a certain property is instantiated within our experience or whether they are facts about the objects around us. We need, in addition to sensation, an interest in properties of certain types (such as colour hue) in the first place, although sensory experience will be needed to determine just what colour contents fill our colour space, while in the case of enduring physical objects, we need a set of object concepts which essentially transcend any actual experience. This is because thinking of something as a physical object is to endow it with causal or dispositional properties – to think of it as being disposed to behave in certain ways and to have those dispositions even at times when they are not being manifested or exercised. Hence, physical object statements support the truth of counter-factual conditional statements about what would have happened had those dispositions been activated at times when they were not, and this is something that is necessarily beyond the power of any possible sensory evidence to prove. Thus my senses alone are quite unable to assure me that what I am now perceiving as my dog would have barked had someone passed a moment ago or would have jumped up had I stopped writing a few moments ago. Yet these and hosts of similar counter-factual truths about the past, and corresponding expectations for the future directly follow from seeing things as enduring physical objects endowed with specific dispositional properties.

What needs to be examined, and what James's account leaves out altogether, is the way in which our basic physical object perceptions and judgments are related to the sensations on which they are based.

The first point to notice is that a judgment that there is a table in my room, although it does not follow from my currently having the visual impression of a table before me, does explain my having that visual impression. This is because, among the dispositional properties of tables, is the property of causing in normally sighted observers in normal conditions of perception, the visual impression of tables. So the impression and the object can be seen to be related as explicandum and explicans. This in itself is not enough to justify my belief that there is a table. My visual impression could perhaps be explained in other ways. Certainly in principle it would only be a matter of ingenuity to devise alternative explanatory hypotheses. However, the physical object explanation does in this case have a number of points in its favour over possible competitors.

In the first place it can be drafted so as to fulfil two important criteria for satisfactory explanations which have been noted by Popper (1979, pp. 192-3). The first criterion is independent testability, which is required to ensure that an alleged explicans is not simply another way of referring to the explicandum, which it would be if the only evidence for it were the explicandum itself. To take Popper's own example, it would be vacuous to explain a sea storm by saying that Poseidon was angry, if the only possible evidence for Poseidon's anger was the storm itself. Obviously saying that there is a table here and that tables cause visual impressions of tables has many other consequences over and above *my* having visual impressions of a table, most notably consequences about the visual impressions of others and consequences for one's other senses. Popper's second condition for a good explanation is that it should make use of universal statements or laws of nature asserting that all members of a certain class have seen property, or, failing that, that a certain proportion of them do. The point of this condition is to rule out the appending of an irrelevant independently testable statement to a vacuous explicans in order to fulfil the first condition (for example: there is a storm at sea because Poseidon is angry and ravens are black). In a satisfactory explanation, the natural law statements, together with statements of the relevant initial conditions, will allow us to interpret the explicandum as an instance of a reproducible effect, deducible from or shown to be at least probabilistically related to the other two statements. Thus, in the case of our visual impression of the table, it would follow from and be explained by the universal statement 'Whenever normal observers in normal conditions of observation and attention have a table in their visual field, they will have a visual impression of a table' together with the initial conditions statement 'There is a table currently in my visual field and I am a normal observer in normal conditions.' (We will examine shortly some of the complexities and implications of the references to normal observers and conditions.)

From the initial conditions statement, it follows that there is a table in my environment, and hence that cross checking is possible from my other senses, and from other observers, hence both the universal and the initial conditions statement are further testable independently of my current visual impression, which is another way of saying that they transcend it. The question obviously arises, why accept *these* statements as providing the correct explanations of what my senses currently assure me of? To say that this explanation satisfies certain formal conditions for explanations is not to say very much, for doubtless other explanations also satisfying the formal conditions could be devised (for example, 'whenever conjurors so arrange things as to create the illusion of a table, normal observers in normal conditions have the visual impression of a table' and 'a conjuror is currently so arranging things and I am a normal observer in normal conditions', etc.).

Moreover, the universal statement mentioning tables may also be, on occasion, apparently falsified, for example, when a normal observer in normal conditions did indeed have a table in his visual field, but failed to register any corresponding visual impression because his attention was completely taken up by other things in his environment, such as a fire or a naked person, or even because he was from a different culture that had no concept of a table. However, the table explanation does have advantages over the conjuror explanation. It is more highly confirmed by virtue of its other independently testable consequences being verified, while the apparent exceptions to the universal law statement about tables can be explained away by appeal to testable psychological theories about the relationships between such things as attention and concept possession, on the one hand, and perception, on the other.

(The point about concept possession becomes particularly important when what is being observed is something like a microscopic
organism that needs practice and training to be seen for what it is at
all. We shall consider later how much support the point about a
training in perception can give to the religious account of religious
experience.) So, the table explanation is more highly confirmed
than the conjuror explanation. In other words, relevant tests other
than my current visual impressions corroborate both the initial
conditions statement and the universal statement in the table
explanation, while the initial conditions statement in the conjuror
explanation fails the most obvious tests, and can be saved in the
present case only by postulating a conjuror of almost superhuman
ability and extreme deviousness, amounting almost to invisibility.
This suggests a further desideratum in explanatory schemes: that
the more an explanation requires additional explanatory hypotheses
to explain its failure to survive its further testing, the less good it is.
In general, then, where there are two competing explanations, the
one that needs less saving is the better.

It will be observed that the table explanation, in both the
universal and the initial conditions statements, makes use of the
concept of normal observers and normal conditions, and that this is
clearly something highly theoretical relative to my present sensory
input, as are any theories about attention and perception which are
invoked to explain apparent failures of the universal statements.
This does not, of course, give the conjuror explanation any
advantage, for it too uses the same concepts and theories.
Nevertheless it is clear that the table explanation, in utilizing such
notions is very far from being self-contained, and actually relies on
a number of very general ideas about the conditions and causes of
perception about what counts as normal in this context, about what
sorts of perceptions are had in what sorts of conditions, about the
characteristics of perceivers, their psychology and attention, about
the things that cause perceptions and the future experiences those
things will cause, and about the sorts of cases, emphasized by
Goodman (1978, pp. 72-83), where one's perception gives a highly
misleading picture of what is actually before one. Neither the
generality nor the inter-relatedness of these ideas ought to be
considered a disadvantage. First, we have learned from Popper that
the more general a theory is, the more likelihood there is of its
being falsified if it is false. Many of the theories covering perception

are in addition highly precise, explaining in detail both the causes and the extent of deviations from perceptual norms, both in observers themselves and in non-normal conditions. Thus, for example, we have a good understanding of the causes and consequences of phenomena such as short-sightedness and astigmatism on the one hand, while on the other it is possible to explain why sticks appear bent in water and why the sun looks bigger on the horizon than it does at midday. It is worth mentioning that explanation in terms of illusion is still an explanation of why we have the experience we do, and is expressible in the same way as the standard physical object explanations: 'whenever normal observers in normal conditions have (for example) a straight stick half immersed in water in their visual field, they will have the impression of a bent stick' and the normal initial conditions statement. Note, incidentally, that the illusion explanation still refers to physical objects. Second, we should stress that the interrelatedness of the theories explaining experience should not be regarded as a disadvantage. When an inter-related system of theories includes many theories which make precise, corroborated predictions, it is surely reasonable to prefer the system as a whole to competing systems which contain more problematic theories. Thus, to take an example from physics, the Copernican astronomical system would be regarded as preferable to the Ptolemaic on the grounds of needing fewer *ad hoc* auxiliary hypotheses to save the phenomena.

We began by asking about the epistemological relationship between our experiences and physical objects, and the answer is in terms of the explanatory role played by physical objects. Statements and theories which imply the existence of physical objects explain why I have the experiences I do according to the criteria we have laid down for good explanatory theories: independent testability, law likeness, generality, precision, systems of mutual support.[2] In the foregoing, we have concentrated on the level of common sense theorizing about what it is we perceive and theories of perception, but the explanatory model will naturally take us into science, for science is only the attempt to refine, correct, extend and further explain lower levels of explanation, and must itself be assessed ultimately in terms of its explanatory and predictive power relative to our experience.

Does the explanatory role played by physical objects in

explaining our experiences in any way justify all or any of our common sense talk of physical objects? To answer this question, it is necessary to realize first that there is no general theory of physical objects as such in competition with some alternative way of structuring our experience which makes no appeal to physical objects. What we do have as Putnam has pointed out (1975, pp. 343-5), are various thing-theories of various types in specific areas, and these specific theories can, with greater or lesser plausibility, be regarded as explaining some of our experiences. As Putnam puts it:

> with some care in making explicit additional auxiliary hypo-
> theses connecting thing-events with the events one could
> describe in a sensation or appearance language, one can even
> make out that these hypotheses, laws, garden variety empirical
> statements, etc., together with these auxiliary hypotheses
> explain the phenomena that would be described in a sensation or
> appearance language.

It is at the level of specific theories that the procedures of inductive testing, theory comparison and so on can get to work. Thus, although there is no direct inductive proof that material objects exist, there may be inductive or quasi-inductive proof that tables exist, molecules exist, electrons exist, or at least inductive or quasi-inductive proofs of the theories and statements in which there is talk of tables, molecules and electrons. In so far as there is support from our sensory experience for specific theories entailing the existence of specific material objects, there is thus indirect support for the general proposition that there are material objects, because to deny that is to repudiate at the same time all those theories which imply it. In saying that our experiences support and are explained by material object talk, I am not saying that we *infer* objects from experience or that there is some process whereby we first have sensory experiences and then transform them into experiences of objects, nor am I unaware that most of our observational talk is actually in terms of objects rather than in terms of sensations (which would be a further reason for declining to speak of belief in material objects as if it were an inductively supported theory). But what I am interested in, in order to assess the comparison made by James between religious experience and everyday experience is analyzing the epistemological relationships between statements closest to the experiential periphery of our conceptual scheme (which, given the scheme, require little more than an immediate experience for their verification), and those, including talk of objects, which are more remote from the periphery. As already mentioned, I have argued elsewhere (1980, pp. 80-5) that the ability to classify sensations depends on the existence of enduring physical objects. In other words, a conceptual scheme that consisted only of sensation descriptions would be an impossibility (because it would be inherently unstable). Nevertheless, within a conceptual scheme that permits talk both of objects and of sensory experience of them, and of the causal relations between them, it is clear that *particular* judgments about sensations require less in the way of experiential verification than *particular* judgments about enduring objects, and this is all that my present point amounts to. My criticism of James is precisely that in the Mysticism passage he fails to see that once we are able to deploy the distinction between our experiences and the objects we are taking them to be experiences of, the justification for our beliefs about the existence of what we think they are experiences of cannot be simply in terms of clarity, immediacy or apparent directness of the experiences.

Naturally, the fact that a given set of theories explains certain experiences is not a conclusive proof that any or all of the theories are true, however much the theories satisfy the criteria we have laid down for good explanation. But – and this is a crucial point also urged by Putnam – given that there is no alternative explanation, it is a strong reason for accepting the theories, at least provisionally to the extent that they work well for us. What is quite clear is that although there are frequently alternative theories at the level of theoretical physics, we have no viable alternative to our material object talk at what Putnam called the garden variety empirical level. This, combined with the fact of its very high level of success, is as good a reason as we are likely to find for our common sense empirical talk, given that it cannot be conclusively proved either on the basis of sense experience or pure reason (which is the lesson to be drawn from the failures of epistemologies which seek to found knowledge on a firm and unquestionable basis).

What I am arguing here is that in empirical matters, epistemo-logical justification goes hand in hand with explanatory power, and that the primary data to be explained are our sensory experiences. In taking some data to be primary, I avoid the objection of arbitrariness that can be urged against some versions of what might be called explanationism in epistemology that regard no statement as unsacrificeable if it stands in the way of an elegant explanatory system. (There is more than a hint of this strategy in Quine's 'Two Dogmas of Empiricism' (cf. Quine, 1953, p. 43).) Taken to an extreme, high explanatory power could easily and cheaply be achieved in a system of statements simply by denying the truth of all unexplained or inexplicable statements, so that everything accepted in the system is perfectly explained (cf. Lehrer, 1974, pp. 170-1). The insistence on the primacy of people's sensory data clearly blocks such a deletion strategy. Even if we say sometimes that people's sensory data are mistaken, we will still have the job of explaining how the mistake came about, and this will presumably involve us in formulating theories of perception to explain the mistakes and illusions, so there is no short cut to explanatory power by simple strategies of rejection. In taking sensory data as the most basic things that have to be explained, I am very far from regarding them as not open to criticism, however. Apart from cases where we learn to regard particular sensory experiences as illusory, as I pointed out earlier, classifying sensory data requires frames of classification, innate and learned. There is nothing to prevent us regarding initial schemes of classification as dispensable or even potentially misleading for more advanced theoretical purposes. This is the sense in which the world of physics is colourless, though to make such an assertion is itself to demand a search for a two-fold explanation, first of the physics and physiology of colour vision and secondly of the (evolutionary?) reason for our being genetically endowed with colour vision. None the less, the fact that we (or many of us) do perceive things as coloured is something that must be taken as given and cannot itself be denied, however much it is explained away.

There is a further line of objection to seeing epistemological justification in terms of explanation, and that is that there can be justifications of individual beliefs which are not explanatory. Thus Lehrer (1974, p. 178) says that a man would be justified in believing that a mouse was five feet from an owl by a combination of a general statement (Pythagoras's theorem) and the initial conditions statements that the owl was on top of a three foot pole and the mouse was four feet from the bottom of the pole. Lehrer also uses this example to suggest that there can be cases of deduction from premises consisting of universal statements and initial conditions statements which are not explanatory, for we still have to have it explained why the mouse is five feet from the owl. Is Lehrer correct, however, in assuming that there is no explanatory power in this deduction? Surely Pythagoras's theorem does explain exactly why, given the facts recorded in the initial conditions, the mouse cannot but be five feet from the owl. Saying that, given the initial conditions, the conclusion has to be is just the role the universal statement is supposed to play in an explanation, and, as Putnam has argued in another context, there are certainly cases where geometrical rather than causal or physical explanations can be just what we are looking for – if, for example, we want to explain why square pegs cannot go into round holes. What Pythagoras' theorem does not explain is the peculiar set-up described in Lehrer's initial conditions, but then no explanation scheme can do that for its own initial conditions. There is nothing about the deduction in question to prevent anyone giving further and possibly more interesting or relevant explanations of the set-up. All that the model of explanation presented here does is to say that any genuine explanation of a state of affairs will either be deductive in form, consisting of a universal statement, and a statement of initial conditions from which the explicandum is deduced or a probabilistic inference along similar lines. It does not say that all such explanations are of equal value, interest or power for all purposes.

Lehrer (1974, pp. 178-80) gives another type of example of supposed justification without explanation, and it is where people have come to believe something true simply by observation or by some evidence that is not explained by the belief. Thus, we might see a dead man and affirm on that evidence that he was once conceived, without his conception explaining his death, or come to believe that Pythagoras' theorem was true by observation alone. The reply here is surely that mere hunch or observation of past regularity on their own is no justification for a belief at all. Thus without understanding the explanatory connections between the theorem and its proof, and between death and life and conception, the beliefs, though true, are hardly justified. In the case of the dead man, the reason why we are justified in believing that he was conceived is because of two suppressed general truths ('All dead men were once alive' and 'All live men were once conceived'), which we regard as being part of the explanation of the existence of the corpse. The reason why we regard these general truths as having an explanatory relevance to the corpse is because we have noticed that there are no dead men who had not at one time lived and no live men who had not been conceived, together with the hypothesis that these observed regularities are not due to biased or inadequate samples, but reflect the way the world actually is. In other words, as Harman has persuasively argued (1965), enumerative induction is warranted only when we regard the general fact induced as a more likely explanation of our observation that all observed A's are B's than that our observations are in some way distorted by bias or inadequate sampling. There is, of course, an implicit appeal in such an assumption to our total evidence, in the light of which competing explanations of observations will have to be ranked for likelihood. Obviously this ranking can only be provisional and can go wrong. Therefore whatever assurance is given by our total evidence will also be provisional. But this is unavoidable, and is only another aspect of the inter-relatedness of the theories making up the scheme which enables us to transform our sensory data into a picture of a world we are in contact with.

I have been arguing that the relation between sensory input and factual judgments from those of common sense through to theoretical physics is one of explicandum to explicans: that factual judgments are warranted if they provide the best available explanation of the data to be explained. In the case of garden variety empirical judgments this goes almost by default, since there is no genuine competitor. Although there is admittedly much discussion of how competing explanatory theories are to be ranked, it is clear that the qualities of generality and predictive success are going to feature in any set of criteria for ranking. It is also clear that particular judgments about specific data are related to other theories, in particular to theories of perception and to more general theories which imply (or fail to imply) those judgments. This is the sense in which there is indeed a web of belief, and, of course, a web of believers, for built into our theories of perception are ideas of mutual corroboration of observers and observations. In the web of belief, there are thus explanations of the experiences of individuals, which are highly complex and ramified, but in which each successful prediction of an individual experience increases the degree to which the whole system is corroborated. Conversely, altering an element in the system can have widespread repercussions, and this would be particularly marked if an alteration were proposed to one of the theories of perception on which our ideas of normality and objectivity of perception are based.

It is perhaps worth stressing that even if it is true, as many have argued, that understanding another culture involves understanding their concepts, and that the deductive model of explanation is of no help in this, it remains the case that in establishing a historical matter of fact, such as the occurrence of a specific event or the existence of a person we will have to make use of the same theories of perception as we use in our everyday judgments, supplemented no doubt by canons of historical evidence, which will also be expressible in the form of lawlike statements. There will often be considerable difficulty in knowing whether with a particular bit of historical evidence the relevant initial conditions statement is satisfied, but the important point is that as far as the establishing of matters of historical fact goes, the same basic scheme will apply as in other areas: that the factual judgment that such and such an event happened is the best available explanation of the available data. (That we are often not in a position to decide which is the best of the competing explanations on the available data does not detract from the general validity of the scheme.)

It has also been claimed recently by Davidson (cf. e.g., 1980, p. 224) that, for various theoretical reasons, there can be no strict laws (presumably even of a statistical sort) enabling us to predict and explain mental phenomena. Would this mean, on my view, that our ordinary psychological talk about mental phenomena (beliefs, desires, sensations, perceptions, and so on) is not genuinely explanatory? Without going into Davidson's reasons for his claim (which I touch on again in Ch. 4), I simply say this here. Even without strict laws for mental phenomena, the strength of our explanations of people's behaviour through appeal to their psychological states (whether these are long-term dispositions like jealousy or short-term states like their perceiving a red traffic light) depends on our having and sharing general, if not strictly quantifiable ideas of the likely causes and effects of such states. At a basic level, the explanations we give of behaviour in psychological terms clearly depend on an assumption of the truth of such ideas, even if there is much more to psychological explanations than that, in the way they enable us to draw up a coherent, rational account of a man's actions, and so on. But we would not be able to make any practical use of such accounts in controlling and predicting behaviour if the general ideas about the causes and effects of being in various psychological states were not to a large extent empirically confirmed. (That *some* types of psychological 'explanation' are not empirically grounded in this way is, of course, an explanation of their practical uselessness, and, I would say, of their lack of genuine explanatory power.) So, even if, for various reasons, such as those of Davidson, or perhaps for more general considerations to do with freedom of the will, our general ideas about the physical causes and effects of psychological states cannot be made precise or strictly lawlike, their explanatory power depends on their being based on a significant degree of regularity and predictability between the physical and the psychological. Furthermore, even if Davidson's claim about the unavailability of strict laws in the psychological realm entailed something stronger about the non-existence of regularity of any sort in the mental (which it surely does not), it could hardly benefit James or those religious believers who want to appeal directly to religious experience, because, at least implicitly, what they are doing is to suggest an analogy between the explanatory schemes operating in the areas of sensory experience and religious experience, and, as I have been arguing here, sensory experience is properly regarded as objective only when there is a high degree of regularity observable among the supposed objects of that experience.

The relation of matters of fact to sensory evidence is thus far more complicated and interesting than James suggests in his passage on mystical experience. What we now have to do is to examine the analogy drawn by James and others between sensory and religious experience to see whether the two do stand or fall together.

Undoubtedly the strongest motivation in favour of a religious interpretation of what might neutrally be called depth feelings and experiences comes from a sense on the part of the religious man that what he experiences is so profound and meaningful for him that he could not possibly be in error about its sense. In many cases it would clearly be wrong to cast doubt on either the sincerity of the believer or on the profound effects of the experience in the life of the individual concerned. There is, then, a prima facie presumption in favour of taking as genuine the experiential reports of such people as St Teresa of Avila or St John of the Cross. In my discussion of common factual experience, some may have objected to my taking experiential reports as primary data, but we would hardly begin to do justice to the religious case were we to do anything else, for what we have here are the considered accounts of serious and sincere people of what they take to be the most significant experience of their lives.

Having said that the reports of mystics deserve to be taken seriously as primary data is not, however, the same thing as accepting what they imply about transcendent objects as being incorrigible or uncriticizable. The lesson to be derived from our examination of ordinary experience and matters of fact was that no sensory reports are uncriticizable, and that when there is any question of them referring to objects endowed with dispositional properties they are certainly not in themselves incorrigible and are only to be accepted in so far as they explain the experiences adequately in terms of having genuine explanatory power and better than other available explanations. To impose these same conditions on experiential reports which refer to divine beings is not to prejudge matters in favour of physics and common sense and against religion. I am not simply saying that religious reports have to conform to the methods of physics or the sciences generally but rather that the logic of experiential reports is such that whenever they refer to objects with powers beyond what is verifiable in the experiences themselves, something more than the experience on its own is required to justify acceptance of the report.

So a feeling of conviction, however strong, is not sufficient to ground an experiential claim: the further the claim outstrips the experience the greater is the need for support from beyond the experience itself. Unfortunately, in the religious case, the conviction of the believer is usually presented as the most forceful piece of evidence in favour of his interpretation of his experience. Baillie thus rejects 'logical argument of any kind' to establish the truth of religious statements, and appeals instead direct to religious experience (1949, p. 132). While we can have some sympathy with him if what he is intending by this is to say that religious belief cannot be founded on metaphysical argument, such a direct appeal to experience is, in this context, entirely question-begging, once we realize that no experience in itself can ever guarantee the truth of any statement beyond that asserting that the subject of the experience has had such and such an experience. As C.B. Martin has shown admirably in his careful analysis of religious experience (1959, Ch. 5.), one can treat one's experience as incorrigible, but only at the expense of emptying it of what he calls ontological reference: what is incorrigible is only my having had an experience, not that I experienced a table or God or anything else 'out there' beyond my experience. Even the fact, stressed by many writers on religion including James, that people often change their way of life radically after a profound religious experience does not itself show that their interpretation of the experience as emanating from God is actually correct, for to argue that it was would be tantamount to arguing that the truth of a belief was equivalent to its power to motivate. James glosses over an important distinction here when he expresses this position by saying that 'God is real since he produces real effects' (1902, p. 491), for while it is true that our only direct evidence for electrons, say, is the observable effects they are taken to have, the force of the move from effect to postulated reality is entirely vitiated when, as in this case, the effect depends on the psychological state of a human agent and the postulated reality is taken to be something non-psychological. It is only too common for people to be motivated by false beliefs or hopes, and by experiences which are wrongly interpreted.

The real problem with the religious interpretation of religious experience is that it is quite deficient in explanatory power. The judgment that one has had a divine experience is quite unlike the judgment that one has seen a table in that it appears to lead to no testable independent predictions. Moreover, in many religious traditions, it is a key aspect of religious experience that it is unpredictable. Christians, for example, tend to explain this unpredictability by saying that these experiences are a gift of God. This may be so, but saying it certainly weakens attempts to argue from the experience to the reality, as an important element in such arguments is often an ability to relate the experiences to specific and repeatable conditions.

There are, however, religious traditions such as the Buddhist Visuddhimagga, in which religious experience is not thought of as a gift, but is seen more as what is arrived at when, after intense ascetic practices and effort, one has stripped away certain impediments to religious insight. This view of religious experience accords better than the typical Christian one with the idea that there is a religious sense, which is like the other senses, only veiled or dormant before the effect of spiritual exercises. What might be called the Aldous Huxley view, according to which drugs are the doors to perception of the truly real, is in a way only a variant on this theme. In each case, there is held to exist a mode of perception which needs some sort of release or triggering before it can become active.

There need be no fundamental objection to the idea that one can perceive more or better or in a different way by means of drugs or religious practices. After all, in science and everyday life we are familiar with artificial aids to and extensions of our normal perceptual faculties. What we need to examine, however, is the grounds on which drugs or religious practices could be seen as providing windows on to a 'more extensive and inclusive world', to use James's phrase, and this is really tantamount to asking for the grounds on which the religious experiences we have as a result could be regarded as experiences of an objective sort. In the light of our earlier discussion, the answer will have to be in terms of the explanatory power of the hypothesis that religious experiences are due at least in part to the existence and operation of an objective religious reality, rather than due to merely wordly factors, such as features of a person's psychology, chemistry or upbringing.

The likelihood of an objective reality being causally related to certain experiences will be very much increased if (i) we are able to predict accurately further experiences of our own or others due to our assuming the existence of the reality, (ii) some of these future experiences of our own are experiences of senses other than the original sense involved, and (iii) other people can corroborate what we are perceiving. Condition (i) is simply the requirement that a genuine explanation has independently testable consequences. Condition (ii) is based on the lucky evolutionary chance that our various sensory faculties combine so as to enable us to build up a picture of a single coherent world that can be experienced by different sensory means. As has been pointed out by W. W. Bartley, this piece of evolutionary luck itself provides a strong argument in favour of some sort of realism, for, as he puts it

> The various cognitive structures employed by humans, animals and insects make no sense individually or collectively in their mutual integration, in the way in which they complement one

45

another, check and partly compensate for the inadequacies of one another, in their hierarchical arrangements and controls, except by reference to a common external world in which they function, which they attempt in various ways to represent, and in interaction with which they have evolved. (1982, §8)

Condition (iii) reflects the not unreasonable presumption that if something is objectively real, it will have similar effects on other similar observers similarly placed.

The religious interpretation of religious experience, however, comes off quite badly under all three conditions. Even in those religious traditions where future religious experiences are held to be predictable, given the right ascetic preparation, the experiential predictions are not very precise. Indeed, in the *Visuddhimagga* (§508) it says that belonging to the Aryan way *is* the finding of the existence of Nirvana; there is here at least a hint that one criterion of having correctly performed the exercises and training is the having of the experience, so there is in the prediction that one will have the experience given the training, no genuine independence of test. On the second condition, there is never any suggestion that a truly religious experience is correlated with other types of experience. The characteristic position here is that of St Teresa of Avila, who said that in the prayer of union the soul is wholly asleep as regards things of this world and deprived of every feeling: 'she neither sees, hears, nor understands so long as she is united with God' (quoted by James (1902, p. 394)). Failure on the third condition means that it has to be shown why only certain people in and then only in certain states have experiential access to religious reality.

There are, of course, answers to these objections. Religious experience is a gift, which comes and goes in an unpredictable fashion and only to certain individuals who are blessed with something like an extra sense or who have undergone special training in religious perception. The idea that certain individuals have extra senses is not to be dismissed out of hand, as the example of the sighted man in the kingdom of the blind shows, but it is unclear how much support the religious believer can draw from the analogy, because what gives the sighted man his epistemological strength is his ability to anticipate future experiences in a way the blind cannot. Indeed, we could imagine him being able to convince his blind peers that he did have an extra sense because they are able to cross-check some of his predictions with the senses they do have. But this sort of cross-checking with other senses does not apply in the religious case. This does not show that there is no religious sense, of course, nor that the non-religious are right to reject the idea. After all, as Ayer has pointed out (1976, p. 6), the sighted man might have been unable to correlate his visual experiences with tactile or auditory experiences, yet he would still have every right to insist on his extra sense, and the blind people would be wrong to reject his claims. But the argument for such a dissociated sense, giving insight into a real world, even for the sighted man himself, would surely depend on his visual experience having a degree of consistency, regularity and predictability, features which are mostly absent in the case of religious experience. As regards special training in perception, I have already suggested that perception of scientific phenomena may require such training, but once again the analogy hardly favours the religious. The biologist who can see things in his microscope which the rest of us cannot see is enabled to make further predictions on the basis of what he sees, what he sees is embedded in a set of theories that certainly do have microscopic effects and he can repeat his observations and reach agreement on them with his peers. However, even among religious people themselves there is no great consensus on descriptions of the content of their religious experience. Not only are such descriptions often prefaced by talk of the impossibility of talk in this area, but the descriptions vary considerably given the culture and background of the describer, again something that is difficult to explain if what we have is akin to a vision of a real world. Thus, we are told by Walter Otto (1954, p. 232) that the classical Greek 'at every turn of life saw the visage of a god', but what he saw must have been entirely and inexplicably different from what was experienced by Mohammed or by Ignatius of Loyola – and it is unclear why in terms of experience, one set of experiences is to be preferred to either of the others.

I do not want to suggest that a religious explanation and interpretation of religious experience is necessarily incorrect, or that there could not be circumstances in which such an explanation was more probable than any other. If people, after praying to a particular God or within a particular religious tradition, often had fairly specific experiences, internal visions and the like, of the divine beings of that religion, the probability that the experiences emanated from those beings would be greater than if the experiences were inconsistent and irregular. The probability of the divine origin of the experiences would be increased if, as a result of the experiences, the believers came to have knowledge of themselves and the world, which was beyond their normal powers and which was at least sometimes later corroborated by other means. The probability of the religious explanation would perhaps be stronger still either if it was only in one religious tradition that such clear and corroborated experiences occurred or if believers from other traditions surprisingly had experiences very similar in content to those had by believers in the favoured religion.

Any or all of these factors would increase the strength of an argument from religious experience to an objective reality although, as I shall suggest shortly, if religious experience became too much like sensory experience and too closely connected to it, there is a danger that it would lack some religiously important features, and the source of the experience would begin to resemble the paranormal of psychic research. However, in practice in religious experience, none of the features of objective experience appears to be present. Religious experiences are not generally predictable, repeatable, nor do they have independently testable consequences or even agree among themselves when they are at all specific. Furthermore, we know that people in states of sensory deprivation or lack of food or under drugs frequently have visions and experiences of an hallucinatory sort. At the same time, we know that people can be moved by very intense feelings as a result of music or some personal relationship or by experiences of nature. In these cases, the feelings need have no specific religious content and those who have the feelings often feel no drive to interpret them religiously. No doubt, the religious believer could argue that these other feelings are really religious experiences, only not perceived as such, but the strength of this line of argument will depend entirely on the plausibility of *his* interpretation of explicitly religious experiences as experiences of an objective reality.

What I am suggesting, then, is first, that religious experiences lack either that degree of independent testability or the degree of regularity which in the case of sensory experience allows us to speak of the experiences supporting our physical object scheme. Second, very similar types of experience to religious experience are known to occur outside specifically religious contexts. Both these points seem to me to weaken very much the religious interpretation of religious experience, and this is something that should be conceded by the religious themselves after they have reflected on what goes to make up objectivity of experience. If it is found, further, that the experiences of loss of self and sensation combined with some sort of ecstasy which are frequently part of a deep religious experience can be produced by bringing about brain activity of a specific sort, and that mystics are in this sort of brain state when in mystical rapture, given the lack of specific content in most such rapture, it might well be possible to explain even the mystical state in terms of brain activity.

The aim of this chapter so far has been to explore the extent to which there is any analogy between religious experience and sensory experience, which would provide some sort of argument from religious experience to a belief in something transcendent. The upshot has been to suggest that sensory experience is related to statements about the physical world and physical objects as explicandum to explicans, the physical world statements at once explaining our sensations and being independently testable, but that this is not so in the religious case. The absence of any independent testability of the statements about the divine which supposedly explain religious experience is almost total. These statements neither lead to future testable predictions, nor are they cross-checkable by others or by other senses. Finally, the experiences themselves are not regular or predictable.

The argument so far has been highly abstract. When we come down to concrete cases and consider specific types of religious experience, we find an important distinction which throws some further light on the relationship between religious experience and religious knowledge, and explains to some degree why religious experience has to be different in some respects from sensory if it is indeed to be religious. The distinction is that between those religious experiences which are conceived of (as in Ignatius of Loyola's *Spiritual Exercises*) as emanating unpredictably and gratuitously from a transcendent divine person, and those which are seen as experiences of some ever-present and ever-available reality, a God beyond attributes, Brahman, the ground of our being, or whatever. Clearly experiences of the first sort cannot be totally regular and predictable. The characterization of their source precludes this. This is tantamount to saying that the religious experiences freely and unpredictably vouchsafed to believers by the God of the orthodox Judaeo-Christian believer, for example, can never have the regularity of ordinary sensory experience nor could they be seen as falling under anything like the laws of physics. If they were like that, they would not be experiences of God suddenly breaking in on you and taking you into Him which St Paul, St Ignatius of Loyola, St Teresa of Avila and the rest thought they had. On the other hand, an experience conceived of as making contact with a permanently present, only ordinarily unperceived, deeper level of reality need have no implications of gratuitousness and unpredictability about it. It is conceivable, despite what I said earlier about the *Visuddhimagga* that techniques might be discovered that, with some degree of success, regularly put adepts in contact with this reality. But then, on this picture, the reality in question is being conceived of fundamentally as open to investigation of an empirical or quasi-empirical sort. A reality that could be regularly and predictably reached in experience ought, one feels, to be taken account of by empirical science, particularly if reaching it leads to further testable consequences; the limits of the scientific should be extended to deal with the most basic force manifested in the universe, of experience, however this is conceived.

What I have just been saying means that either religious experience can never be seen as regular and predictable as sensory experience, or, if it is regular and predictable in this way, it becomes something to be investigated empirically. At the very least, we would want to frame laws covering the regular revelations of some deep level of existence. Of such regular experience of a deeper level of reality, we would naturally ask whether such an ultimate force in the universe could be both within the province of physics and a fit object of religious veneration? Anticipating what will be said at greater length in later chapters on religious explanations, it must be said that this is hard to accept, for while empirical explanations of how things are always end with a substantive determinate reality of a specific sort about which further questions could be asked, religion always seems to be looking for an explanation which is in some sense ultimate about which further questions cannot be put. On the face of it, a reality which, like a psychic force, is conceived of as being experienced regularly and predictably, and hence as subject to empirical investigation is one about which very many more questions could reasonably be asked, about why it is like it is, why it has the content it does and is experienced in the manner in which it is experienced, and so on. Something attainable and experienceable in this sort of way would be neither the ultimate, transcendent and humanly impenetrable divine will which some believers see as the end of explanation, nor is it the propertyless ground of being, the not-this, not-that which religious thinkers from many other traditions postulate as being the only fitting end to questioning and explanation.

The distinction which I have just been drawing has been aptly dubbed by Peter Munz as the two faces of God (cf. Munz, 1981). The point of the distinction is to suggest that there is a tension between two rather different conceptions religious people (and sometimes the same religious people) have of God, or of whatever they are conceiving the ultimate religious reality to be. One of God's faces presents him as a personal being of infinite power and will, who is and remains separate from his creation. In his will, which is ultimately impenetrable and hidden to human beings, is contained the reason for whatever is, and its ultimate direction and purpose. This face reaches its ultimate expression in the voluntarism of Islam, in which human happiness is seen in terms of submission to the divine will, but the underlying picture is shared by orthodox Judaism and Christianity. In God's other face, the radical polarization between God and the world is denied. God is seen as the ground of the world's being, the soil from which the world springs, the world itself sometimes being represented as an emanation from the divine reality. In this conception, the divine reality is characteristically seen as without positive attributes of its own, for any positive attribute would contaminate the purity of that from which all attributes and all things spring. Any positive attribute attached to a specific divine manifestation is regarded as a secondary expression of the divine essence, rather than the essence itself, which is beyond those specific qualities or properties about which further questions might legitimately be asked. God as being itself, and hence indeterminate, from which the world and all determinate beings emerge, and into which they will return is, of course, very much the face of God revealed in Hinduism and Indian thought generally. Nevertheless, the distinction between the two faces does not allow us to categorize religions into two distinct camps, because in all major religious traditions, both faces are recognized. There is a mystical, gnostic tendency in the great monotheisms, while there are specifically dualistic interpretations of Hinduism. And, as I shall suggest in Ch. 6, this is not surprising, for if religion is to be the ultimate stopping point of explanation, both faces are necessary. The great monotheisms in a sense provide a stopping point for further questioning, by appealing to the inscrutable will of God, but this can seem too arbitrary a stopping point, and it is natural to attempt to soften the sheer givenness of the divine will by reinterpreting the divine as something beyond specific willings, as being-itself. On the other hand, seeing God as being-itself, which, in a sense because of the very emptiness of the characterization, raises no further questions of its own, because of that very emptiness fails to explain in any way why the world is as it is; and moreover seeing ourselves as part of Brahman tends to undervalue our sense of our own identity. So Brahman comes to be viewed as not just being-itself, but as something with a will and a personality, and distinct from us.

A further examination of the two faces of God will be made in Ch. 6, but what is clear at this point is that a reality that was regularly and predictably encounterable in experience could not be Brahman, the God beyond attributes, for no experience could be an experience of something beyond all attributes. Any divine manifestation within this context would have to be of some intermediary of the ultimate reality, and not of the reality itself, knowledge of which would have to come from other sources. On the other hand, an experience of the inscrutable God of the monotheistic religions would have to be a gratuitous, and hence unpredictable act of grace on the part of that God, and this is indeed how the great Christian mystics have understood their experiences. However, it could be that even if our experiences of the transcendent Person of the great monotheisms of Judaism, Christianity and Islam were not themselves regular, we were still able to establish some sort of knowledge on the basis of them, because explanations of the experiences in terms of such a Person led to independently testable consequences. The situation here would have some affinity with the situation where a miracle was treated as a sign of the divine Person. For, in both cases we would have events which were necessarily outside the normal causal processes of nature and, hence, unpredictable. (If they were not, then they would be part of the proper subject-matter of the empirical sciences, and not something that we would wish to attribute directly to the intervention of a transcendent God.) From a theistic perspective, there needs to be no insuperable objection to such intervention, but from the human point of view we would have to establish that such an event actually occurred. In the case of a miracle, we would have to establish with reasonable probability that the event was an exception to the normal course of nature, which would seem a reasonable position to take in at least some imaginable cases. An event of this sort could still reasonably be held to have happened if it was observed by numbers of reliable observers and if its effects were checkable by other types of test and systems of observation. In the case of a private religious experience, however, this type of checking would not be possible, and the only independent test that seems to be available would be if the mystic was able, on the basis of the experience, to make testable predictions which we would not think he or she otherwise could. The situation here would be similar to that which obtains in the case of dowsers, mediums, clairvoyants and prophets of various sorts, where a preliminary estimate of the veridicality of the experience in question can be made by cross-checking the predictions that are made on the basis of them, but religious experiences rarely have even that degree of specificity and potential testability. So it seems that in practice, if not in theory, religious experiences emanating from a transcendent divine Person do not, on their own, provide a basis for knowledge of such a Person.

There would, in fact, be a danger for religion in religious experiences which were too fully integrated with ordinary sensory experience. If the experiences were both predictable in themselves and had consequences cross-checkable by empirical means, religion would become in some respects similar to psychic research, in which the aim of many researchers is not so much to establish a transcendent realm as to widen the scope of the empirical sciences. The hope is that the experiences and events themselves will be seen as lawfully predictable and that physical theory will be extended so as to accommodate hitherto paranormal events within its laws. If religious experience became too regular and too closely integrated within the world of ordinary empirical experience, then it would be hard to resist the conclusion that the source of such predictable and empirically effective experience was itself really part of the physical world. But, as I have suggested, religious experience could begin to establish itself as objective without being itself predictable, so long as it led to some testable consequences in the physical world. The fact that it does not means that we cannot use the fact of religious experience to justify or support a belief in God.

It seems, then, that on one main view of religious knowledge – where the object of religious knowledge was beyond attributes – no experience could be an experience of that, while on the other view – where the object of religious knowledge is a transcendent divine will – the experiences believers have do not in fact provide the basis for the independent testing which would give some grounds for thinking of the experiences as veridical. So, on neither view of the ultimate end of religious knowledge can actual religious experience be seen as providing the basis for that knowledge or any guarantee that one is in contact with one of God's ultimate faces, and this despite the fact that we have shown that some features of objective empirical experience would necessarily be absent in the religious case. There is, however, a final position that could be adopted concerning religious experience and religious knowledge, and that is to say that religious experience is not a source of knowledge of anything at all, transcendent or otherwise, but rather a state in which men learn to see and accept the world for what it is and to overcome their own cravings and weaknesses. Some forms of Buddhism would appear to take this attitude to meditation, which would be entirely consistent with the Buddha's repudiation of all metaphysical and theological speculation. With this approach to religious experience, there can be no quarrel from an epistemological point of view, as there are no claims of an epistemological sort made here. Where appeals to religious experience are suspect is when they are used to bolster claims to religious knowledge. For either the claims are such that they either defeat any attempt to talk of experience in their case, or the experiences are such as to defeat any attempt to erect a system of knowledge on them. Our conclusion must be that those who have hoped to by-pass metaphysical argument in religion by a direct appeal to religious experience have failed to understand the logic of empirical support.

NOTES

1   It might be interesting to compare what James says in this passage with his later

Essays on Radical Empiricism (1912). There he asserts, in line with the naive position that seems to be implicit in the passage just quoted, that we see the room and the book before us immediately 'just as they physically exist' (p. 8). But, at the same time, he wants to hold that there is a neutral, primal stuff, neither physical nor mental, neither inner nor outer, but prior to such distinctions, out of which our picture of the world, including the distinctions mentioned, is built. He also goes on to say that a merely hallucinatory experience may not differ in quality from an experience of a physical oject (pp. 17-18). The latter experiences are marked as experiences of physical objects by virtue of their regularity and connections with other experiences. In this, what he says, so far as it goes, is not altogether different from what I argue below in criticism of the 'Mysticism' passage. Indeed, his realization in *Essays on Radical Empiricism* that 'face to face presentation of what seems immediately to exist' are *not* in themselves enough to base rational beliefs makes it especially curious that he was apparently prepared to allow that they might be in *Varieties of Religious Experience*. Of course, even if James himself can be exonerated from this criticism, and it can be shown that he did actually require more from religious experience than that it should be both vivid and have an effect on the lives of those who underwent it (cf. below, p. 44) what I say about what he appears to be arguing in the 'Mysticism' passage will still hold against all those who do attempt to base religious belief on the strength and psychological effects of religious experience, apart from considerations of the sort demanded here.

2   These criteria are intended to be necessary conditions for good explanations, but they are not sufficient, because we could envisage explanations satisfying all these criteria yet still being useless because they failed to be relevant to our interest in seeking an explanation in a given case. My criticism of James's account of religious experience on analogy with sensory experience will be that it fails to satisfy even these purely formal criteria for good explanatory schemes.

3

Religion, Truth and Morality

In this chapter, I will consider the often expressed view that certain fundamental human dispositions presuppose or in some other way make sense only given the existence of a transcendent deity. The particular cases I will focus on concern human intellectual activity and morality. The argument in each case is that there is something about the human practices concerned which makes an appeal to a divine standard of correctness or goodness. It is not always clear whether the argument is supposed to itself be a proof of God's existence, which is taken to follow, given the existence of the human practice, or whether the argument is intended to show that, without a God, the practice would be futile or senseless. Indeed, both types of claim can be found in the literature. Either way, the challenge is for the non-believer to show how the practices involved are not futile in a godless world, but that they can derive all the support and validation they need from features of human nature and the world in which they exist. If this can be shown, and the non-futility of the search for knowledge and of morality in a godless world established, then clearly it cannot be claimed that the existence of the practices provides any proof of the existence of God, so by taking the weaker of the two claims, we may be able to dispose of both at once.

In what follows, I will attempt to show that there is something in the futility claim, that the existence of God could provide a background of intelligibility for morality at least. Nevertheless, I shall argue that there are also purely secular viewpoints from which knowledge and morality can be established at least sufficiently firmly to render them possible and worthwhile even on the assumption that there is no God. Hence the argument fails in both cases, although it has something to teach us and should not be dismissed out of hand, as non-believers are sometimes inclined to do.

Section 1 Knowledge and truth

In this section I shall consider two distinct claims, both of which attempt to show that our cognitive activity requires the existence of God. There is first the claim that our search for knowledge and understanding is ultimately directed towards an infinite being. Then, second, it has been argued that we cannot meaningfully speak of truth if there is no God.

The first of the two claims will be familiar to anyone versed in twentieth-century neo-Thomist thought, but probably unfamiliar to others. Versions of the claim can be found in the writings of Karl Rahner (1968, 1969), Bernard Lonergan (1957), Gaston Isaye (1953) and many others who owe a debt, direct or indirect, to Joseph Maréchal's *Le Point de départ de la métaphysique* (1927-49) and, ultimately, of course, to St Thomas Aquinas himself. There are important differences in the thought of the writers I have mentioned, even regarding the claim about knowledge. Nevertheless, they all share a certain number of assumptions and the overall strategy is the same in each case. So I hope that I will not be distorting what is important in the argument if I present it in a composite version of my own, in which I believe its essence will become clear. That what I am doing is not to travesty the position completely is, let us hope, ensured by basing what I say on a text of Aquinas himself, in which it is claimed that our mind has a natural tendency to reach out to the infinite.

Aquinas writes as follows in the *Summa contra Gentiles* (1.43.10):

> Our mind in its understanding reaches out to the infinite. A sign of this is that whatever finite quality is given, the mind can conceive a greater. Now this orientation of the mind to the infinite would be in vain unless there were an infinite intelligible thing. There must therefore be an infinite intelligible reality, which must be the supreme being, and this we call God.

It is significant that Fr. Copleston (1955, p. 257) glosses 'in vain' in this passage as 'unintelligible and inexplicable', for an immediate reaction to what Aquinas says might be to say that it is not impossible that some aspects of our mental life might simply be 'in vain' in the sense that they are doomed to unfulfilment (for example, and relevantly, the pervasive intellectual desire to find a causal explanation for all phenomena). The argument requires not just 'in vain' in the sense of having an unfulfillable goal, but some more thoroughgoing incoherence, and this is what the neo-Thomists claim to be able to discern. One approach here is to say, following Karl Rahner, that in every judgment we make we are in fact implicitly grasping the Infinite, which would indeed be incoherent were there no such thing. A problem in understanding this claim, however, is that there is a crucial ambiguity in the notion of an anticipating grasp of the Infinite which is not resolved by Rahner's own terminology. (He speaks of a *Vorgriff.*) Does this mean an actual grasping, a real acquaintance, or is it a purely conceptual matter – a grasp of the *concept* of the infinite or of some notion of unlimited existence? If the latter, there is still a need to explain why, in the case of *this* goal, the intellect could not be striving after something unreal. Why is this goal different from attempts to find an elixir of life or a perpetual motion machine? The argument that is then usually given by those who do not see us having straight off an actual grasp of the Infinite amounts to a claim that reality must be completely intelligible or everything that we do in affirming its intelligibility is fundamentally flawed. The complete intelligibility of reality is taken to consist in part in its ability to satisfy the dynamism of our intellect towards the Infinite, and for a total explanation of everything that requires further explanation, which, it is held, can only be provided by an infinite intellect, while we are held to be pre-supposing and affirming this complete intelligibility of reality by the very fact that we find it worthwhile to engage in rational activities, such as seeking for explanations of physical phenomena, discussing theology, and so on. Questioning of this sort is taken to be evidence for the complete intelligibility of reality.

It might be objected at this point that our particular individual rational activities do not presuppose or affirm any view that reality is completely intelligible, nor do they have any dynamism towards the Infinite. Examining the reasons that are given for these claims will perhaps suggest why neo-Thomists find it so central to rationality to assert that God exists and that, as Aquinas puts it, He is known implicitly in everything we know (cf. *De Veritate*, 22, 2 ad 1), but it will also show that there is something fundamentally mistaken in the underlying account of knowledge. According to some versions of this account, whatever we perceive in the world, we perceive as existing. However, *what* we affirm to exist, when we make a judgment that some individual exists, is always something that is perceived as limited, either in the sense that it is merely finite or in the sense that it is not the answer to all the questions we could put either about it or about other things. According to Rahner, in fact (1969, pp. 183-7), it is actually a condition of seeing some object as limited that we have an implicit grasp of some positively infinite being. Every time we encounter a limit of being or a limit of intelligibility, the dynamism of our intellect drives us to transcend the limits we encounter. This is because, although we apply the predicate of existence to all the things we encounter, we are never able in the world to apply it unrestrictedly. Rahner speaks characteristically of infinite being as the unobjective Horizon of every act of affirmation. Equally, from the side of understanding, no explanation we ever find is the total explanation of everything or totally intelligible in itself. What we are after is pure Being and total intelligibility – something which just is, which requires no further explanation for itself, but which is the ground of everything else we encounter, which is limited and never fully intelligible. In the words of Joseph Donceel:

> What our intellect is really after in every one of its activities is: to meet and to grasp a reality which fully deserves the predicate IS, a reality which is not merely this or that, a reality which simply IS, without any specification, determination, negation, or limitation. (1973, p. 169)

Lonergan's position is somewhat more complicated and somewhat different from the Rahner-Donceel talk of grasping the Infinite, or seeing God as the Horizon of all our intellectual activity. Indeed, according to Lonergan, we do not grasp God at all in any direct way; we can only reason indirectly to his being the natural end of our intellectual activity. Nevertheless, Lonergan's argument amounts in the end to the same sort of claim as that presented in the other neo-Thomists we are considering.

According to Lonergan, in our restricted inquiries about specific things, we are giving evidence of a quite general and unrestricted desire to know: a desire to understand completely. Lonergan calls the arbitrary closing-off of questioning at any point obscurantism, and argues that the universe appears to the various levels and perspectives implied by different sorts of human intellectual activity by being intelligible in the ways implied by those perspectives (scientific, mathematical, and so on), and ultimately by being completely intelligible. This desire we have for a complete understanding of everything is for Lonergan nothing other than a desire to answer the quite general question 'What is being?', for everything that is, is being, and apart from being, there is nothing. Thus the core of all our thought and intentionality is being. Although in our particular inquiries, we prescind from tackling the question 'What is being?', admitting the naturalness and force of this most general and pervasive question is the only way to stave off obscurantism. In a key passage, Lonergan writes:

> Being is the objective of the unrestricted desire to know.
> Therefore, the idea of being is the content of an unrestricted act of understanding. Again, apart from being there is nothing.
> Therefore, the idea of being is the content of an act of understanding that leaves nothing to be understood, no further questions to be asked. But one cannot go beyond an act of understanding that leaves no questions to be asked, and so the idea of being is absolutely transcendent. (1957, p. 644)

It is true that, unlike Donceel, Lonergan does not speak of the notion of being as lacking all specifications and determinations. On the contrary, he goes on to speak of the idea of being as 'the content of an understanding that grasps everything about everything', and being itself as an immaterial and unrestricted unity, whose primary activity is total and instantaneous self-knowledge, and which grasps everything about everything by grasping itself. This sort of characterization of God (for Lonergan goes on to identify being with God) clearly derives from the Aristotelian strains in the thought of Aquinas, some of the specific problems concerning which we will examine in later chapters. Nevertheless, it is worth saying here that the idea that something could be completely and instantaneously self-conscious seems to involve the difficulty of explaining how an introspecting agent could, while introspecting, introspect its current act of introspection. Nor is it clear how, simply by introspecting, God could know everything about everything else if, as Christian theists like Lonergan hold, some beings in the universe have an existence that is not completely pre-determined by the mind of God (cf. below, pp. 218-19).

However, where Lonergan's analysis of judgment is most open to question, and what leads me to say that it is in fact close to those of Rahner, Donceel and the others, is in the way he takes being as such to be the object of the unrestricted desire to know. My objection here is that a desire to know everything completely is entirely misconstrued by being thought of as a desire to know being, for knowing being would be to know something so general as to know nothing at all. This is presumably the reason why Lonergan is able to claim, in the passage quoted above, that the idea of being leaves no further questions to be asked. It could leave no further questions to be asked only because it is in itself so general or 'transcendent' that it raises no further questions. But it is precisely because of the empty generality of the notion of being (whatever is, is being) that Lonergan can with any semblance of plausibility identify our search for explanations of everything with a desire to answer the question 'What is being?'. That, despite his later attempts to concretize the idea of being, Lonergan never really escapes from the empty contentless notion of being is suggested by the way he insists on being as a simple, single, unchanging unity. Change and complexity would presumably make being over-specific, and difficult to see it as the self-explanatory ground of all else, for changes and complexities would inevitably raise questions as to why they were as they were. On the other hand, as we shall see in Ch. 4, Section 4, it is hard to see how a non-changing being could have knowledge of this world of free agents. Lonergan is in fact involved in the same difficulties as Aquinas in trying to have God as pure being, simple and unchanging and hence as raising no further questions, on the one hand, and as a person, entering into genuine relationships with people in the world, on the other. So, while Lonergan does show some awareness of the emptiness involved in talk of having the idea of being as the content of a complete act of understanding (by insisting that such an understanding would in fact grasp everything about everything), his argument to taking the idea of being as having such a content only appears to work at all because he takes being as the most general thing there is, a category under which everything is included. Only thus could it possibly seem plausible that knowing everything about everything could be achieved in one single, unitary and unchanging perception, even on the part of God, rather than through the grasp of a great many extremely complicated propositions. It is, in any case, entirely to misunderstand our search for explanations of whatever exists to think of it as pointing logically and inevitably towards such a single and simple act of understanding, rather than towards grasping ever more detailed and more precise aggregates of facts and laws.

What is central to the neo-Thomist position, then, is the idea that the dynamism of our intellect is to attempt to move away from limits, in the direction of *pure* being, to something unrestricted, undetermined. Whatever we are acquainted with *is*, so what we are really after is existence pure and simple. The unrestricted desire to know of Lonergan turns out to be a desire to know something as unrestricted as being itself. In these subtle shifts are contained what is most seriously wrong with the position. For when we reflect on knowledge, we see that there could be no knowledge that fails to define (and hence to limit) its object in some way. Propositional knowledge, knowledge that something is the case, is clearly logically dependent on the understanding of *what* it is that is the case, and this presupposes a grasp of something definite and determinate. Even when I might be said to know a thing or a person by acquaintance, my perception of that person or thing is always a perception of it under some category or class of thing. Of course, this defining of the thing means marking it off from what surrounds it, but it is quite unclear why what surrounds it should be regarded as actually infinite, as Rahner claims. Moreover, when we speak of attempting to transcend the limits of our knowledge, this should not be understood as attempting to wipe away what is clear and distinct in our knowledge, or in terms of seeing our knowledge in terms of answering the question 'What is being?', but rather in terms of making our knowledge less inadequate, and this means making it *more* precise or bringing more things under more specific descriptions. In doing the latter, of course, we are embarking on the programme of natural science, and, as Popper and many other writers on natural science have demonstrated, claims to be extending our knowledge by postulating general laws and descriptions for whole categories of apparently different types of phenomena must always be judged and assessed in terms of their precise predictive power, otherwise the lumping together of different things will be a questionable gain in understanding their true nature. This is precisely why saying that all our knowledge is of being or of beings is so empty, because from the fact that whatever is, is a being, or is understood as being a being absolutely no predictions whatsoever follow about the behaviour of any individual. Contrast this with the type of case common in natural science where apparently unconnected natural kinds, such as whales and horses, are shown, surprisingly, to be classsifiable as members of the same zoological class. From that knowledge and from knowledge of the class, we will be able to make plenty of precise predictions of the future behaviour of individual whales and horses, and we will have attached a clear sense to the claim that we now understand them better. In a demonstrable way, we will have transcended the limits of our knowledge, but in doing it what we know has gained, rather than lost, in clarity and distinctness.

We do, of course, seek ever more fundamental explanations. This is what is right in talk of the dynamism of human knowledge, and of an unrestricted desire to know. At times, even, we do this in a disinterested way, beyond what could have any immediate practical applicability. Human beings do indeed have a sense of wonder and curiosity for its own sake. But it is a travesty of the drive for understanding to construe it as a desire for knowledge of what simply IS. 'Knowing' that there is (a) pure being provides no explanation of what actually is. It cannot explain why things that exist have the specific properties they do in a causal way, or even in a teleological way. For (a) pure being can hardly be credited with such anthropomorphic traits as intentions or even with attractiveness to worldly things, for in attributing such qualities to it we are thereby contaminating its purity. More radically, it is extremely unclear how speaking of something that simply IS is to convey anything at all. Some definite thing or quality or description can be said informatively to exist in the sense of being actually instantiated in the world. Thus 'Moses existed', 'roses exist' or 'The king of France exists' are informative, because here what is at issue in these cases is the instantiation of some specific being or description or property. But 'There exists something' or 'This exists' or 'Kashkei exists' convey nothing at all about what it is that exists – unless we know what sort of thing the something is, or what type of thing the demonstrative or name is referring to. It is a travesty of our intellectual dynamism to read it as entailing that what we are really after in our knowledge is something so vague (a reality that simply IS with no other identifying feature) that talk of it is of doubtful significance. As Hegel had clearly seen, the notion of being, abstracted from all particular determinations of beings, is exactly equivalent to nothingness, with or without a capital 'N' (cf. Scruton, 1981, p. 170).

Many neo-Thomists will naturally follow Aquinas himself and surreptitiously identify the God of their natural theology, even if that God turns out to be the reality that simply IS, with that which all men call God, with all God's traditional properties. Many people have seen *this* being as having considerable explanatory power, and this is a claim that we will consider in detail in the next chapter. But in so far as God is allowed to be powerful, knowing, loving and so on he is hardly the unspecific, undetermined being that will be arrived at if we remove all determinations (or 'limitations') from the things that we do know. It might be said that we *have* to speak of God as unspecific and undetermined because any attempt to specify or determine what He is, will distort His true superhuman nature. This is doubtless Aquinas's motivation in saying that we can say of God only what he is not and not what he is. But how far this act of reverence is consistent with Christian belief is open to question: more to the present point, if we can ascribe no properties to God in any way at all it will be disastrous to both theology and religion, for we will be left with no idea at all of what it is we are speaking about or worshipping. We will in fact be left in a situation where the unintentionally perceptive remark of the Japanese Buddhist to Heidegger, that 'to us, the Void is highest name for what you like to express by the word "Being"', will be equally apposite to this qualityless God, who just IS. (This might seem funny rather than tragic, were it not for the fact that such a conception does indeed appear to govern the lives and thinking of many contemporary theologians.)

The tendency of Thomists is to see our intellectual strivings as being futile if they do not lead to something infinite, pure being or total intelligibility. The notion of pure being is, as we have seen, entirely empty of content. Total intelligibility, in the sense of a final and ultimate explanation of everything is, on examination, equally puzzling, and, in the hands of Aquinas, turns out to involve a notion of a pure being, whose essence is to exist. Lonergan, it is true, does not say this, but does speak of God, the object of our unrestricted desire to know, as self-explanatory. The reason why a self-explanatory explanation of everything, including itself, is puzzling is because every explanation of one phenomenon (the explicandum) works by explaining it in terms of something else (the explicans). Even if the explicans is psychologically more familiar than the explicandum (which is often not the case with scientific explanations in which very peculiar things indeed are held to explain visible phenomena), the explanation itself cannot contain an explanation of the explicans. For that another explanation will be needed, in which the old explicans features as a new explicandum. This is why, logically, no explanation is ever a complete one, and why science has no natural end, which could logically be perceived as the point at which no further questions can be asked. However basic we get in science, we can always ask further questions about why the most fundamental level of matter we have reached is as it is, and if we did by chance stumble on the most basic facts about matter, we would never actually succeed in finding a scientific explanation for them because there would not be one, but this would not stop us being able to ask why the ultimate facts are as they are.

The theologian might see this as the chance for him to introduce appeals to God and his intentions to explain why matter is as it is, but on the face of it, we could equally well ask questions about why God is as he is, and why he has the intentions he does. Far from partial explanations being futile unless based in a 'total' explanation, the notion of a total explanation is itself a logical absurdity, involving as it does an explicans which explains itself. It is no doubt due to a realization of the absurdity of a *self*-explanatory explanation that Aquinas insists in his cosmological arguments that God is a completely different type of cause from anything else (for further causal questions could surely be asked about God if he was an ordinary cause), and, in an attempt to make his existence self-explanatory, goes on to speak of his *essence* being to exist, and says that the name 'God' 'does not signify any particular form, but existence itself (ipsum esse)' (*Summa Theologiae*, la. 13, 11). But far from this talk pointing to an ultimate explanation, it is precisely an assertion of the 'pure' being that is so empty of content as to refer to nothing at all. Whether Aquinas, despite his words here, believed all the time that God is just pure existence in the sense of being without any form is open to question, as one of the main planks of his system is the doctrine that perfections such as wisdom and goodness can be meaningfully and truly ascribed to God, by means of analogy. It is hard to see how God's purity of being is preserved if he is actually a personality with various perfections and intentions. What may be happening here is that Aquinas realized the importance of maintaining that God is causally independent, and requires no cause for his existence, and this is what leads him to speak of God as the being whose essence it is to exist. This is perhaps strange even from his own point of view, as he is quite clear about rejecting the ontological argument, according to which we cannot deny that God exists once we perceive that his essence is to exist, but more damaging philosophically in leading him to refer to 'God' as signifying no form but existence itself, which is no doubt the cue from which the modern neo-Thomists take their doctrine of a reality which simply IS, without any specification, determination, negation or limitation. (These points about being and Aquinas's views on God's essence will be taken up again when we consider God as necessarily existing, in Ch. 4, Part 3.)

So we should not construe our intellectual dynamism as leading us to require a pure being, whose function is to stop all further search for explanations. 'Pure' existence could do this only in the Zen sense of being a concept to boggle and paralyse the mind, and we have seen that the reason for this is that talk of existence is logically empty unless wedded to some idea of the sort of thing whose existence is in question. The notion of being as self-explanatory is additionally problematic, involving as it does the obscurity of a self-explanatory explanation. However, these negative conclusions about the neo-Thomist view of the end or goal of our intellectual activity should not lead us to overlook the fact that there is an important insight underlying their talk of an intellectual dynamism. This is precisely the fact that no particular judgment or explanation can be self-sufficient. To put it another way, none of our judgments or explanations can be satisfactorily regarded as ultimate. In this sense, there is indeed a horizon, which is forever receding, against which we might indeed speak of all our knowledge as limited, so long as this does not lead us to think that there could ever actually be total explanations of experience which would legitimately close off all further demand for explanation. Although, in order to live, there comes a point at which each individual person has to stop his or her own questioning and learn to live with a brute, unexplained fact or set of facts, it is sobering to be reminded that in themselves the 'facts' on which we base our lives are always uncertain, provisional and in a sense in need of further explanation, even if this is a need we personally learn not to feel. Talk of all our knowledge as limited can certainly help us to appreciate the provisional nature of our knowledge and the intermediate status of our explanations, though it must be added that total intelligibility is necessarily unrealizable (which is actually part of the reason for the intermediate status of any actually existing explanation).

The realization that no explanation can ever be ultimate does not, of course, mean that particular explanations are not useful for all sorts of purposes or sources of wonder and amazement. Relative to particular interests, a partial explanation may be perfectly satisfying, even if, as the neo-Thomists insist, it can never close off all questioning. But it would be a strange, almost diseased, cast of mind which regarded, say, all biological and geological accounts of specific phenomena as useless because we do not know the reasons for the Big Bang, or even whether there was such a thing. Nor do we need to assert, as Lonergan apparently does, that partial explanations are possible only given a total explanation. For we know from experience that partial explanations are possible and, on reflection, we see that a total explanation is logically impossible. Moreover, our search for explanations, although an unendable quest, is not less worthwhile or valid because it is unending. As has already been said, the quest continually leads to all sorts of useful and fascinating discoveries, which people find fascinating and useful enough without feeling any need to compare them with the chimerical total explanation.

The impossibility of ultimate explanations, and the hope (or desire) that an Infinite being might be the means to overcoming the impossibility connects closely with the idea that without some ultimate and self-validating standard of truth (again seen in divine terms), it is meaningless to speak of truth. This idea has been discussed by Leszek Kolakowski (1982, pp. 82-90), in a way which clearly brings out its implications. According to Kolakowski, the legitimate application of the predicate 'true' to any of our beliefs requires the existence of some Absolute standard of truth, or there can be no foundation for talk of truth because we will have no guarantee that the concept has any genuine application. Our own procedures of justification fall foul of the traditional sceptical arguments, and fail to show us that anything we believe to be true really is the case independently of our thinking it true. Any standard we use can itself be questioned for its correctness, so we are faced with the unsatisfactory choice of either an infinite regress of justifications or an arbitrary and unjustifiable decision to close off further questioning at some point. To defend our standards of justification by appeal to the technological success of our science will be unavailing. To regard truth as efficacy is not logically absurd, but it is actually an example of an epistemologically arbitrary decision, because we cannot justify the belief that what works well for us is actually true, irrespective of our own faith that it is. In fact, according to Kolakowski, science can proceed quite well without a notion of truth; 'logically it does not need to presuppose that what is acceptable according to its criteria should also be true' (1982, p. 84). This indeed is part of the sceptic's position – that talk of truth can be dispensed with for all practical purposes, and, in view of the widely recognized failure of epistemologists to find any fully justified standard of truth, would be better being dropped. So, finding the sceptical dilemma unanswerable, Kolakowski holds that meaningful talk of truth requires an assurance that something is true. We cannot be sure that any of our beliefs are true. Only an omniscient subject could have that assurance, because only such a subject could be sure that his own knowledge of reality would not be undermined by a wider perspective. So only if such a subject exists, do any beliefs guaranteed to be true exist. Hence, on Kolakowski's view, talk of truth requires the existence of an omniscient being. 'Either God or a cognitive nihilism, there is nothing in between' (1982, p. 90).

It is true that Kolakowski does not regard these reflections on truth as a proof of God's existence. Rather he sees them as exposing a dire consequence of non-belief, similar to the ethical nihilism Dostoyevksy and Nietzsche see as the consequence of atheism. Nor does Kolakowski make a simple and erroneous conflation of criteria for truth and what truth is. He defines truth as correspondence with what actually is, and does not assert that the existence of an omniscient being gives us fallible creatures any standard by which to judge truth. What the existence of God is held to provide us with is not knowledge of which things are true, but knowledge that there are true beliefs, at least in God's mind. What Kolakowski's argument appears to be resting on is a principle to the effect that for a concept to be meaningful, we have to think of it as having some justified applications.

It is by no means clear that any such principle is valid. We can surely speak meaningfully of such things as the intra-Mercurial planet or the philosophers' stone or the cure for the common cold, though we firmly believe that there are no justified applications of any of these concepts. It might be urged that these concepts are meaningful to us because we have some idea of the conditions under which they might be justifiably applied. But this is not Kolakowski's position on truth. He does not think that knowing of God's perfect knowledge will actually help us to know the conditions under which our beliefs might be true. In any case, in a perfectly straightforward sense we do know the conditions under which our beliefs are true. 'Snow is white' is true if and only if snow is white, 'Grass is green', is true if and only if grass is green, and so on, for all our beliefs.

The semantic theory of truth, alluded to in the last sentence, shows us clearly what the truth-conditions are for any sentence in any language we understand. If we regard the law of excluded middle (p or not - p) as applying to all, or at least to some of the sentences in our language (and we surely do believe this), then we know that for those sentences to which the law applies, either they or their negations are true. So, in the case of the host of disjunctions to which we regard the law of excluded middle as applying, we know that the predicate true applies to one or other of the disjuncts. So we know that truth does have an application to our language, even before we raise any epistemological questions about how we might know which of the disjuncts is true.

Thus, on purely logical grounds we can see that truth does have both an application and a meaning, without invoking omniscient beings, or indeed any epistemological considerations at all. To that extent, what Kolakowski says about truth must appear simply confused, as it is based on epistemological scepticism. What he might say at this point is that what we are really interested in when we speak of truth is not its formal logical properties, but its actual application, and this is why epistemological theses are relevant. What is the use of speaking of truth, if we can never be sure of when we have grasped it or when we are approaching it? However, if he did say this, we could point out that, on his own admission, God's possession of justified standards of judgment is not in itself going to help us to discover what those standards might be.

So the question both for Kolakowski and the non-believer is actually exactly the same. Does the fact that we know some propositions are true (one disjunct from each of the members of a certain set of disjuncts, or those propositions accepted by God as true) have any genuine role when purely human standards of judgment cannot be an infallible guide to truth? This way of putting the question seems to me to be the right way, because it shows that whether one is a believer in an omniscient being or not, we have no standards for judging truth other than our own. Even what a preacher claims are messages from God would have to be assessed by us for their divine credentials, so direct appeal to God cannot help us here. We can, of course, regard truth as a regulative ideal, but saying this is of very little point unless it could be shown to be an ideal which we might on some occasions justifiably regard ourselves as getting nearer to. To attempt to show this is to do nothing less than embark on a whole programme of epistemology. Without actually attempting anything of this sort, one can suggest that the stark dilemma posed by Kolakowski can be somewhat softened by pointing out that the infinite regress of justifications is only a theoretical infinite regress, and then one can provisionally stop it at the points where we find strategies which have proved to work well up to now in increasing our knowledge of the world and its mechanisms, subject of course to the same strategies delivering the goods in the future. Thus, for example, we might regard survival of severe tests as one of the standards by which scientific theories are to be judged. And to say this is not to conflate scientific truth with efficacy, because implicit in the claim that severe testing is important to science is the recognition that for all practical purposes, plenty of theories that have failed severe tests are extremely efficacious for technological purposes. But from the point of view of the claims of Kolakowski, what is significant is that we have shown that the non-believer can attach a perfectly good meaning to the concept of truth and even specify cases where it applies, while the believer does not escape from the limitations of human knowledge and the consequent need to examine and assess its claims while all the time remaining within a human perspective, simply because he is assured that an omniscient being exists and is sure of what he knows.

Section 2   Religion and morality

Plato's *Euthyphro* raises the question of the relationship between
morality and religion by means of a famous dilemma. The dilemma
consists of asking whether what is holy is holy because the gods
love it or whether the gods love the holy because it is holy. Each
horn of the dilemma has problems. If the holy is what it is because
the gods love it, this seems to suggest that when the gods love the
holy they are simply loving what they love, which is singularly
uninformative. If, on the other hand, the gods love the holy
because of its holiness, this suggests there is some god-independent
criterion of holiness which, in the dialogue, Euthyphro is unable to
specify.

The Platonic dialogue is much more problematic than it seems at
first sight. For one thing it is complicated by the fact that the gods
referred to in it are not themselves particularly holy. Moreover
there are difficulties in interpreting the Greek idea of holiness.
Finally, Socrates' strategy in the dialogue is one of exposing his
protagonist's inability to come up with a satisfactory formal definition of the concept at issue; but that this inability demonstrates an
incoherence in the concept itself or in anyone's grasp of the
concept has been dubbed by Geach (1969, p. 40) 'Socrates' fallacy',
on the grounds that there are plenty of concepts we use every day
without misunderstanding, but which we could not define.

Rather than examining the minutiae of the dialogue, it would be
better to rephrase the dilemma in a way in which it bears directly
on contemporary moral and religious thinking. We can ask
whether the moral good is good because God has willed it, or
whether God has willed the good because it is good. The first horn
of the dilemma makes goodness dependent on God, but seems to
introduce an arbitrariness into the matter, by excluding any
questions that might appear reasonable to ask about the goodness
of God's will. Moreover, it seems to make our recognition of
something as morally good dependent on recognizing it as willed
by God, whereas, since Kant at least, it has been customary to
claim that part of what is involved in recognizing something as a
revealed expression of God's will is the independent recognition
that it is good. So the Kantian tradition would push us towards the
second horn of the dilemma. Accepting that God wills what he
wills because it is good implies that there is an independent
criterion of goodness which God is bound by. It also suggests that

we, as human beings, set ourselves up in judgment of God's deeds in the light of our understanding of the independent criterion. While this may be a calmly rational position, it is not one that commends itself to religious thinkers who would not wish God's ways to be judged by human criteria. Isaiah, Kierkegaard and the whole of Islamic thought would regard such pretensions as shallow in the extreme. Who are we to understand the mysteries of divine goodness? Why should we be able to perceive God's intentions or his plans? Is it not blasphemous to suppose we could? But to say this leaves us unable to do anything but accept that what God is revealed as wanting and doing must be morally good. If God tells us not to eat pork, eating pork is bad, even if there is no humanly perceptible reason for such a prohibition. If, as in the case of Abraham, we are told by God to kill our children, well, as Kierkegaard insists, that must be good too. And it is at this point, of course, that most people begin to turn back to the Kantian position. Surely there are some things that we know in advance of any revelation of God, that a good God would not order or permit, and we bring this knowledge with us when we assess the claims of a revelation or the worthiness of a divine being to be worshipped.

A way out of the dilemma has been suggested by a number of philosophers, following in the footsteps of Hobbes, notably P.T. Geach (1969, Ch. 9) and Hugo Meynell (1972). Hobbes said that 'God declareth his laws by the dictates of natural reason.' Following this hint, it is possible to analyse the situation like this. Men, by rational reflection, are able to see that certain types of act are good and others bad. Using this natural knowledge, they are thus able to consider and judge purported revelations in which God is said to speak. Having decided that a certain revelation is a revelation of the true God, they may then discover further facts about what God has decided morally and so refine and embellish their natural knowledge of morality. In this way the epistemological primacy insisted on by Kant of human judgment over revelation is preserved. Men do and should use their natural knowledge of good and evil to scrutinize religious claims. However, this epistemological primacy of reason does not mean that God is subject to some external moral constraint, because human reason and what it perceives as good and bad is part of God's creation and a reflection of his will. In this way a religious philosopher can accept part of each horn of the dilemma, while avoiding the religiously unpalatable consequences of either horn.

Neat as this resolution of the dilemma is, it still leaves some problems for us. Morality is seen from the perspective of Geach and Meynell as directly dependent on God's will and commands, even though it may not initially appear as such. It is true that Meynell defines moral goodness in terms of what contributes to human happiness and fulfilment, but for this to fit in with his analysis of the dilemma, it must be understood in terms of what God has intended to count as human happiness and fulfilment, or God would be subject to some criterion of goodness that was not dependent on him. But there is always the possibility that men might take a different view of their fulfilment, as Satan did in *Paradise Lost* or indeed as Adam did in wanting to taste the tree of knowledge. The religious view would regard human nature as something given to us by God and not as something for men to make something of. In making something of it, they might wish to go against the divine blueprint, certainly as it is laid down in revelation, but such a desire must appear the ultimate hubris to the religious.

Geach is perhaps more candid, for he moves straight from the Hobbes quotation to dealing with the question 'Why should I obey God's law?' The answer given by Geach is that it would be sheer insanity to defy an almighty God, and in reply to a supposed objector who says that this is plain power-worship, he says

> So it is: but it is worship of the Supreme power, and as such is
> wholly different from, and does not carry with it, a cringing
> attitude towards earthly powers. An earthly potentate does not
> compete with God, even unsuccessfully: he may threaten all
> manner of afflictions, but only from God's hands can any
> affliction actually come upon us. If we fully realize this, then we
> shall have such fear of God as destroys all earthly fear.
> (1969, p. 127)

So the fulfilment that God has in mind for us is one that is reinforced by what Geach later refers to as 'an ultimate suasion'. Both Geach and Meynell, incidentally, argue that without such a suasion, morality would be profoundly senseless. Geach says that the only 'relevant and rational' reply to the question 'Why shouldn't I?' is an appeal to something the questioner wants, while

Meynell (like Kant) speaks of moral tragedy resulting from the non-existence of God, for in this world, the wicked often flourish and suffering triumphs. What the non-believer has to do in the face of such claims is to show how without any ultimate suasion or divine redressing of balances, morality can still be a viable project.

Whatever might be said in the end about the basis of attempts to resolve the Euthyphro dilemma, examination of the dilemma does show that there can be no straightforward reduction of morality to divine commands, accepted as such independently of human perception of good and evil. Such a reduction would make morality into a submissive obedience to a power that could not in any other way be regarded as good. But this would be a very one-sided picture of morality, for a large part of what is involved in morality is the cultivation of attitudes of respect for other people and the consideration of what might contribute to their good. We want to leave open what logical space is required to be able to rebel on moral grounds against a supreme power whose edicts could in no way be regarded as leading to some hoped-for good for human beings, and this certainly involves making a logical distinction between a divine command and a judgment that it is morally good.

Insisting on the logical distinction between morality and divine commands however, does not do anything like full justice to the widespread feeling that morality and religion are so intimately connected that without religion, moral obligation will appear less than absolute and morality itself will lack any ultimate rationale. It is unfortunate that this feeling is often analysed in terms of a religionless morality lacking an ultimate sanction, for if this was all that there was to the matter it could perhaps be dismissed as involving a view of morality as dependent on rewards and punishments, and hence as indistinguishable in the long term from prudence. Once again, one wants to be able to say that whether one chooses to act on moral grounds or on prudential grounds, there must be logically a potential distinction between what it is in my own interest to do and what is demanded by a consideration of what is morally right. Moreover, not all religions involve a belief in a life after death in which the good will be rewarded and the wicked punished. Some of those that do not still provide a framework within which morality is given a religious foundation by being seen as part of a scheme that transcends the limits of human lives and concerns. Thus there is in rabbinical thought a considerable degree of agnosticism and even scepticism concerning an afterlife, but men are still expected to act with dignity befitting those made in God's image. The Buddha, too, rejected all speculation about an afterlife. Even if we regard karma and the quest for Nirvana as implying some sort of moral sanction, in Mahayana Buddhism there is great regard for the bodhisattvas, those who forego Nirvana, so as to be born again to help future men to enlightenment.

Although it is unfortunate that we tend to see the interconnection between religion and morality in terms of the connection between Christianity and morality, because of the centrality of reward and punishment in Christianity, there are, even in Christianity, elements of a less prudential and more other-regarding approach to morality, encapsulated in the notion that all men are sons of God and should be treated accordingly. What we need to consider now is the way in which religions typically provide a metaphysical setting from which specific moral attitudes to other people and to the world itself follow naturally, and to consider how far the absence of such a setting might undermine what we would regard as basic moral attitudes. The temptation for the non-religious is that having considered the Euthyphro dilemma and concluded that moral judgments are in some sense logically distinct from factual beliefs, even beliefs about divine commands, one will regard oneself as in a position to choose whatever morality one likes, even a basically Christian one, overlooking the fact that many of the moral values of Christianity derive from fundamentally religious beliefs about the nature of man as God's creation, the consequent sanctity of life and so on – even if a philosophically enlightened Christian might regard himself as choosing his moral values in abstraction from what he saw as God's direct and revealed commands. The fact is that even if value judgments are logically independent of factual judgments, beliefs about what one regards as facts about the nature and destiny of men inevitably provide the conceptual background for one's moral attitudes. Thus, for example, one's attitudes to abortion and euthanasia would inevitably be coloured by a belief that life is a sacred gift from God, and also by a belief that human life has no non-biological source. Equally, one's attitude to capital punishment and to war will be affected through and through by what one thinks about an afterlife. (For a non-believer there can be no

Crusade or Holy War, as this has been understood in some theistic religions.) It is not that these beliefs *determine* one's moral attitudes, it is rather that they will necessarily form part of the argumentative framework in which one will formulate and justify one's moral positions. In this sense a moral discussion between a Buddhist and a Thomist theologian on the rights and wrongs of killing animals to eat (to take another example) may very well never really get under way at that level, because of the absence of any shared belief between the two protagonists on the nature of life and the universe.

Nietzsche's irony regarding the moral attitudes of some nineteenth-century English atheists is not undeserved:

> They have got rid of the Christian God, and now feel obliged to cling all the more firmly to Christian morality: that is *English* consistency. . . . If the English really do believe they know, of their own accord, 'intuitively', what is good and evil; if they consequently think they no longer have need of Christianity as a guarantee of morality; that is merely the *consequence* of the ascendancy of Christian evaluation and an expression of the *strength* and *depth* of that ascendancy: so that the origin of English morality has been forgotten, so that the highly conditional nature of its right to exist is no longer felt. For the Englishman morality is not yet a problem. . . . (1888, pp. 69-70)

The point is that Christianity, with its beliefs about human destiny, about what is good for man and what will promote human happiness (summed up in Augustine's 'our hearts are restless till they rest in Thee') presents the believer with a context in which submission to God's will and the attitudes such as compassion and charity which follow from this submission can readily be seen as promoting a harmonious life, both for the individual and society. But once the beliefs have gone, the grounding in which these particular virtues have been seen as promoting human well-being has been taken away, and something more than moralizing intuition is needed to justify them. Indeed, one suspects that the intuitions may be no more than the penumbra of reverence that attaches to the virtues even when their metaphysical underpinning has been removed.

Some, concerned to stress the objectivity of morality, have seen it not as stemming either directly or indirectly from the divine will, but as deriving from an objectively existing Platonic good, or from non-natural moral properties. The good is seen as really existing and also, like Goethe's eternal feminine, as leading us on, and moral knowledge is seen as insight into and attraction by the good. Clearly such a transcendent object or set of properties are extremely hard to justify empirically, and so is explaining how they are connected to the natural features of good and bad actions, for on this view the natural fact that gratuitous cruelty causes suffering, say, cannot alone be the reason for its moral wrongness, which presumably stems from its participation in the bad or its possession of non-natural badness, but it might be supposed that a religious belief in a transcendent spiritual realm could provide a context for Platonic forms or for non-natural values. Certainly such things look very much like religious objects, with their supposed transcendence of human desire and their intrinsic desirability.

Nietzsche says in *The Genealogy of Morals* (§24) that if there is no God, everything is permitted. This may seem too stark an account of the relationship between religion and morality, and suspiciously close to the view that without rewards and punishments after death there could be no reason for men to devise moral codes and to follow them in their own conduct. Any human society will require standards of conduct from its members, and there can be arguments and discussion about what these standards should be and how they should be passed on to the young. It is possible to imagine well-regulated societies such as that of Regulus in which each member of the society will feel that, as a member of that society, he has a personal reason for abiding by the precepts of the society, even if he could sometimes get away with breaking them. People can feel committed to interests wider than their own private well-being, even when there is no question of any ultimate sanction. Nevertheless, it might be said both by a religious believer and by his Nietzschean shadow that in the absence of any transcendent perspective on human life, in which each human being is seen, say, as a son (or daughter) of God, or as embodying a divine spark, it is hard to see why people are to be regarded as worthy of the individual respect and consideration moral theorists characteristically insist on. A purely biological perspective will give no grounding to individual rights, and might tend to a sort of Social Darwinism, in which individuals would be seen in terms of their contribution to the survival and improvement of the species or society, while appealing to the fact that human beings are centres of consciousness and of pleasure and pain will not serve as a basis for any rights we are not equally prepared to accord animals. (Whatever we think of the notion of animals rights, there are, as I shall indicate, morally important features of human life not shared by animals.)

The reason why a traditional hierarchical society is attractive to many people is not simply that in it an authority gives out orders to the majority. It is rather that everyone in the society, including the authorities, can see themselves as fulfilling a role in some overall scheme of things, a scheme which is not regarded as subject to whim or arbitrary alteration, but which one is part of by virtue of one's birth and from which each person derives a sense of who he or she is, the terms in which he or she is to define his or her identity and the end to which he or she is to be seen as progressing in life. Alasdair MacIntyre in *After Virtue* (esp. Ch. 15) has argued strongly that the ability to see one's life in terms of a unified narrative or quest, defined by one's social position and consequent duties and roles in a traditional society or even by a religious viewpoint, is crucial to any moral system which is to be undermined by what he sees as the inevitable fragmentation of life and moral arbitrariness of modern individualism. He says that unless moral values are grounded in some coherently structured and socially oriented account of the good life (such as that given by Aristotle), a man's moral beliefs turn out in the end to be no more than expressions of his own feelings, while the very notion of personal identity cannot be satisfactorily elucidated unless one is able to see one's whole life in terms of a unified narrative defined in terms of a single telos or end which one is striving towards throughout one's life. Whether or not MacIntyre is right to think that without a teleological view of human life there can be no morality that is more than rationalization and will to power (and we shall return to this later), clearly a religious view of the whole world will be able to provide for the believer just this sense of his life as a narrative or a quest, which MacIntyre is looking for. It is a horizon against which people locate their own position in life, and on the basis of which they are able to define the appropriate way to treat others (not always as equally worthy of respect and compassion, incidentally). In Nietzsche's view, the abolition of religious belief is to be seen precisely as a wiping away of the horizon:

How have we done it? How were we able to drink up the sea?
Who gave us the sponge to wipe away the whole horizon? What
did we do when we loosened this earth from its sun? Whither
does it now move? Whither do we move? Away from all suns?
Do we not wash on unceasingly? Backwards, sideways,
forward, in all directions? Is there still an above and below? Do
we not stray, as through infinite nothingness? (1882, §125)

The problem for the non-believer is to show how, in the absence of
a religious horizon, any purely natural basis can be solid and
convincing enough to found morality. J.P. Stern, in commenting
on Nietzsche, claims that

Where men have abandoned their belief in an immortal soul, the
destruction they visit on others has become more heedless and
complete than before; and where they act in the conviction . . .
that there is no authority to appeal to, their style of life is more
troubled and more sordid than before. (1978, p. 97)

Whether this is true as a matter of historical fact, what the believer
is challenging the non-believer to do is to show what a God-less
morality might be based on, and whether it would have the
psychological hold on people that God-directed codes have, and it
is to this challenge that the rest of this chapter is addressed.

It is certainly true that a secular system of values unlike a
religious one will take as its starting point the way in which human
beings are seen as masters of their own destiny and the source of
whatever value they place on individual lives and rights. Thus,
Nietzsche is quite right to stress the wiping away of a horizon when
religion goes. But is the upshot of this necessarily to be what he
calls elsewhere a 'pandemonium' of all free spirits? No doubt, for
many, there will be a sense of loss, but joyful submission to the
divine order of things is not the only response to a divine horizon.
There is also the assertion of human experience and enjoyment in
the face of what must appear the essentially capricious divine law,
capricious because it is willed by another:

> . . . ille potens sui
> laetusque deget, cui licet in diem
> dixisse' vixi: cras vel atra
> nube polum Pater occupato

vel sole puro; non tamen irritum
quodcumque retro est, efficiet neque
diffinget infectumque reddet,
quod fugiens semel hora vexit.'

(Horace, Ode III, 29)

(Horace is saying in effect that whatever the gods do in the
future, they can't wipe away the enjoyment of life we had
today.)

Divine suns can be overwhelmingly stifling and claustrophobic,
producing feelings of rebellion, inadequacy and guilt as often as
more positive responses.

Nietzsche himself, as always, went to the extreme, when in his
madness he said that he could tolerate the existence of God only if
he himself was God. Perhaps more importantly, it is not clear why
free spirits have to be in pandemonium. Saying that human beings
are the source of value, and that there is no superhuman telos,
deriving from God or some other transcendent source, is not to say
that values thereby become totally arbitrary, or that there could not
be purely human structures of moral support and education.

While it is true that morality cannot exist in a factual or
ideological vacuum, and that a will uninformed by or deliberately
blind to any of the relevant facts about human nature and human
needs is likely to find itself lacking rational criteria for moral
choice, religious facts are not the only type of facts which one could
appeal to, to make moral choices non-arbitrary. Thus one could,
starting from the position that there is no God, observe that human
beings are creatures with certain types of strength and weakness,
with specific needs and psychologies, and that natural resources in
the world are limited in various ways. Moral discourse could then
be seen as making appeal to the principles on which, given these
various facts, human life could be made tolerable. Speaking of life
being made tolerable is emphatically not to imply that the only
basis for morality is the Hobbesian picture of the individual
surviving better as an individual in a group than on his own. For
although, as Mackie has shown, a morality that does not fully
recognize the centrality of egoism and self-interest in human
motivation and consequent limits to unrestricted altruism is

unlikely to have much practical applicability, even egoism should not be conceived in purely individualistic terms (Mackie, 1977, passim). Men, in all times and places, want to engage in and define themselves through those competitive and co-operative projects such as raising families, engaging in trade, crafts, education, games, and so on, which require for their satisfactory development a basis of mutual respect and rights among the participants, and a sense that the projects themselves have standards and goals internal to them. Moreover (and this suggestion is one of the most interesting features of Mackie's work on ethics), the fact of egoism itself – the idea that people naturally want to pursue what they see as their own happiness – suggests that a society in which people can flourish will be one in which some form of property rights and a right to non-interference are admitted, as a guarantee of liberty and property will provide the best conditions for individuals to pursue their own ends. In other words, even a society in which individuals who are largely self-seeking and generally capable only of limited altruism wish to engage in shared activities will also have to be a society in which individuals are accorded certain rights, to allow for the pursuit both of egoism and of shared projects. In addition, as part of their psychology, perhaps partly for evolutionary reasons, in that in those societies in which people generally do have moral feelings, individuals will naturally tend to do better than those in which there is no genuine co-operation, most people do have a conscience regarding the suffering or well-being of others; as well as a sense that promises should be kept, truth told, and so on; thus, as Mackie again suggests, for most people 'what *is* prudent is then not the same as what would be prudent if (they) did not have moral feelings' (1977, p. 192). To go against one's moral feelings in one's actions will, of course, result in psychological disturbance. The point is that if, by nature or upbringing, we have moral tendencies, by virtue of that very fact being moral becomes part of what it is in our own interest to do. So, both in terms of the sorts of things human beings characteristically do and in their psychological make-up, we can find a basis for a life style which is not just a matter of solitary individuals deciding on how best to survive as solitary individuals. In so far as anything may be described as natural to all human society, the existence of shared projects and of moral feelings can be.

The social and ethical implications of the existence of shared

81

projects among human beings have been well analysed by MacIntyre (1981, Ch. 14). He speaks in this context of a practice as a

> coherent and complex form of socially established cooperative human activity through which goods internal to that form of activity are realised in the course of trying to achieve those standards of excellence which are appropriate to, and partially definitive of, that form of activity, with the result that human powers to achieve excellence, and human conceptions of the ends and goods involved, are systematically extended. (p. 175)

Examples of practices in this sense are games, farming, physics, chemistry and biology, history, painting, music, and even politics. A key feature of all these activities is that newcomers, if they want to succeed in them, have first to master the standards internal to the activities, and this in turn means that ideally they should define their relationships with other practitioners in terms of those standards, rather than in terms of personal likes or dislikes. Practices, then, can flourish only if their practitioners display the virtues of justice and respect for truth, and, in addition, that degree of courage to be able to put the interests of the practice above that of immediate personal gain. So the existence of shared human projects immediately opens up horizons beyond those of narrow self-interest.

What I am suggesting is that certain facts about human psychology and about human activities provide a basis for at least a limited application of such virtues as sympathy, justice, truthfulness and courage. If these facts were different, if human beings generally lacked moral feelings and if they never shared projects, it is possible that nothing we would regard as morality would have any role in human life. If this dependence of morality on certain contingent facts is what the religious theorist means when he says that in the absence of a belief in God, moral obligation would be less than absolute, he is right. But given these facts, which are deeply reflected in the language we use to evaluate people, and given further the essentially contemporary facts about worldwide inter-dependence and scarcity of resources, we do have a context in which principles of an impartial and general moral sort could be generated so as to allow best for the flourishing of human lives and of the multifarious and inter-connected practices in which human beings characteristically engage. Further, basing the principles on an understanding of human activity and psychology and on aspects of the contemporary world situation would give them a greater chance of gaining practical acceptance than if they were simply based on some divine revelation or pulled out of the blue of pure reasoning.

The approach to morality I am suggesting here does not appeal to any divine perspective or superhuman telos. It is based entirely on a combination of human nature, human tradition and human choice, although it is worth stressing that a type of objectivity is secured in this approach by stressing that neither nature nor tradition is entirely plastic. Certain concerns and feelings are given to us by nature, while others are embedded in our language, our modes of description, and social institutions and rituals, and these culture-dependent facts are what provide us with those concepts and modes of perception that initially endow our lives and experiences with meaning. As Putnam (1981, pp. 211-6) has argued, any discussion about what one ought to do must necessarily begin from and make appeal to (what is at any time) 'ordinary moral discourse', which has certain values internal to it. Equally we cannot invent a totally new morality, without, as he puts it, 'arbitrarily wrenching certain values out of their context while ignoring others'. MacIntyre, however, is insistent that without some overall goal being ascribed to human activity, even given the nature of practices as he has analysed them, the virtues and goods internal to those practices and the ranking of the practices in degree of importance to us will appear ultimately to depend on our choices, and hence 'the modern self with its criterionless choices apparently reappears' (1981, p. 188). Not only do our references to human nature and tradition prevent total arbitrariness here, but it is unclear where, without a religious perspective, a telos that was not dependent on human choice could come from, (and, apart from expressing dissatisfaction with Aristotelian biology, MacIntyre does not enlighten us on this point). I have expanded elsewhere (1981) on the dangers of an uncritical acceptance of anyone's claim to know the true end of human life, on how this too easily leads to political repression, false enlightenment and a distortion of life, which honest writers at least will always give witness to. What I am suggesting is that what we need and all we can reasonably ask for is something much more modest than a clear concept of *the* end of human existence.

Men are naturally social. They want to co-operate and live in societies not only for mutual protection, but also because living in society enables them to undertake the various projects and practices which make life worth living, as well as providing in its language and institutions a context of shared meanings for their lives. For a society of people engaging in shared projects and practices to work at all, the members of the society will have to accept and be guided by principles respecting the other members of the society as potential contributors to the projects and practices. Thus such virtues as truthfulness, justice and respect for the property and autonomy of others will naturally be valued in such a society, and extend and build on the scope of whatever purely natural feelings of sympathy people have for each other, as well as being reflected in the descriptions we give of other people as loyal, considerate, mean, weak-willed and so on.

At one time, it might have been possible to see the world in terms of isolated societies, and to regard virtuous attitudes as applicable only to members of one's own society. Historically, no doubt, the world religions have played a large part in breaking down the idea that barbarians are outside the moral pale. It is just possible that the considerations relating to shared projects and practices and their reflection in our assessments of others could be regarded as providing a basis for co-operation and moral attitudes only within societies, and not across societies, although some of the practices themselves (such as physics, trade and painting) may lead people to want to transcend national barriers. However that may be, we are now long past the stage at which the world can satisfactorily be run as groups of warring or non-co-operating societies. This alone is enough to suggest very strongly the need for seeking to extend the scope of the virtues necessary within societies through the whole world, to regard the whole world in fact as one society. From this perspective, it can be urged that regarding each member of the human race as having an entitlement to a degree of respect is the best basis for the well-being and continued survival of the whole human race, for only in this way can disastrous and destructive conflicts be averted. In the light of this, it is essential that we emphasize, in education and elsewhere, the sympathetic aspects of human nature at the expense of aggressive ones, something that might not have been so easy to justify in earlier times before the world was not so clearly a single, inter-dependent entity, and when aggression could more plausibly have been an important element in the survival of groups and societies.

Would any of this present a reply to Nietzsche? What has been said about the other regarding aspects of human life does present the germs of a reply along these lines. Nietzsche, in effect, presents us with an either – or. Either a divine horizon or a solitary will, seeking to dominate. The notion of a practice, or a shared project, suggests that much of human activity is not to be conceived of in terms of solitary wills seeking to dominate other wills. Of course, Nietzschean 'great men' may seek to use practices in this way, but in doing so they subvert the standards and goals of the practices. If the practices are to survive, they must be able to resist the incursions of great men, as poetry survived Nero's self-declared victory at Olympia in 67 AD. MacIntyre is quite right to draw our attention to Nietzsche's own portrait of the great man:

> A great man – a man whom nature has constructed and invented in the grand style – what is he? . . . If he cannot lead, he goes alone; then it can happen that he may snarl at some things he meets on his way. . . . He wants no 'sympathetic' heart, but servants, tools; in his intercourse with men he is always intent on making something out of them. He knows he is incommunicable; he finds it tasteless to be familiar, and when one thinks he is, he usually is not. When not speaking to himself, he wears a mask. He rather lies than tells the truth; it requires more spirit and will. There is a solitude within him that is inaccessible to praise or blame, his own justice that is beyond appeal. (*Will to Power*, §962)

Such a man could never be a true scientist or artist or anything that required a submission to objective standards outside himself and of course he would place himself outside our current moral discourse. If he is a sane man at all, he is either a primitive despot or a modern dictator – but is he not in truth more like a God? (Aristotle indeed had referred long before this to the man outside society as being either a beast or a god.) The most effective reply of the non-religious moral theorist to Nietzsche is precisely to reject his either – or, and to suggest first that Nietzsche's view of human activity as will-to-power is grossly inadequate as an account of human practices. Furthermore, it is extremely dubious that a world consisting of warring hero-supermen could any longer be viable as a world, however much romantic classicists may regret the passing of such Homeric possibilities. There is definitely a sense in which, as Nietzsche saw, men such as Cesare Borgia and Lorenzo de Medici are anachronisms. History since Nietzsche has simply served to reinforce the view that a politics of the will to power can now lead only to total mutual disaster.

In suggesting that it might be possible to ground morality in facts about human activity and psychology, existing moral discourse and in facts about the contemporary world, it could be argued that I am confusing factual questions and questions concerning possible motivation with questions about what is actually right and wrong. My reply to this has to be that I accept part of the Nietzschean perspective: that there is no clear distinction in moral reasoning between what is right and wrong, and how men think in the light of their current view of the world and their current moral judgments. Moreover, the condition of the world and of society does have an effect on the delineation of what is right and wrong. The arguments I have advanced about the inter-connectedness of the contemporary world simply would not have applied in the world of the *Iliad*. To have told Agamemnon that he ought to care about the fate of starving Chinese peasants would have been about as sensible as telling someone today that he ought to care about the fate of suffering beings on the other side of the universe, and for the same reason: that there is as little actual relation between the two in the one case as in the other.

It might also be said that it would have been senseless to suggest to the warring parties in the *Iliad* that they should have extended their natural sense of sympathy from those of their own side to their opponents. The honour-shame axis of Homeric society, it would be said, limited sympathy to sympathy for one's own kind. But, if this is so, then the poet belongs to a later stage of moral development than that of his characters, for the *Iliad* takes on a tragic and universal grandeur in Book 24, in the scene of reconciliation between Achilles and Priam when it is clear that both men are at one in grief, and their susceptibility to mortality. Whether or not MacIntyre is right in suggesting (1981, pp. 120-1) that Achilles is unable to see both himself and Priam as equal in suffering from the war, this is certainly how Homer portrays them to us. It is clear that once this sense of mutual suffering and shared mortality begins to exist between men of different tribes a new moral dimension can also begin to exist (though as the story of Alexander the Great demonstrates, not all devotees of the *Iliad* have appreciated this). The key point here is that the natural sense of sympathy will, if unimpeded by social constraints, extend itself naturally to any who are perceived as victims of tragedy or disaster. Thus there may be in human sensibility itself a strong tendency uniting men and breaking down social barriers between them. This tendency can, of course, combine with the tendency to sharing activity and the facts about global inter-dependence to promoting in individuals the sense of all other individuals in the world as being entitled to moral respect.

I have suggested a non-religious perspective from which moral principles may be drawn. The perspective is one which is based on features of human nature and activity, and also on facts about the world. The question remains, however, as to whether such a conception of morality could be strong enough to prevail generally in the world. After all, there are in each of us aggressive as well as sympathetic tendencies, and there are people who are barely susceptible to moral or humane considerations. It is here that the religious moralist may seem to have the advantage, for, as we saw with Stern, he can appeal to something higher and, as he would put it, 'more absolute' than 'merely human' considerations. Whether or not such appeals actually have any measurable effect may be open to doubt when one considers such episodes as the Fourth Crusade and the history of medieval Europe generally. However this may be, the non-religious will, of course, simply admit that he has nothing higher to appeal to than the characteristics of human beings and the state of the world but in this admission there could be an important lesson. If there is nothing higher to appeal to, the onus is placed squarely on our shoulders to ensure that the morality we choose should be seen to be reasonable and also that it does in the main prevail. What this means in practice is, first, that the moral principles we do fix on should be seen as stemming from those facts about human nature I have indicated, together with our mutual need to share the resources of the planet so as to prevent global catastrophe or even something less total (due to the greed of the rich, the resentment of the dispossessed and so on). Then, second, and most important, we should all be extremely concerned to devise and defend institutions, national and international, which will make it extremely difficult for individuals ever to be crushed by the power lust of the immoral. I remarked earlier that in a society governed by moral feelings, all individuals will do better. But, of course, some of the individuals who profit from living in a moral society will be immoral, and will not respect morality themselves. What we have to prevent is the subverting and eventual destruction of our 'conspiracy of doves' from within. Moral education and argument may not realistically be expected to convince everyone, but we can by political and institutional means hope to minimize the depredations of future Alexanders and Hitlers. If the removal of divine sanctions from the picture helps us to see the urgency of this task, and the sense in which it will be a continuing struggle to maintain and improve any institutions we do devise, eventual dissociation of the morality from religion, assuming it comes about generally, may, despite the fears of those political establishments which strive to prevent it, actually turn out to be a significant step forward for mankind.

4

Religious Explanations

In this chapter, I intend to consider claims to the effect that
religious explanations are either on a par with or more satisfying
than scientific and common sense explanations in various respects.
In doing this, I will show first that *if* science or common sense rest
on unprovable foundations, this can be of little comfort to
theologians; second, that the claim that religious explanations
provide a more fitting terminus to explanation than materialistic
ones is at best unproven; third, that the idea of God as a necessary
being is radically incoherent; and fourth, that the god of process
theology stands more in need of explanation than it is able to
explain.

Section 1   The religious 'tu quoque'

In this section we will look at what is a fairly widespread
theological response to scepticism: that things you the sceptic
believe are no better off epistemologically than what you criticize
us for believing. In other words, if we are sinning, so are you too
(*tu quoque*).

One of the most common religious *tu quoque* arguments is to
suggest that the scientific enterprise rests on faith as much as a belief
in God, because science requires a principle of induction or a belief
in the uniformity of nature, neither of which can be rationally
justified. A good example of a claim of this sort is to be found in
F.R. Tennant's *Philosophical Theology*. Tennant first asserts that
'nothing logical constitutes the "probability" of science's pre-
suppositions; it is constituted simply by faith.' He goes on to
explain this by speaking of faith as 'venture dictated by human

interest' and saying that 'science postulates what is requisite to make the world amenable to the kind of thought that conceives of the structure of the universe, and its orderedness according to quantitative laws' (1928, pp. 297-9)

What Tennant is claiming is that science is a practical activity, aimed at showing that the world is governed by quantitatively expressible causal laws. That it can succeed is the faith that underlies it. This faith is itself a reflection of the human need to find quantitative regularities. (In all this, his attitude to science shows a striking anticipation of the later Wittgenstein, who also saw the physical sciences as symptomatic of a deep human need.) Tennant goes on to compare the faith that in his view underlies science with religious faith, which answers the human desire to find meaning and purpose in the universe. The point of the comparison is presumably to show that science, with its assumption of regularity in nature is as much an enterprise based on faith and deep-rooted tendencies of the human mind as is religion, with its assumption of purpose.

While it is true that science and indeed everyday life depend for their success on the disclosure of regularities in nature, it is not at all clear that this makes either science or everyday living a matter of faith, or in any way analogous to religious faith. For the assumption that we can learn from experience, that what we *have* experienced is likely to be a guide to what we will experience in the future is obviously indispensable to the rational conduct of life and, probably, to survival as well. We could hardly hope to live long if we did not have some knowledge of what types of things are likely to nourish us, to protect us, to endanger us and so on, and all such knowledge must rest ultimately on persisting regularities in experience. (Blind instinct would have survival value only if it corresponded at least in part to the way things actually were.) Science can quite plausibly be regarded as simply the refinement of the everyday search for regularity. Our expectation of regularity in experience is so pervasive and basic to our lives that it has been described as instinctive, the implication being that we are born looking for, and expecting to find, particular regularities of specific sorts, as well as having a predisposition to search for regularity in general. Some have regarded the instinctiveness of our regularity-seeking as meaning that talk of a faith in regularity is inappropriate (cf. Brown, 1973, p. 36). Saying that regularity seeking in everyday life is instinctive or has instinctive roots, however, hardly settles the question as to whether the explicit assumption of regularity that underlies scientific research should be regarded as a faith. A faith is something that carries with it a definite cognitive commitment that something is or will be the case; an instinct, on the other hand, is simply a behavioural response, which carries cognitive commitment only by way of redescription. (The sucking baby acts *as if* he believes he will get milk; but there is no more to the belief than the behaviour.) The claim that Tennant is making is that scientists make a definite cognitive commitment to the regularity of nature, and that this might be regarded as a faith.

There is certainly something to be said for the second part of the claim, that nothing in reason or experience can assure us of the regularity of nature. As Hume showed once and for all, there is nothing inconsistent in holding that nature is not uniform, while any argument from experience to the effect that it is presupposes its own truth. You cannot conclude that because your experience has been of regularities and uniformities, your future experience will be similarly regular, without assuming that there is a uniformity between your past experience and what you have not so far experienced – which is just what has to be shown. Nevertheless, the crucial questions are not whether we (or scientists) have any grounds for a belief in natural regularity, but rather whether scientists have to have such a belief in order to do science, and whether, if they do, they would have to hold it in any way like a religious faith.

Philosophers of science in the Popperian tradition have tried to show that science can proceed without any inductive assumptions, that reasons can be found for preferring theories which have nothing to do with induction and which do not rely on any assumption to the effect that the future will resemble the past. These arguments have, of course, been hotly disputed (see, e.g., Salmon, 1981; O'Hear, 1980, Ch. 3-4). Nevertheless, Popper himself contends that science is an attempt to uncover a pattern of regularity in nature, and also that if our world was as irregular as some worlds or parts of the universe might be, the acquisition of knowledge by physical means would be impossible (cf. Popper, 1974, p. 1027). So even Popper agrees that the scientific enterprise can succeed only given a degree of natural regularity. What non-Popperians can learn from Popper's hostility to inductive assumptions in any form is that there is no guarantee in logic or experience that the world in which science is possible – our world – will continue for any specific length of time. Some cataclysmic event even in the next moment might bring it all to an end. Our survival, our culture and our science would all disappear. This much can readily be conceded to Tennant.

But why should any scientist, even a believer in inductive logic, not agree with the Popperian insight that there is no guarantee of regularity in nature? What Tennant would like to see in response to this is scientists filling in the no-guarantee gap with an act of faith, but it is quite unclear that any such act is required or desirable. It is not required, because all that is needed for science is the *provisional* assumption or conjecture that some sort of regularity in the universe may correspond to our drive to seek regularities, and that *if* there are any such regularities, the rigorous and controlled methods of science are the best chance we have of finding them. We can, if we like, add to this the fact that our methods have worked reasonably well up to now, but this should be regarded as at most giving us a psychological boost. Looked at from the perspective of reality as a whole, the debate between those philosophers of science who reject any inductive assumptions (Popperians) and those who do not (inductivists) should not be seen as being over a supposed act of faith in the continuance of regularity in the universe, because no rational inductivist would go so far as to make so groundless a claim, but rather a series of disputes about the types of consideration that should be brought into theory preference and the type of conclusion that we should draw from these preferences. According to Popper, we do not (should not) rely in our future behaviour on past regularities, and past evidence should not be seen as *supporting* our theories; according to inductivists we cannot do otherwise and past evidence does support our theories. Nevertheless, both Popper and the inductivists agree that it is rational to act on previously successful theories, and whether or not this is described as reliance or seen in terms of support is perhaps not particularly significant.

What is really at issue between Tennant and those philosophers of science who would disagree with him is whether our un-grounded assumption that our science does reveal present and future reality is to be seen as an act of faith. Saying that an act of faith is not required here is just to say that we can continue our science in a sort of provisional hope that it will continue to succeed, without *faith* that it will, for faith can hardly be conjectural. Faith in natural regularity would presumably persist through whatever upsets our present expectations of regularity suffer (assuming what is very doubtful, that we were actually able to survive any widespread breakdown in the present order of things). Of course, there is a sense in which we have to rely on experience and have to assume the continuance of past regularities, but we can at the same time and perhaps should continue to regard this as epistemologically risky. It is this latter point that seems to me to make a *faith* in natural regularity undesirable, for it will tend to draw attention away from the fact that our methods for survival, including of course our everyday expectations and our science, are just that: *our* methods. From our point of view, there is nothing else, no other means of acquiring knowledge, but it can be only salutary to realize that there is nothing sacrosanct or guaranteed about them. We need to be conscious that our past successes and experiences of regularity may fail us in new areas of experience, and also that the world as a whole, including our own corner of it, may change, even radically. A faith that the world will correspond to our cognitive drives and processes may make us all too complacent, and disposed disastrously to overlook symptoms of breakdowns in our theories, and signs of problems with previously successful methods. Realizing this sort of thing might just allow us to readjust and to save ourselves. Hence, even though we are unable to *do* otherwise than (provisionally) rely on (suitably examined) past experience, it would not be desirable to have any blind faith in methods which have worked well for us up to now.

What I am suggesting here is that it would be extremely irrational to put anything like religious faith in any methods and theories just because they have done well for us. Whatever our instincts may be regarding future behaviour and expectations, a study of evolution clearly demonstrates the fallibility of instinct, and the need to be ready to modify our instinctive attitudes in the face of changing circumstances. Tennant's attitude to science makes what should be conjectural and provisional enquiry into something like a religious faith or hope that there really are universal laws, operative throughout nature, to mirror the universal theories our science strives to formulate.

A similar line to that taken by Tennant has been put more recently by Hans Küng (1980, pp. 461-77). Küng picks on certain statements by philosophers of science, in particular Popper (cf. 1966, pp. 230-1) and Wolfgang Stegmüller (1969, pp. 168-9), in which there is talk of an irrational faith in reason. Both Popper and Stegmüller believe that any attempt to argue or to produce evidence in favour of our rational activities is bound to produce a vicious circle, because in arguing and bringing forward evidence we are assuming the validity of just those reasoning procedures whose credentials are in question. For Popper, the only way out of the impasse is to defend his rationalism (=reliance on argument and evidence) on ethical grounds; for him there can be no non-circular rational vindication of rationalism. Stegmüller speaks of a 'pre-rational primordial decision' in favour of accepting evidence and reasons in argument, which he thinks is a 'personal decision of conscience'. The problem raised by Popper's talk of an irrational faith in reason and by Stegmüller's personal decision of conscience in favour of scientific evidence is that, as Bartley has amply demonstrated (cf. Bartley, 1962), although these scientific rationalists might thereby escape the charge of vicious circularity, they leave themselves with no ammunition against an irrationalist opponent who makes a primordial decision in favour of racial or class feeling, or some alleged divine inspiration. There is at the bottom of their philosophies as much of a retreat to commitment as there is with the Nazi or the religious fundamentalist. The immediate problem with basing science on an ethical decision alone is that *if* science is based on irrational trust, then religion may be no *worse* off than science, but, by the same token, it is no *better* off than any other type of personal or ideological commitment, which would be a somewhat dubious basis on which to rest for a belief in the ultimate intelligibility and rationality of the universe.

Küng is not apparently worried by this aspect of his *tu quoque*. Instead he goes on to claim that

> the fundamental trust in the identity, meaningfulness and value
> of reality, which is the presupposition of human science and
> autonomous ethics, is justified in the last resort only if reality
> itself – of which man is also a part – is not groundless,
> unsupported and aimless. (1980, p. 476)

What he is saying here is that as science is based on a fundamental trust, we should take the ultimate implication of such trust to be that reality itself is trustworthy, in the sense that there is a God sustaining the whole. It is not clear to me why, just because we make a qualified act of trust (to accept that science can partially reveal to us how the world is), we are thereby *more* rational to go the whole hog and conclude that the world as a whole is governed by a good God. It might be equally rational to make our trust in the intelligibility of the world highly qualified, and to extend it no further than the degree to which our actual scientific theories provide successful predictions for us. Moreover, if Küng is serious in taking the Popper-Stegmüller view as a demonstration of the non-rationality of argument as such, one might wonder by what licence Küng thinks he is entitled to *argue* from such a demonstration to the need for a fundamental trust in reality. But without deciding on these points, what needs closer examination is the nature of the trust that is supposed to underlie rational use of argument and attention to evidence.

The argument in favour of the supposed lack of rationality in being guided by argument and evidence, which is presented by Popper and Stegmüller, is that any argument for the validity of the use of argument and evidence will, *as an argument*, itself assume the validity of argument and evidence. Leaving aside doubts about the legitimacy of arguing *against* argument, the circularity of arguing in favour of the use of argument and evidence is supposed to entail that the use of argument and evidence must be based on something non-rational, like a free decision of conscience. Against this, it must be stressed that the 'decision' (if that is what it is) to use argument and evidence is not at all on the same level as a decision to accept Christ as the Son of God or Lenin as the authentic voice of the Russian proletariat or even that $e = mc^2$. For these are all particular beliefs in specific propositions, which are only intelligible as beliefs given that their holders can plausibly be seen as understanding what it is to believe, and, in particular, this means grasping the close link between having a belief and seeing the relevance to it of appropriate argument and evidence. In other words, for someone to be seen as holding particular beliefs pre-supposes that he is also seen as entering into the practices of argument and evidence-collecting. For it is part of what is meant by my having a belief that I think it true, and act appropriately to it being true. Now part of what acting appropriately will involve in the case of a belief is being ready to consider its connection with the truth; in general terms, this means being ready to consider argument and evidence relevant to it. If I never cared about the truth of my beliefs, in the sense that I continuously disregarded or ignored counter-evidence and counter-arguments, there would be a serious question as to whether I understood what it was to believe at all. What I am suggesting here is that it is part of one's grasp of what it is to have beliefs that one sees the importance of considering arguments and evidence relevant to the truth of the propositions believed. To opt out of the practices of arguing and considering evidence is tantamount to opting out of the practice of believing. On the other hand, without attributing beliefs to a man, we would be unable to see him as a language speaker, for involved in understanding the meaning of a man's words is bringing what we take him to be presupposing in his various speech acts (and hence believing) into some sort of rational consistency with his behaviour and his other psychological states (cf. Davidson, 1980, Ch. 12). The conclusion to be drawn from this is that although one may not be able to argue at a general level in favour of using argument and considering evidence, someone who did not engage in these practices would in effect be opting out of human social life, including everything connected with language.

What we can, of course, do is to argue in favour of or against *particular* types of argument and evidence, by showing how the general aim of argument and evidence (i.e. the transmission and discovery of truth) is served by particular means. The claims of Popper and Stegmüller concerning the irrationality of rationalism perhaps get more credence than they deserve, because we read them in the light of other things they say, as expressions of epistemological doubt concerning our particular ways of arguing and collecting evidence. But they are not that. They are, in both cases, explicit appeals to the vicious circularity of arguing in favour of rational procedures in general. But the conclusion to be drawn from this vicious circularity is not that we have to make some sort of irrational commitment to argument and evidence, but rather that practices of arguing and considering evidence are presupposed by speaking or having beliefs at all.

A sceptic might say at this point that none of our practices of arguing or looking at evidence actually leads us to the truth. Applied to simple deductive logic, it may be doubted whether such a claim makes sense at all, for in simple arguments in logic, we can simply see that truth is transmitted from conclusion to premises in the case of valid arguments, and that falsity is transmitted from conclusion to premises in invalid arguments. On our search for empirical truths, there is perhaps more to be said in favour of the sceptic, particularly when scientific theories are held to be supported by inductive evidence. But if this is what is behind Küng's claim that trust is a pre-supposition of human science, his position is the same as Tennant's and so is our answer to it. Certainly we can engage in science quite properly without any *pre-supposition* (as opposed to hope) that the world is governed by universal laws, let alone that it is meaningful in some more theological sense.

Küng, however, does add something to doubts about induction in his consideration of scientific rationality, and that is to appeal to the view made fashionable by T.S. Kuhn and Paul Feyerabend that the history of science consists in the replacement of one paradigm or general theory by another, and that the replacement process is irrational. The reasons for this irrationality vary. Kuhn often stresses the inconclusiveness of procedures on scientific falsification, while Feyerabend tends to emphasize incommensurability between competing paradigms. Each paradigm is supposed to determine the way in which scientists working within the paradigm interpret the evidence. Hence there is no neutral ground from which to compare competitors. Küng is not alone among theologians in appealing to the Kuhn-Feyerabend view of science. I.G. Barbour has done so explicitly (1974, esp. pp. 134-6), while Ian T. Ramsey may be said to have done so in an anticipatory spirit in speaking of religion in terms of models (1964, p. 17). Indeed, Kuhn himself has spoken of scientists moving from one paradigm to another as a matter of a conversion experience, rather than of proof (1962, p. 150), and of a decision to work with a new paradigm as an act of faith (1962, p. 157).

Let us assume for a moment that the Kuhn-Feyerabend view is correct and that progress in science does involve scientists making rationally unjustifiable decisions between incommensurable competing paradigms. Would anything follow from this that could in any way support or comfort the religious? It is hard to see how it would. In general, objections to religious belief do not rest on specific scientific findings. Problems with evil and suffering have nothing to do with science, nor do many of the shortcomings of traditional arguments for the existence of God. It is true that some scientific advances have threatened particular religious conceptions, such as the cases of Galileo and Darwin, but religious believers have been able to show without total implausibility that these threats can be avoided or at least mitigated by a more sophisticated understanding of the conceptions in question. It may well be true, however, that something like a scientific picture of the world stands in some sort of tension with a religious one, in that in science we do not look for interventions in the universe as a whole, or in this world in particular from transcendent personal beings. Indeed, the scientific conception of the world is a fundamentally impersonal one and in that sense in some tension with religious views, as we will see further in Ch. 6. But, saying that science and religion suggest alternative conceptions of the world, and adding that there is something at root arbitrary about the scientific one does nothing to add credibility to the religious one. One might feel that if this were the case, the reasonable thing to do would be to suspend judgment on both until something positive was said in support of one or the other. Proving the irrationality of science cannot by itself make religion any more rational than it is on its own merits, and it is just this that tends to get lost sight of when people talk about 'the scientific paradigm' and 'religious models'. In fact, regarding religion as a model or paradigm one can adopt if it suits is surely to adopt a thoroughly frivolous attitude to something whose claims and implications are so momentous, far more so than any scientific claims, which, after all, relate only to specific events in this life.

In fact, of course, the Kuhn-Feyerabend view of science as a matter of jumping from one incommensurable paradigm to another is one that has found little favour with most philosophers of science, and the issue is far from settled in its favour. Even Kuhn's historiography is open to serious question, as Peter Munz has shown (1980). For the historian has to select his data from the mass of material available, and this is no less true in the case of historians of science than in the case of any other type of history. This means that the historian of science has to have a philosophical theory about what constitutes the significant aspects of scientists' activity. The suspicion is that Kuhn, in appealing to history to support his philosophy, is in fact looking at history in terms of his philosophical paradigm (though, like many relativists, Kuhn does not apply his relativism to his own work). I cannot, however, discuss the merits and complexities of the Kuhn–Feyerabend view here, beyond saying that reflection on the type of data appealed to by Kuhn and Feyerabend might lead one to regard rationality in science not as non-existent, but as something which develops and refines itself in the history of science and through the actions of scientists (cf. Putnam, 1981). However, instead of pursuing this interesting line of thought here, I will simply attempt to evaluate the extent of any parallel that may be drawn between religious explanatory models and scientific models, even on a relativistic view of the latter.

Relativists about scientific theory do not as a rule say that just anything could be acceptable as science. What they assert (and scientific rationalists deny) is that there is no sense to be attached to the idea that one paradigm might objectively be better than another in the sense of reflecting the real world more accurately, but to say this is not to imply that there might not be other occasions where theories or explanations do not even begin to meet the criteria for scientific explanations. Indeed, Newton-Smith (1981, pp. 112-13) has discerned in Kuhn himself five important elements in any 'good' scientific theory: predictive accuracy, consistency both internally and with other currently accepted theories, independent testability, simplicity and fruitfulness regarding new research findings. Now, for religious beliefs to be seen as explanatory models in the scientific sense of the term, they will have to be seen to have at least some of these features, or analogies of them. It is hardly a matter of controversy to say that religious beliefs do not make accurate predictions about specific events, nor that they are not independently testable. They may in a sense be simple, in that they refer all phenomena to a single source, and this is a claim which we will have to examine further (cf. Section 2 below). It is unclear that they are fruitful of new research findings; although they do provide us with a way of addressing experience in general, they hardly lead to any specific results. Whether or not they are consistent, internally or externally, is part of what we are considering throughout the book.

The conclusion seems to be that religious explanations are very unlike scientific explanations, particularly at the key points of lacking independent testability and of leading to no specific new predictions. This type of criticizability has no role in religious thought, a point we will examine further in Ch. 6, when I suggest

that religious believers, unlike scientists, typically and characteristically seek to preserve their favoured models from criticism *at all
costs* and *in the face of whatever difficulties* they encounter – something
that would certainly be seen as irrational in a scientist. Even a
relativistic philosopher of science, such as Kuhn, is prepared to
admit that within science a particular paradigm can become so
disreputable and problematic that it would be 'stubborn and
pigheaded' (1962, p. 151) to continue to work with it because of its
empirical and methodological difficulties, although he will maintain his epistemological relativism by declining to express this in
terms of the paradigm's lack of fit with the world. The absence of
such a feeling for irrationality with respect to religious dogmas
does not, of course, mean that we may not be entitled to speak of
religious explanations in some sense. But it does mean that there is
little for the religious in any comparison between religious and
scientific explanations, and certainly not enough to support the
claim that religion and science can be regarded as both providing
explanatory models or paradigms, except in a highly ambiguous
sense of those terms.

Although defenders of religious belief have tended to employ *tu
quoque* arguments in connection with inductive and scientific
reasoning, a most original and challenging version of the *tu quoque*
is presented by Alvin Plantinga in his *God and Other Minds* (1967).[1]
One of Plantinga's aims in that book is to show that while
traditional arguments for the existence of God are flawed, the
teleological argument is epistemologically in much the same state
as belief in other minds (i.e. that we are surrounded by people like
ourselves with feelings, intentions and so on, rather than by robots,
stuffed dummies or other simulacra). In particular, the teleological
argument and belief in other minds both rely on highly dubious
appeals to analogical reasoning. In both cases, the evidence, such as
it is, often points against as much as in favour of the desired
conclusion. Thus, if we accept that the universe is designed, what
we know of designers might as well lead us to suppose that it is the
work of several of them, that the designers are embodied, less than
omnipotent and did not create the matter on which they worked,
just as much as the traditional theistic positions on these matters.

With respect to other minds, Plantinga argues at length that the
only plausible justification for this belief is some version of an
argument from analogy, from the fact of my own experiences and
their connections with my bodily behaviour, to the conclusion that

other beings that manifest similar behaviour also have similar experiences. Thus, we want to show, by analogy, that (a) I am not the only being that feels pain, and that (b) there are some pains I do not feel. We will presumably base our argument here on the fact that all cases of non-feigned pain behaviour, for which I can determine by observation whether or not they are accompanied by pain (i.e. mine), are so accompanied. Hence, we might argue, other people's pain behaviour (where I cannot observe the pain) probably is also accompanied by pain too. But such an argument would be patently silly, for it would allow in an inference to epistemological idealism, by arguing from the premiss that every physical object of which it has been determined whether or not it has ever been conceived (i.e. conceived or thought of) has been conceived, to the conclusion that there are probably no unconceived objects. For an acceptable analogical argument, our sample class must include at least the possibility of counter-examples. If we are arguing from the fact that all observed A's have B to the fact that all A's have B, we must be able to determine by observation that some A's do not have B (and, also, to avoid other problematic inferences, that they have or do not have each of the properties that go to constitute B-ness). However, this stipulation (A') wrecks the inference from my experience of a correlation between my pain behaviour and pain, because I never manifest non-feigned pain behaviour without observing pain, and it is presumably impossible that I should do so. However, dropping A' so as to allow the original inference to (a) and (b) would open the gates, as Plantinga puts it, to an argument from the fact that every pain which is such that I have determined by observation whether or not it was felt by me, was felt by me, to the conclusion that every pain is felt by me. Even if we keep A', and so avoid this unfortunate conclusion, other parts of the 'other minds' position are equally vulnerable to moves of this sort. Thus, assuming that it is logically possible to discover that some pains I can observe directly are not in my body and that I am not certain to start with that they might not be so, and determining by observation that all the pains I can observe directly are in my body, I might conclude that all pains are in my body. Plantinga's conclusion, after considering many more examples, is that keeping A' blocks any acceptable inference from my experience to other minds, while dropping it allows analogical arguments both for and against other minds.

The reason why Plantinga discusses the belief in the existence of other minds in connection with belief in God is because he wants to show that there are ways in which the two are on the same footing epistemologically. In both cases believers may be said to believe without proof. In neither case do they look for proofs in order to convince themselves of what they believe. They believe first and then look for justifications of what they believe (1967, pp. 218-9). In both cases, believers may (even with justification) claim to *see* that others are in pain, or, impressed with the beauty of the universe, to *see* that God exists (1967, pp. 188-9). According to Plantinga, however, these beliefs cannot be supported epistemologically. The best argument for God is the teleological argument and the best for other minds in the analogical, but neither is successful. Does this mean that these beliefs are *irrational*? Strangely, perhaps, this is just what Plantinga wants to deny. What he wants to get us to accept in the case of other minds is that

> a man may rationally hold a contingent, corrigible belief even if there is no answer to the relevant epistemological question.
> (1967, pp. 269-70)

and that if this is so in this case, it should be so equally in the case of belief in God, which is also unsupported. He concludes his book by saying that

> of course there may be other reasons for supposing that although rational belief in other minds does not require an answer to the epistemological question, rational belief in the existence of God does. But it is certainly hard to see what those reasons might be. Hence my tentative conclusion: if my belief in other minds is rational, so is my belief in God. But obviously the former is rational; so therefore, is the latter. (1967, p. 271)

In reaction to this, however, one wonders just why, in view of what he has said, Plantinga finds it so obvious that belief in other minds is rational. What, in the absence of some sort of rational defence of the belief, entitles him to say this? An effective criticism of Plantinga's conclusion, and his overall strategy in *God and Other Minds* would be to show that there is a sense in which belief in other minds is rationally defensible, and to question whether a belief in God can be defended in the same sense.

It will be remembered that in our discussion of religious experience in Ch. 2, it was suggested that theories could be defended in terms of their explanatory power, and that a partial justification of a general belief in physical objects could be based on the explanatory power of particular theories which implied the existence of such objects. What I am now going to suggest, following Putnam (1975, pp. 342-61) and Ayer (1976, pp. 133-6), is that the same sort of approach can be applied to the existence of other minds. Belief in other minds is not like, nor is it to be justified in terms of, attributing to others a special feature which one knows from one's own case, but which one cannot directly observe in others (such as a hidden birth-mark in a part of one's body that is always clothed). Any such analogy would be weak in the extreme, as well as falling prey to the types of objections put forward by Plantinga. But saying that someone else has a mind is not like saying that he has an unobservable birth-mark. It is rather to see his activity in terms of a whole network of explanatory concepts and theories, to see him as jealous, intelligent, prone to anger, injudicious, sensitive, and the rest. It is, moreover, to see his speech as expressive of intentions to communicate information on one occasion, to deceive on another, to provoke on another, and so on, as well as intelligible against a background of beliefs and desires we attribute to him. In other words, attribution of a mind to someone is implied as part of the way we see, explain and predict what they do. It is not in itself an empirical theory about them, as it is not tested, like ordinary empirical theories, in competition with other theories; moreover, the observations we make of others are predominantly made in psychological terms. Nevertheless, belief in other minds receives indirect support from the innumerable occasions on which our particular psychological accounts of others do have predictive success and explanatory power. Above all, the rationality of belief in other minds can be defended on the grounds that there is no alternative explanation of the behaviour of other people in the field, nor can we even envisage how such an alternative would work, unless it traded on our psychological accounts (e.g. by translating psychological talk into neuro-physiological talk and back again).

Of course, saying that the sceptic about other minds has provided no viable alternative to the assumption that there are other minds does not mean that he could not, nor does it mean that he might not be right in some deep sense. But it does give us a reason for deciding against him at least until he is able to come up with an alternative. Strangely, in *God and Other Minds*, Plantinga does not consider the type of defence of other minds suggested here, beyond saying that to call belief in other minds a well-confirmed scientific hypothesis is a case of *obscuram per obscuras*, because the relationship between scientific hypotheses and their grounds remains 'a black and boundless mystery' (1967, p. 269); nor does he suggest an alternative to belief in other minds. One can certainly concede to Plantinga that there is much that is mysterious in the philosophy of science, and that many of the key concepts in it, such as simplicity, plausibility and verisimilitude are far from well understood. But, as remarked earlier, it is clear that any scientific theory worthy of the name will have a high degree of predictive accuracy, consistency and fruitfulness. However, it is also clear that other minds talk is not a scientific theory, nor does it lead to scientific theories in the same way that material object talk might be said to lead to the theories of physics. As things stand, 'scientific' psychology is largely distinguished by its meagreness of attainment and lack of any theory of human nature that is both comprehensive and predictively powerful. If Davidson is right, it is in the nature of psychological concepts that they *could* not be worked into strict deductive – nomological shape. Certainly if they could, our attitude to other people with its assumptions about their autonomy, their unpredictability and their opacity to each other would have to undergo a radical review. However, even if for better or worse, psychological talk is not even embryonically scientific, this does not mean that it does not have considerable explanatory and predictive power, in the sense that it can be used to make the past and future behaviour of ourselves and others intelligible to us and, within certain limits, predictable, as we noticed in Ch. 2. Whether or not this is why Plantinga is so sure that talk of other minds is rational, it certainly does yield a sense in which such talk is rational, which, incidentally, is not based on finding epistemological foundations for it.

I have based the rationality of belief in other minds on its explanatory usefulness and the lack of my viable competitor. Plantinga might jib at this last point because he has actually claimed that there *is* a competitor: that only I have a mind and the others are actually the mindless puppets of Descartes's familiar evil genius (cf.

Plantinga, 1965a). However, as Putnam has argued in response to this suggestion, the details of the evil genius hypothesis have not been worked out; moreover, the hypothesis is too silly to be taken seriously (Putnam, 1975, pp. 359-61). On the first point Plantinga could take two courses. He could either begin to work out the evil genius hypothesis in enough detail to specify some empirical difference between it and the common sense view in which case we could test between them, and settle the matter. Or, as is more likely, he would build into the evil genius view the proviso that there will be no empirical difference between it and the other minds supposition. Now, while we cannot falsify the evil genius view directly (unless someone else holds it about *us*, so as to deny *our* mental activity), we can argue that whatever empirical success it has in allowing us to predict and explain the behaviour of others will depend on our grasp and application of 'other minds' hypotheses, for we will have to treat them *as if* they were people with minds. The hypothesis that behind the other minds lurks an evil puppeteer seems a redundant and unnecessary complication which adds nothing to whatever understanding our psychological accounts give us of specific actions, and, for that reason, it is not reasonable to hold (even if, nevertheless, true). Is it, in addition, just silly as Putnam claims? It no doubt is, but to use this as an answer to Plantinga is in effect to play into his hands, for he will now inquire into the foundations of our a priori plausibility/implausibility orderings, and it may well be that there is nothing rational about this. However, so long as the evil genius view remains a merely metaphysical conceit, parasitic upon the common-sense view and making no difference in practice, there is a clear sense in which it is less rational than the common-sense view of other people.

So, in response to Plantinga's *tu quoque*, we can argue that a belief in other minds does have some rational support in view of its explanatory power and the absence of any competitor with such potential, even if, as Plantinga believes, it can get no support from more direct epistemological arguments. Can the same be said of any of the traditional ways of conceiving God? Does postulating God as creator or designer have any explanatory power? Are there any competitors to these hypotheses? To these questions we will turn in the next section.

Section 2 Cosmological and teleological arguments

Some version of the cosmological and teleological arguments for the existence of God will undoubtedly be familiar to most people, as arguments of these sorts do seem to correspond to deep-seated tendencies in the human mind. A cosmological argument is one which postulates God as the ultimate cause of the universe, a cause outside the universe and lacking the contingency and corruptibility of things within the universe, while a teleological argument sees the complexity and orderliness of the universe or things within it as requiring explanation in terms of a divine designer or orderer. The deep-seated tendency of the mind reflected in the cosmological argument is the search for causal explanation, while teleological thinking reflects our appreciation of order and the human tendency to see personal intentions underlying natural phenomena. It is not surprising that people who have done no philosophy in any formal way often have thoughts and aspirations couched in cosmological or teleological terms, for these terms promise an answer to the ultimate questions of life and existence. I do not want to argue that the arguments are totally without plausibility or persuasive power. The questions they address themselves to, which concern the origins and nature of the universe, are undoubtedly fascinating and troubling; too quick a dismissal of them may indicate a lack of imagination or depth. Nevertheless, the answers supplied by the arguments seem to me to be no more than subjectively persuasive. For the person who is not inclined to believe in God, rejection of the arguments and their answers is neither irrational nor without justification.

Although Aquinas is generally associated with the cosmological argument – in fact he proposed at least three versions of it – his writing on the subject is largely vitiated by its dependence on medieval physics and by what appear to be strangely slipshod logical errors. (For details, cf. Kenny, 1969.) In fact the argument can be presented in a way free of these defects. All it requires initially is an appeal to a principle of sufficient reason, according to which there is some sort of sufficient reason or explanation for everything that exists. This is a principle which is certainly applied in everyday life, and in science. We do not like to think that things happen randomly, or for no reason at all, and science can be seen as the attempt to eradicate such unintelligibility from the world. It is true that many theories in current physics are indeterministic: they cannot predict the behaviour of individual particles but only of populations of particles. Some, such as Einstein, would regard this as a defect of explanation, and an indicator of the state of our ignorance. However, even if Einstein was wrong, and the universe is in some deep sense indeterministic, probabilistic theories can provide a sufficient reason for the behaviour of populations of particles, and to that extent conform to our faith in the principle of sufficient reason. The cosmological argument attempts to apply the principle of sufficient reason beyond particular events or states of affairs within the universe. For any event within the universe, we can seek for its explanation, in terms of its causal antecedents and the relevant laws of nature. In principle there is no reason why such a search cannot be endlessly regressive. Any causal antecedent of a specific event will have its own antecedents, and they theirs in turn, and so on. Equally, any particular covering law may turn out to be an instance of some more general feature of matter or the universe. These potentially regressive chains of explanations may, of course, have an actual terminus. There may have been a temporally first event – a Big Bang – in which case, we will be unable to find any causal antecedent for that. Some properties of matter – perhaps the second law of thermodynamics or the relationship between matter and energy – may actually be ultimate brute facts, with nothing more general in the structure of things to explain them. First events and ultimate brute facts are, of course, grist to the cosmological arguer's mill. Surely, he will say, such things cry out for an explanation. The universe cannot suddenly have sprung into existence for no reason, nor can things just be such and such with no explanation. But even if we believe the universe to be infinite in time or chains of explanation in terms of properties of matter to have no natural end, the principle of sufficient reason can still be invoked to pose questions as to why the universe has the properties it has, which transcend any answer which can be given in terms of a yet earlier event or a yet more general covering law.

Many philosophers, following Hume, have argued that if you have an explanation of *each* member of a series, you need no explanation over and above that of the series as a whole, and there are examples for which this is true. To cite one, given by Paul Edwards (1958), a series of five Eskimos on the corner of Sixth

Avenue and Fiftieth Street would be completely explained by giving the reason why each of the five happened to be there. But, in giving this explanation, we would, of course, be appealing to facts that were not themselves part of the series of events to be explained. The presence of the five Eskimos would not be fully or satisfactorily explained if we were told that four of them were there because they wanted to meet the fifth, if no explanation was forthcoming of the fifth's being there. Following Richard Swinburne (1979, p. 124), I conclude that a series is fully explained only if the explanation appeals to some fact or facts outside the series. Hence, even if a series of causal antecedents or of ever more general physical laws is in practice never-ending, we do not explain the *series* by appealing to ever earlier antecedents or ever more general laws. Would the possibility that the series was infinite make any difference to the principle that no series can be completely explained in terms of its own members? It is hard to see why it should. In the case of the universe, its having infinite duration in time hardly renders empty the question as to why it has infinite duration, while endless chains of covering laws will not stop us asking why the series of laws has the general form it does. Moreover, neither infinite duration nor endless series of laws can give a sufficient reason for why there is anything at all, or even why there is just so much matter in the universe and no more. So, the principle of sufficient reason certainly leads us naturally to ask questions about the existence of the universe, which cannot be answered from within the universe, and this is the case whether or not we think there is a first event or ultimate facts about the nature of matter.

Saying that the principle of sufficient reason leads us to ask questions about the series of events and regularities that go to make up the universe, which cannot be answered from within the universe, does not, of course, mean that it is logically necessary that there should actually be a transcendent being or anything else to answer to these questions. It is hard to see that the principle of sufficient reason is itself *logically* necessary. It is not inconceivable that even within the world there might not be brute facts incapable of explanation, nor is it inconceivable that the world should just exist, without any further explanation, however much we might *feel* that these states of affairs are unsatisfactory. Moreover, even if we move outside the universe to God and so explain the universe, questions can still be asked about the reason why God exists or why he has created the universe in the way he has. God himself and his intentions are in fact taken by many believers to be ultimate brute facts, and there is something right in doing this. Some might, of course, want to maintain that God's existence is logically necessary, and this view will be examined in the next section. However, even if God's existence is logically necessary, by virtue of the fact that it is logically necessary, it cannot explain the contingent fact of the existence of the world, which is what the cosmological argument is attempting to do. I am assuming here that there is a clear sense in which the existence of the universe is contingent, namely the sense in which we would *imagine* a universe quite different from this actual universe. To assert that the universe logically could not have been other than it is would be to collapse entirely the distinction between necessary and contingent truths, something not even Leibniz was prepared to do. Significantly, some of those theists, such as Hartshorne, who see God as having to create *something*, stress that God has created only one of the many possible universes open to him to create. So it seems that if the cosmological argument is setting out to explain the existence and nature of the world, its terminus of explanation cannot be a logically necessary truth. It must be something, such as the Big Bang, or God's intentions or existence, which is regarded as a brute fact in the sense that it is not logically necessary and presumably also such that there is no sufficient reason for it. Hence then principle of sufficient reason cannot be of universal applicability, even for the defender of the cosmological argument, for his own argument ought to end in something that has no sufficient reason. So the principle can hardly be invoked to make it *logically* necessary that it has an application in a specific case, even when that case is the existence of the universe itself.

It is not logically necessary that the universe has an extra-mundane cause, just as it is not logically necessary that God's existence or intentions have some sufficient reason. But the consequence of this fact, that the cosmological argument cannot therefore deductively imply the existence of God, does not mean that it is thereby valueless. For, as has been persuasively argued by Richard Swinburne (1979), the various arguments for the existence of God should be viewed not as so many weak deductions, but as attempts to show that certain features of the world make God's existence more probable than his non-existence. They can do this by suggesting that the phenomena in question are better explained by postulating that they are brought about by an all-powerful personal God, than they would be if there was no God.

Swinburne uses Bayes's theorem as his tool for comparing competing explanations. Where h is a hypothesis, e a particular piece of evidence we are interested in, k our background knowledge apart from that piece of evidence and P (h / e.k) is read as the probability of h given the conjunction of e and h, Bayes's theorem reads:

$$P (h / e.k) = \frac{P (e / h.k)}{P (e / k)} \times P (h / k)$$

It will be noted that the theorem makes the probability of a hypothesis, given all our evidence and our background knowledge, (its posterior probability), *increase* the higher the probability of the evidence is, given the hypothesis plus our background knowledge, and the higher the probability of the hypothesis is given our background knowledge alone (the prior probability of the hypothesis), while the posterior probability of the hypothesis is *decreased* the more probable the evidence is on background knowledge minus our hypothesis. Bayesians claim that this theorem (which can be derived from the axioms of the probability calculus) systematizes many of our insights concerning scientific testing. Thus, e will give more support to h when it is a severe test of h (i.e. when the probability of e would not be high given k alone); equally e gives more support to h the nearer e comes to being deducible from h and k. In the case of universal scientific theories, where e is deducible from h, P (e / h.k), is, of course, equal to 1. So Bayes's theorem will tell us that an originally unlikely consequence of such a theory can give it considerable support, which is what we would expect. A further plausible consequence of Bayes's theorem is that a hypothesis h is confirmed by evidence e if, and only if, the evidence is more likely to occur if the hypothesis is true than if it is false, (i.e. P (h / e.k > P (h / k) iff P (e / h.k) > P (e / – h.k)). That is, the evidence must be in a strong sense relevant to the truth of the hypothesis. A more controversial aspect of Bayes's theorem, however, is the implication that the prior probability of the theory contributes positively to its posterior probability, in such a way that, of two competing theories both supported by the same evidence, the one with the greater prior probability will be given the greater posterior probability. This is controversial because, as is well known, Popper does not regard high prior probability as in any way to a theory's credit. Indeed, he sees it as simply an indication of low empirical content: for him, the more a theory initially predicts, the less probable it is. Swinburne, on the other hand, reads prior probability not as a measure of empirical content at all, but rather as an indication of a theory's probability relative to the rest of what we know. Popper claims to be unimpressed by plausibility of this sort, preferring instead theories that are bold and initially implausible. To go further in this dispute would be out of place here, and in any case unnecessary, because what will emerge from Swinburne's application of Bayes's theorem to arguments for the existence of God is the highly subjective nature of his assessment of the prior probabilities of theism and atheism, on which, as we shall see, the inductive support for theism from the cosmological and teleological arguments largely rests.

In applying Bayes's theorem to the cosmological argument, h will be the hypothesis that God exists. A lot is going to depend on how e and k are interpreted, but in order to give the argument its strongest possible form we will take e to be not just the existence of any finite object, but to be the existence of this complex physical universe over a period of time. In view of this, there is no observational evidence left for k to be, so the relevant background knowledge becomes what is generally known as tautological evidence, and P (e / k) and P (h / k) will refer to the intrinsic probabilities of e and h, respectively. Swinburne says, correctly it seems to me, that the probability of God creating a universe such as this one (P (e / h.k)) is not very high. As the traditional view of theism has it, God has no overriding reason to create a universe at all, and, even if he does decide to create one, no overriding reason to create one similar in complexity and content to this one. (It is, of course, open to anyone to attempt to show that God would have an overriding reason to create, but to argue this will be to argue a need, and hence a dependence, in God, which is why traditional theists, keen to preserve divine independence, have always been wary of such a suggestion.) As P (e / h.k) is going to be fairly low in this case, (though not, according to Swinburne, completely negligible[2]), the support that h can get is going to come mostly from showing that the hypothesis is fairly probable in itself (i.e. P (h / k) is fairly high), while the evidence is not very probable on its own (i.e. P (e / k) is low). Showing that the support comes from the evidence, rather than from the hypothesis alone, it will be remembered, is going to depend on showing that P (e / h.k) > P (e / – h.k). Swinburne argues that all these conditions are satisfied, by showing first that P (h / k) is higher than many other hypotheses about what there is, including P (e /k), where e is this world without God. Largely on the basis of what he establishes in doing this he then argues that the probability of this world without the hypothesis of God (i.e. P (e / -h.k) is far lower than the probability that this world is dependent on God (i.e. P (e /h.k).

We will take what he says about P (h / k) first. According to Swinburne, the prior probability of any theory is to be assessed primarily in terms of its fit with our background knowledge and its simplicity (1979, p. 52). In the case of the cosmological argument, where, because we are taking the existence of the whole world to be evidence, background knowledge is merely tautological evidence, and the simplicity of theism becomes the crucial factor in determining its prior probability. Swinburne argues that theism is an extremely simple hypothesis in three important respects. First, it postulates a person of a very simple kind, a creator who is omniscient, omnipotent, free, eternal, good and incorporeal. Second, its terminus of explanation is the activity of God. This contributes to the simplicity of theism in two ways; first, the choice of an agent is 'the most natural kind of stopping-place for explanation', and, second, placing our terminus of explanation in God's personal intentions means that the apparent dualism we get in everyday life between explanations in scientific terms and explanations in terms of people's intentions is ultimately resolved, because scientific laws are shown to be, in fact, expressions of divine choice. The final way in which theism is an extremely simple hypothesis is that it postulates that all things depend on God while God depends on nothing. So it is the end of all explanation. The intrinsic simplicity of theism is thus very high. Why should this contribute to its intrinsic probability? According to Swinburne,

perhaps it seems *a priori* vastly improbable if one thinks about it, that there should exist anything at all logically contingent. But, given that there does exist something, the simple is more likely to exist than the complex. (1979, p. 106)

So, even if P (h / k) may not be terribly high in itself, relative to other hypotheses about what might exist, where the existent is not simple, it is very high 'because of the great simplicity of the hypothesis of theism'.

Swinburne claims a high degree of simplicity for theism, first on the grounds that the God postulated is a simple entity. One wonders what entitles him to say this. From some points of view, God seems highly complex, far more complex than human beings, who are said by many to be the most complex beings on earth. Is God less complex than one of the simple, changeless objects postulated in Wittgenstein's *Tractatus*? In so far as God has a large number of attributes, and acts and wills in time, he might be said to be considerably more complex than an indivisible, unchanging atom; even though Swinburne would say that God's various attributes fit together, God is still multiple and complex compared with the atoms of logical atomism. (As we shall see in Section 4 below, attempts to think of God as unchanging are fraught with problems.) Then, according to Swinburne, an ultimate explanation in terms of personal agency is more simple than an unresolved dualism of explanations of a scientific and a personal sort, as well as being more satisfactory than an ultimately scientific account, because appeal to personal agency is the most natural stopping-point of explanation. Swinburne is right to say that an explanatory scheme with two radically different kinds of explanation is in that respect less simple than one which shows that one kind of explanation can be accounted for in terms of the other, although in other respects explanatory dualism might be simpler, if, for example, the resolving of the dualism was extremely complicated. But his belief that personal explanation is the most natural stopping-place for explanation is not likely to be accepted by everyone, particularly in this case, where God's decision to create is being taken as a basic datum not to be further explained. Is postulating an inscrutable act of will as the ultimate brute fact any more natural than postulating some facts about matter as no further explicable? Even though, as Swinburne says, we are aware from our own experience of ourselves as the sources of things being this rather than that, this does not mean that we are often satisfied with

113

our acts of will as the terminus of explanation. As human beings we characteristically look for further explanations of our acts of will. Finally, one wonders if postulating an independent cause of the universe outside the universe is more or less simple than sticking with the universe alone. Certainly, talking of God *and* the universe gives us a radical dualism of ontological types, where some might find it simpler to settle at this point for things of one type only.

I do not think that these questions show that Swinburne is definitely wrong to say that theism is a simpler explanation or account of the universe than other accounts which leave us with an unresolved complexity of things and always, not ultimately stemming from something very simple in various respects. But they do show that if there are ways in which theism is simpler than atheism, there are other respects in which atheistic alternatives might be simpler. The trouble with assessments of the simplicity of explanations is that they are indeterminate unless the respects in which theories are being compared for simplicity are carefully laid down, and even then we can say at most that one explanation is more simple than another in those respects. It is unclear that explanations are ever more or less simple per se. Thus nineteenth-century atomism might have been very simple in respect of numbers of type of basic particle, but far less simple than modern physics in its need for auxiliary hypotheses to save the phenomena. Again, modern physics may be very simple in some of its formulae (e.g. $e = mc^2$) but very complicated in the way these formulae are related to the world of experience. The trouble with Swinburne's comparisons of the relative simplicity of theism and atheism is that he has not specified the types of consideration which are to count as relevant to his determining the relative simplicity of the two. As such, his conclusion that theism is the most simple alternative has a highly subjective air.

However, more damaging to his case than reservations about his claim that theism is a simple hypothesis is his assumption that such simplicity has a bearing on its probability. Even if his simplicity assessment was not in part based on subjective considerations (such as what he finds the most natural stopping-place for an explanation), one is entitled to ask why, *in this case*, simplicity contributes to probability. It is true that scientists often prefer the mathematically simpler of two competing hypotheses, both of which cover all the known data, but the reason for this is not that the simpler hypothesis is necessarily the truer, or even likely to be the truer. It is rather that science aims at more than truth; it aims also at a system of simple and wide-ranging hypotheses. Without such a preference, scientists would have no reason for preferring theories that postulate underlying unifying causes for diverse phenomena, rather than remaining content with mere summaries or digests of past observations. For similar reasons, preference may be accorded theories which postulate one entity, rather than many, one kind of entity rather than many kinds, and zero or infinite degrees of a given quality, rather than some intermediate figure. Some may indeed be prepared to mark these preferences by according theories which are simpler in these respects greater degrees of prior probability, and this is obviously what underlies Swinburne's readiness to do the same in respect of theism. Caution is required at this point, however. Not all philosophers of science regard such simplicity as increasing prior probability, if, as seems likely, hypotheses simpler in the respects mentioned are also likely to be bolder in the sense of making more wide-ranging and striking new predictions than a theory that is a mere digest of past observations. Both Popperians and Carnapians would agree on this point, although they would differ in their attitude to the desirability or otherwise of the low prior probability accorded a simple but bold theory.

What in fact we need to ask at this point is why Swinburne or anyone else should be ready to argue that simplicity in general increases prior probability, meaning by that, that a simple theory is in general more likely to be true than a complex one, and this question needs to be sharply distinguished from the no doubt valid reasons of other sorts scientists have for preferring to formulate and test simple theories. The most that I think can be said here is that if two theories were empirically *equivalent* in the sense of making exactly the same predictions, then we would generally prefer the one that was simpler just because there is no decidable empirical difference between the two, and the simple theory is more in line with what we are aiming at in science. But this type of case is rare. If, as is more likely, we had two theories, both of which covered past data with a more or less similar degree of success, but which diverged on as yet untested predictions, we might well prefer the simpler theory for all sorts of reasons, but I do not see why it is more likely, a priori, to be true. If, to mark our preference, we decided to honour the simpler theory by according it a greater prior probability, this honour would appear to be entirely conditional on its future predictive success. Its future predictive success would in fact be the account on which the higher prior probability cheque was being drawn, but the fact that sometimes people may get away with writing cheques that they cannot yet honour should not make the practice of over-drawing in this way more acceptable in science or in business. Indeed, in science generally prior probability assessments derive their justification from our expectations as to future outcomes in the light of our background knowledge, and it is quite unclear that background knowledge suggests that, generally speaking, nature is likely to behave in what we regard as simple ways rather than in complex ways. But even if we could be sure that nature does conform generally to our assessments of simplicity, a crucial element is missing in the case of the contribution the simplicity of theism is to make to its prior probability. Swinburne does show that theism is a simple hypothesis in various respects, but in this case, as opposed to scientific cases, there is no question of arguing that its prior probability is greater than that of the arguably more complex hypothesis of atheism because our background knowledge assures us that its predictions are more likely than those of its rivals, for neither theism nor atheism make any specific predictions. In other words the ground on which prior probability assessments are made, justified and tested in science is entirely lacking in these cases, and what we are left with is just the bald claim that if anything is fundamental in the world, it is more likely to be something simple than something complex.

It is then, no surprise to find that Swinburne's only defence of his attempt to show why the supposed simplicity of theism contributes to its probability appears to rest in his claim that 'given that there does exist something, the simple is more likely to exist than the complex'. One wonders on what basis such a claim can be made; against what standard of probability can we possibly judge in general terms what type of thing is most likely to exist? If experience is anything to go by, and what is *likely* to exist in the abstract is rather like what we do have experience of as existing, then we will have to conclude that what is likely to exist is rather more complex than it need be. (We can easily imagine possible worlds a lot simpler than ours such as a Parmenidean, block universe.) If, on the other hand, we do not take our actual experience into account, we might wonder what the probability assessment is being based on. It hardly seems reasonable to say, in the absence of any evidence, that what is most likely to exist is that possible world which the human mind finds more simple. Indeed, in the absence of any way of deciding what is correct here, one doubts whether the question has any meaning at all. In a way, the point being made here is the old one made by Peirce, that universes are not as plentiful as blackberries, that, in other words, we have no sample of universes to inspect to infer what is a priori likely or unlikely in an actual world. In view of the impossibility of establishing whether something simple or complex is more likely in itself to exist and of the indeterminacy of the notions of simplicity and complexity outside strictly defined contexts, as well as the inconclusiveness of appeals to simplicity when not allied to expectations of predictive success, we have to conclude that Swinburne's claim that the prior probability of theism (P h / k) is higher than the prior probability of the existence of this fairly complex world on its own, without a divine creator or some other transcendent source, because of the higher comparative simplicity of simplicity of theism, fails. This failure in turn vitiates his attempt to show that the cosmological argument is a good inductive argument, because that attempt relies crucially on the assessments of P (h / k), and P (e / k).

The main reason why Swinburne thinks that the cosmological argument gives inductive support to the existence of God is that he thinks that while God – a simple object – might exist uncaused, it is much more unlikely that such a complex object as the universe should exist uncaused. In other words, P (e / k)< P (h / k). That the cause of the universe, if there is one, is likely to be the cause specified by h, rather than something else (i.e. P (e / h.k)> P (e / -h.k)), Swinburne suggests by arguing, not perhaps unreasonably, that the universe is less likely to be brought about by one or several non-omnipotent being or beings than by one omnipotent being. We may overlook the details of this at this point, because what is really at issue here is deciding whether the universe requires, or is made more comprehensible by, *any* explanation at all in terms of a transcendent cause or set of causes. Swinburne is correct to say that the existence of the universe is 'strange and puzzling'; to deny this argues altogether too flat and unimaginative an attitude to

---

existence. But to agree with Swinburne here is not at all to go along with him when he says that the existence of the universe 'can be made comprehensible if we suppose that it is brought about by God' (1979, pp. 131-2).

Whatever we might think about divine simplicity, what we have to ask at this point is whether the notion of a divine creator for the universe is one that is at all probable in itself, relative to our background knowledge. As J.L. Mackie has argued:

> the very notion of a non-embodied spirit, let alone an infinite one, is intrinsically improbable in relation to our background knowledge, in that our experience reveals nothing of the sort. (1982, p. 100)

All the knowledge we have of personal agency is of finite, embodied agents, whereas the theistic hypothesis postulates an infinite, disembodied agent, who brings things about in the world just by willing them, a willing which appears to have no further explanation. Can we make sense of the idea of a pure, unmediated act of will, as a result of which things just happen? It might be claimed that some of our basic bodily movements – of our legs and arms, for example – do constitute examples of acts of will immediately translated into material effect; and that this gives a sense to the idea of action on the part of something disembodied; in this case, the human will. Such a story is, of course, highly disputed as an account of human action, but even if it were accepted as such, it is not clear that it would help the theist. In the first place, it overlooks the way in which most of what we regard ourselves as willing we regard as subject to further explanations of various sorts, whereas God's will is being regarded by the theist as ultimate and inexplicable. Then, second and even more problematic for a theist like Swinburne who wants to maintain a distinction between the creator and his creation, if basic human actions are to be the model for divine agency, the world itself becomes the body of God. There certainly are people who do think like this, but they do so at the expense of denying that distinction between world and God which, for good reason, is a central aspect of traditional theism (as we shall see in Section 4 of this chapter). In sum, the vast difference between God's supposed agency in creating and sustaining the world and the agency of human persons is masked by

Swinburne's characterization of them both as cases of 'personal explanation', so much so that we must agree with Mackie's conclusion that divine 'personal explanation' is not a satisfactory beginning at all for our chains of explanation, and 'certainly not one that is given any initial probability by the ordinary information that we have to take as our background knowledge' (1982, p. 101).

The main reason advanced by Swinburne for the greater comprehensibility of a universe being caused by a personal God, over a universe such as ours existing on its own, is the alleged greater simplicity of God existing uncaused than of the universe existing uncaused. It is because of the complexity of e that he argues against either $P(e / -h.k)$ or $P(e /k)$ being high, while he thinks that $P(e / h.k)$ will be somewhat higher because e is unlikely to occur without divine agency. As $P(e / -h.k) < P(e / h.k)$, we will, on this view, have $P(h / e.k) > P(h / k)$, and so e will confirm h. Aside from the technicalities of Bayesian confirmation theory and the questionable appeals to simplicity, Swinburne is in effect presenting us with the familiar cosmological view, that while the universe is very unlikely to exist without God, it is not so surprising that a creator God should exist uncaused. But in presenting his case, he not only leaves problems for us with his account of simplicity; he also fails to take into account factors which significantly decrease $P(e / h.k)$. We just have no idea how or why a disembodied divine agent is supposed to create a universe at all, and nothing in our experience makes such a thing remotely probable. In view of this, even if Swinburne were correct in what he says about the greater simplicity of theism over atheism, it is not at all clear that he is justified in claiming that $P(e / h.k) > P(e / -h.k)$, and without this, on Bayes's theorem, he is not justified in claiming that e confirms h.

Swinburne's presentation of the cosmological argument rests too much on a questionable analysis and application of the notion of simplicity. For another account of why the universe on its own is less probable than a universe created by a divine first cause, we can turn to the defence of the argument given by Richard Taylor in Ch. 7 of his *Metaphysics* (1963). According to Taylor, the principle of sufficient reason requires that we look for explanations for the existence of what we find in experience, and he takes this to include the existence of the world itself. Although we can say that the world exists by accident or that it is an inherently necessary being, existing by its own nature, Taylor finds neither of these things very convincing. We do not readily accept that anything that exists *in* the world is either purely accidental, or necessary, so why should we think that either of these things might be true of the world as a whole? Taylor agrees that it is not logically necessary that the totality of things should not be different in kind from the members making up the totality, but says that in the case of world as a whole it is quite implausible to think of it as being necessary. We can easily think of it not existing, just as easily as we can think of anything in it not existing. There is nothing in the world that is eternal and imperishable, so why should the world itself be? This being so, we are naturally driven to seek a reason for the world's existence. Why should the perishable things that make up the world exist at all? The principle of sufficient reason suggests that a series of explanations of perishable beings must terminate in a being that needs no explanation or cause for its own coming into existence. Such a being would be an eternal, imperishable being, which can neither come into existence nor cease to exist, and Taylor speaks of it as non-contingent, self-caused and necessary. He claims that a first cause of this sort would indeed provide a sufficient reason for the universe and everything in it, while not requiring one for itself.

We can agree with Taylor that saying that the world is accidental is less than satisfactory to minds accustomed, as ours are, to operate under the principle of sufficient reason, although it must be emphasized that to say that is not to say that it might not be the case that there just is no further explanation for the existence of the world beyond a Big Bang, or imperishable matter, or whatever. It is at this point that subjectivity once more begins relentlessly to infect the discussion, for whatever one says about the reasons for the world as a whole can have no empirical consequences. Moreover, as I pointed out earlier, there is no logical necessity for the world as a whole to have a sufficient reason for its existence. Whether one finds it plausible that it should depends very much on whether, like Swinburne, one finds explanation in terms of the personal intentions of a disembodied spirit the most natural stopping-place for explanation, or whether, in view of the problems involved in any such hypothesis, one can live with the belief that the world, human beings, and one's own existence are the results of brute material facts, and permeated by chance happenings, through and through. Perhaps what we have here in the end are differences of psychology and character mainfesting themselves in what one does or does not find intellectually acceptable.

Taylor claims further that the world lacks anything necessary, existing of its own nature. God, he claims, is necessary, in the sense that he is neither dependent on anything else for his own existence nor perishable. In comparing the need for further explanation of the world with the absence of such a need in the case of God, Taylor appeals to God's possession of the properties of non-contingency, independence, imperishability, necessity and self-causation. While we can agree that neither the world nor anything in it can be conceived of as non-contingent or self-caused, it is by no means clear that bits of matter or energy might not be eternal or imperishable. Certainly many philosophers and scientists have rejected the idea of the creation of matter out of nothing, while the total annihilation of all matter is extremely hard to conceive. So, supposing that something material is eternal or imperishable, could we find the reason for the world's existence in itself? Surely not; for we could easily conceive of eternal bits of matter as not having existed, and ask questions about their causes. (Theologians are quite right to emphasize in this context that speaking of God as first cause does not imply that he created the world in time.) So imperishability and eternity are not sufficient for non-contingency, but what more is needed? Independence suggests itself, but here we need to distinguish between merely chance independence and something more substantial. If the world existed by chance, it would be independent in the sense of not depending on anything else for its existence, but this would hardly make it non-contingent. What could the more substantial independence be? Self-causation, in the literal sense of bringing oneself into existence is, as Taylor recognizes, absurd; the self-causation he is talking about is just to say that a self-causing being 'can neither come into being nor perish' (1963, p. 93). There could be beings which existed eternally and so *did* neither come into being nor perish, but it would not follow from this that they *could not* perish or have been brought into being. Self-causation, then, is more than eternity, something more like non-contingency, in fact.

The upshot of this discussion is that we can give *a* sense to the ideas of eternal being, imperishable being and independent being. But, despite what Taylor says, in the sense in which they are intelligible, these are not qualities which the world, or elements of

121

it, manifestly lack. Nor, more importantly, are they in any way equivalent to the non-contingency which would satisfy the questioning process initiated by the search for sufficient reasons. Self-causation is a nonsense, strictly speaking, so we are left with necessity and non-contingency itself. The suspicion is that the only type of being about which further questions could not be asked is one that is necessary, not in the sense of being eternal, imperishable and non-dependent, but in the sense of being logically necessary. But, as I have already pointed out, a logically necessary divine being, in addition to being an incoherent idea (as I shall show in the next section), cannot supply a sufficient reason for anything that is not itself logically necessary, and so it could not explain the contingent existence of this world.

In the end, then, Taylor's presentation of the cosmological argument is no more satisfactory than Swinburne's. The qualities he attributes to God to show that God stands less in need of explanation than the world either appear to amount to thinking of God as logically necessary, or they are qualities which foreclose further questioning no more than saying the world just exists does, and which, in any case, might well be found among merely worldly things. A God that stands in as much need of explanation as the world as well as bringing its own problems relating to its agency on the world, can hardly be said to be more probable than the world on its own.

Turning now to the teleological argument, we must first acknowledge that one's *initial* response to it will tend to go hand in hand with one's attitude to the cosmological argument. If one can imagine *a* world existing without a transcendent cause, then one has to imagine something ordered existing without a cause. For, as Hume has pointed out, anything that exists has some sort of order. However, saying this may not significantly weaken a teleological argument in respect of this world, if, for example, it could be shown that this world is a lot more ordered than a merely randomly existing world might have been. As Swinburne puts the argument, 'an appeal to chance to explain order becomes less and less plausible, the more and more order there is' (1979, p. 143 n.). So the principle cited by Hume, that any existing world has to have *some* sort of order is not a sufficient refutation of the argument for the argument concentrates on the nature of the order in *this* world. Nor will pointing to the undoubted truth that any world in which human beings can live and acquire knowledge requires a high degree of orderliness dispose of the argument; for what is at issue is precisely the reason for this world having sufficient orderliness to sustain human life.

So, despite some degree of overlap between the teleological and cosmological arguments, particularly when, as with Swinburne, the complexity of the actual world is brought into a presentation of the cosmological argument, we can distinguish between the two arguments by taking the cosmological argument to be concentrating on the fact of the existence of the world, and the teleological to be concentrating on the rather considerable amount of order to be found in our world. Strictly speaking, one could grant that a world, even one of some complexity, might exist uncaused, while finding it doubtful whether this more ordered world could. This, indeed, is implicit in Swinburne's treatment of the argument. In assessing its probability (P (h / e.k)), he takes the hypothesis to be the existence of a designing God, e to be the degree of order actually to be found in the world, and k to be the existence of any highly complex world. So he is asking what the chances are that a world as complex as ours could show as much order as ours does without its being created by a God. Hume, and many of his successors, including Plantinga (1967, p. 109-10) and Salmon (1978, p. 153), have seen the degree of order in this world as being consistent with the work of many creators and have apparently seen this as a strong objection to the teleological argument. Against this, Swinburne has argued powerfully (1979, p. 142) that we would expect a diversity of designers to produce a diversity of results, whereas so far we have not found different laws operating in different parts of the universe. A diversity of designers view would not just be a needless multiplication of causes, it would also be one for which there is no positive evidence. However, we need not examine this point further, for the main claim of the teleological argument is surely a claim that the world could not be as ordered as it is on purely random principles. To establish what is involved in this claim must be our main task.

Traditionally, proponents of the teleological argument have stressed what they see in the universe as evidence of non-human purposes. Aquinas and Paley both see human beings, and other living animals as functioning organisms in which the parts fulfil purposes within the whole. Thus, the eye is for seeing, the heart for pumping, the liver for cleansing, and so on. However, none of these organs can be regarded as having awareness or intelligence, and, as Aquinas puts it 'nothing however that lacks awareness tends to a goal, except under the direction of someone with awareness and with understanding.' (*Summa Theologiae* 1a, 2, 3). Hence, we have to think of bodies, whose parts are goal-directed, as created by an intelligence, which clearly cannot be a human intelligence. Paley actually sees the reproductive powers of living things as further evidence of their designedness. As is well known, he opens his *Natural Theology* (1802) by saying that a traveller who found a watch on a heath would naturally and correctly infer that what he found was designed by virtue of recognizing that 'its several parts are framed and put together for a purpose' (p. 5). Even if he had not seen such a thing before, this would be a reasonable conclusion on the evidence before him. The inference to a designer would be even stronger if the object he found later turned out to contain within itself 'a mechanism, a system of parts, a mould for instance, or a complex adjustment of lathes, files and other tools evidently and separately calculated for the purpose' of producing 'in the course of its movement, another watch similar to itself' (p. 8). In other words, a machine-making machine would be a very clear example of something produced by a designer. But nature is full of machine-making machines, hence there must be an intelligent creator behind nature, just as we are behind the machine-making machines which increasingly populate our factories.

Both Aquinas and Paley emphasize in their argument the purposefulness or ordering of means to ends which is so noticeable in nature. They can conceive such a thing only in terms of a designer, and this of course is what Paley's assimilation of living organisms to machines is designed to bring out. The validity of this assimilation is just what is contested by post-Darwinian biology, one major aim of which has been to explain purposefulness in nature without invoking any conscious purpose or design on the part of a creator. As Darwin himself put it in his *Autobiography*:

> The old argument from design in nature, as given by Paley, which formerly seemed to me so conclusive, fails, now that the law of natural selection has been discovered. We can no longer argue that, for instance, the beautiful hinge of a bivalve shell must have been made by intelligent being, like the hinge of a door. (pp. 50-1)

What Darwin's 'law of natural selection' attempts to show is that the nature of the species that now live on the earth can be accounted for in terms of the interaction between the environment and earlier species or earlier members of the present species. A key point in Darwinian theory, as modified and corrected by contemporary molecular biology and genetics, is that this sort of interaction is strictly one way. That is to say, the nature of the individuals that are reproduced is determined by their genetic make-up. Parents pass on a selection of their genes to their children, but the genes the parents pass on are in no way altered by the lives or experience of the parents; hence what is given to the children is not affected in any way by what new characteristics their parents have acquired during their life-time,[3] except in the minimal sense that the lives of the parents have enabled them to engage in reproductive activity at all. It is in this sense that the fittest survive: only those beings that are fit enough to reproduce can transmit their genes to offspring. The environment interacts with individuals by not allowing the unsuccessful to reproduce. This is why only 'good' genetic make-ups have a chance of forming populations. Those whose natures are not good enough to allow them to reproduce will never pass on their genes – or their natures.

The interaction between species and environments is a matter of environments weeding out the less successful individuals and, hence, their characteristics. I have said that the nature of new individuals is determined by their genetic make-up, and that this, in turn, is given to them by their parents. But they are not simply carbon-copies of their parents. For one thing, in sexual reproduction, the genes of a new individual are a mix of the genes of both parents. For another, any microscopic process is subject to a degree of instability, and some of these perturbations in the reproduction and transmission of genetic material are sufficient to alter the characteristics of offspring. Both the mixing of genes in sexuality and the mutating of genes are random processes, and this is the second key point of Darwinian theory. Any new characteristics of individuals, any mutations, in other words, are due to random factors. So what the environment weeds out or reinforces is due to chance; the developments brought about by evolution are in effect those randomly produced genetic novelties which survive environmental pressures so as to reproduce and eventually to become dominant within a species or even to form a new species.

Many people, of course, find all this fantastic. How could the process of evolution have led to, say, the elephant or the human hand by means of generations of random alterations to simple organisms? To this, a standard answer is that over a sufficiently long time an amoeba-like creature could eventually have developed into an elephant in the way described. Other biologists have not been satisfied with this standard answer, because of doubts as to whether random genetic changes could possibly explain the relatively smooth way in which anatomical changes in animals appear to answer their behavioural goals (not least because most anatomical changes would be lethal to any organism unfortunate enough to undergo them, because they would not know what to do with them). They have argued that in many cases new genetic mutations do not confront the external environment raw, as it were, but that they are preceded by specific behavioural aims on the part of the organism. It is because an anatomical mutation subserves an existing behavioural tendency on the part of the organism that it is potentially useful rather than lethal. Thus, in an organism for which speed on land is important, mutations leading to longer legs will be preserved, although for other organisms in the same environment who were not aiming for speed, longer legs might be a great handicap. In other words, on this view, changes in anatomical structure are preceded by existing behavioural preferences, in the light of which some anatomical changes are potentially useful and can be recognized as such by the animals in question. (To put it somewhat anthropomorphically, a proto-giraffe would not have known what to do with its longer neck unless it was already aiming to reach the highest branches of trees.) Although the view that behavioural preferences spearhead evolution is a modification of Darwinism, it does little to remove the element of randomness that, as we shall see, makes Darwinism so antithetical to any teleological view of biological evolution. For the mutations that do serve the behavioural preferences (and the genes controlling the preferences themselves) remain the result of random perturbations in the genetic material. It is this view that is clearly inconsistent with the idea that biological evolution *has* to be explained by appeal to an ordering intelligence working to a predetermined end. For the evidence for such an idea could not consist in a process in which the individual stages and hence the ultimate direction were regarded as being so heavily dependent on unpredictable errors of copying at the level of microphysics.

Neither we nor the designers could know just what direction would be taken if it was – as we are assured it is – quite impossible to predict the processes that provide the subject matter for the law of natural selection to work on. The most that might be predicted would be that *if* such and such a mutation occurred at such and such a time in such and such a species, then it would or would not be likely to succeed (although whether it actually succeeded would also presumably depend on all sorts of further chance coincidences concerning the life history of the first individual mutant).

Darwinism and subsequent developments in molecular biology thus make it impossible for us to see clear evidence of the plan of any designing intelligence underlying biological evolution, although saying this does not mean that there might not be a designer juggling the random processes to suit his ends. This might indeed be the case, and it would not necessarily be irrational to believe that it was. But what Darwinism prevents us from doing is drawing any such teleological conclusions from observation of order and function in the biological world. For, according to Darwinism, all such ordering is in a very real sense dependent on chance processes, and this is why, if true, it would destroy the arguments of Aquinas and Paley from biological functioning to a divine orderer. However, we might wonder whether, even in some modified form, Darwinism is true. One set of observations which may appear to cast considerable doubt on the whole programme is the extraordinary similarity of mammalian evolution among both marsupials and placentals. What appears to have been the case is that both marsupial and placental mammals had a common mouse-like ancestor. From this common ancestor, two different modes of reproduction developed at a time before the cutting-off of Australia from the mainland. Only marsupials got to Australia before this happened, while placentals never got there. So we have among mammals two parallel evolutionary processes, one in Australia with marsupials and one elsewhere with placentals. The extraordinary fact is that in Australia we get very good marsupial replicas of many placental species – moles, ant-eaters, flying squirrels, cats and wolves. According to David Attenborough (1979, p. 213) placental and marsupial species of mole and flying squirrel are so similar as to be virtually indistinguishable without handling. As Bartley comments the idea that this parallel and *totally independent* development *just happened to occur* as a matter of random variation in the face of comparable external environments is preposterous (1976, p. 483)

Bartley goes on to argue (following such writers as L.L. Whyte, W.H. Thorpe and L. von Bertalanffy) that these and other cases of parallel evolutions are strongly indicative of internal biological restrictions on posible variations at the molecular and chromo-somal level. This kind of restriction is non-Darwinian, because it is suggesting that there is a degree of internal genetic control and sifting before any competitive selection pressures, behavioural or environmental, are allowed to get to work.

If this view were correct, would it be of any solace to the teleologist? I cannot see that it would, for this reason. What is being added to orthodox Darwinism here is in essence another, albeit considerable grille for sifting random processes. It does nothing, however, to make the actual input to the sifting less random. Thus, while we might now be able to predict that an Australian marsupial occupying the equivalent ecological niche to a European wolf would probably turn out to be anatomically similar to a placental wolf, before its discovery we would have been unable to say with any certainty that there was such a thing at all. At most, the *probability* of there being something anatomically like a wolf would be somewhat higher than on orthodox Darwinian principles, but hardly high enough to make it a good bet. (There are in Australia no marsupial monkeys or horses; nor are there placental kangaroos or wallabies.) Thus, although on the non-Darwinian view we are considering, the effects of randomness are somewhat mitigated, randomness itself is still at the centre of the evolutionary stage, and it is this that makes biological evolution on its own hard to see in terms of conscious design or forethought. Teleology presumably cannot be based on the concept of a dice-playing designer.

There will naturally be those who resist the thought that men and other animals are, in a significant sense, products of chance. One way out, as we have seen, is to see a divine purpose behind *and despite of* the apparently random mutations of genetic material. While this is not in any way absurd, it cannot, of course, be any part of the sort of argument espoused by Aquinas and Paley, because the premise of that argument has to be that design is discernible within and not despite of the biological evidence. Others may wish to reject the whole Darwinian picture, with its 'law of natural selection' operating on random jugglings and changings of genes. It is, of course, open to them to do this, though at the cost of rejecting most of what is known in contemporary microbiology. Some will not find this cost too great as a means of preserving their regard for themselves as beings manifestly and fully intended by a divine creator since the beginning of time, but they should not delude themselves by claiming that some version of creationism is scientifically as respectable as contemporary evolutionary theory. Criticisms of evolution as a scientific theory seem to divide into two not entirely consistent groups. On the one hand, there is the claim that evolution is not, or is not treated as, a falsifiable hypothesis. It is ironic that Popper is sometimes referred to in this context, for while he has denied that there could be a scientific law of evolution (cf. his 1957, pp. 108-9) and has, of course, argued for the demarcation between science and non-science being made in terms of falsifiability, no-one has done more in recent years to argue for the importance of metaphysical research programmes to science in general and for the immense fruitfulness of the Darwinian research programme in particular. A metaphysical research programme is a guiding idea, itself unverifiable and unfalsifiable and quite general in scope, but which nevertheless provides a direction and an impetus for scientific research, for the formulation of precise and testable theories. Examples from physics would be atomism (the ultimate constituents of matter are indivisible particles) and mechanism (there is no action at a distance). Both these ideas have been immensely fruitful in the construction and elaboration of precise theories, though both have now been superseded. Popper regards Darwinism as a research programme in this sense: a theory of evolution, describing the process of biological development from amoeba to man, cannot itself be a law of nature, because what is being described is a unique and highly improbable historical process, whereas scientific laws make assertions concerning all processes of a certain kind. (There is, for example, no guarantee that life on Twin Earth would have evolved in the same way as life on earth.) Moreover, one could add that the 'law of natural selection', as formulated by Darwin, verges on the tautologous, stating as it does that in any struggle for survival 'favourable variations (in species) would tend to be preserved and unfavourable ones to be destroyed' (Darwin's own words).

Nevertheless, the conception of evolution as a process involving environmental selection of randomly instigated innovations (though not itself a scientific theory) is one that has been and is immensely fruitful, not only in leading to detailed and testable theories in biology, genetics and ethology, which have in many cases been confirmed, but also in stimulating intriguing comparisons of different sorts between biological evolution and the growth of knowledge and the spreading of ideas (cf. Popper 1979, Ch. 7; Monod, 1971, pp. 154-5; Dawkins, 1978, Ch. 11). In contrast, the Lamarckian research programme (that acquired characteristics can be passed on by inheritance) has led, by and large, only to falsified theories, while creationism (the idea that biological evolution is a myth, because species are created whole and entire) has led, as would be expected, to no testable theories at all. This brings us to the second line of criticism of evolutionary theory, that it has empirical and theoretical problems of its own. Some of these, indeed, we have already touched on. Others concern the absence of evidence of intermediate evolutionary stages in the fossil record, while others point to the apparently high improbability of life developing at all on the earth, without some intervention from an outside intelligence. We shall return to this last point later, but what the critics of evolutionary theory fail to recognize is that the presence of empirical difficulties for a scientific theory is actually a measure of the theory's initial scientific strength, for it shows that the theory has some empirical bite. Of course, if successive revisions and modifications of the theory fail to account for the counter-evidence, and if a better empirical theory comes up, then counter-evidence for a theory will lead to its overthrow. But the mere existence of counter-evidence need not count against a theory, particularly if, as seems to be the case with some of the difficulties Darwinism is faced with, the modified theories which explain the problems themselves receive empirical confirmation.

I have said that Darwinism does not destroy religion, even a religion such as Christianity which sees the creation and ultimate redemption of the human race as the climax of God's plan for the universe. But it does not destroy it only at the expense of saying that, despite appearances of random genetic mutation, there is still a plan behind it all. Defenders of religion often under-estimate the expense involved in doing this, or fail to realize what is involved at all. Swinburne, for example, writes (1979, p. 135-6) of nature as a machine-making machine similar to the sorts of machine-making machines men make, and hence requiring a creator analogous to the men who design the machine-making machines. Swinburne actually finds this argument weak because of 'the evident paucity of organisms throughout the universe', but claims that, as far as it goes, it is immune to refutation by biological discoveries. But, what biology appears to question is whether nature can be regarded as a machine-making machine at all, in the intended sense. For the machines being made by nature are living organisms, and what is at issue is the extent to which the development of species in nature is like the operation of machine-making machines. At the very least a machine, whether made by a man or another machine, is something that is designed with some pre-determined function, and it is just the notion of design according to a pre-determined function that modern biology has striven to eliminate, without denying the existence of order and function in the natural world.

Because of the problems involved in seeing the development of species in teleological terms, fundamentalist Christians are perhaps wiser than they often realize in fighting against evolution. Evolution is a problem for Christianity not because of the claim that man is descended from ape-like creatures, but because it makes it difficult, though not, to be sure, impossible to see God as having a plan in species development at all. Even though we are not prevented from talking about a plan here altogether, it is very much a question of a plan which is visible only to the eyes of faith. It is certainly not manifest in the biological evidence, as Paley so fervently believed. This at least has been established by modern biology, which, whether its conclusions will stand for all time or not, has presented the most coherent and detailed account available of natural history. Combined with its rejection of teleology, this fact undoubtedly weakens greatly the force of any argument such as those of Aquinas and Paley. We no longer find it inconceivable that the eye should have the function of seeing 'except under the direction of someone with awareness and understanding', nor indeed very improbable.

However, the argument that the world needs a designer does not have to be based on a perception of biological or indeed any other sort of function in the natural world. It is to Swinburne's credit that he has clearly distinguished in this context between what he calls arguments from spatial order and arguments from temporal order. Arguments from spatial order are those which focus on the inter-relatedness of the parts of complex things, particularly biological organisms. However, as we have seen, this inter-relatedness can be and is convincingly explained without postulating any designer for the organism. But doing this does not mean that there might not be other aspects of order in the world which do require the postulation of a designer, and it is this that Swinburne attempts to demonstrate by appeal to what he calls temporal order: the all-pervasiveness of a comparatively few scientific laws throughout as much as we know of the universe, at all times of which we know.

Although one might feel a certain oddity about a God who creates a vastly ordered universe and then plays dice in one part of it (life on earth), Swinburne's claim that the 'overwhelmingly striking fact' of temporal order in the universe strongly requires explanation by appeal to a designer deserves careful attention on its own merits. The point of the claim is to insist that the 'all-pervasive' regularities of succession which we find in the universe in themselves constitute an insoluble problem for science, over and above the actual existence of the world. Even if we could imagine a world existing with no cause, we could not so easily imagine a world so ordered without a designer. Science itself can only report the fact and nature of the order: it cannot explain why nature should conform so well to 'formulae recorded in the scientific laws formulated by men' (1979, p. 148). What Swinburne finds 'incredible' (p. 145) is the suggestion that physical objects should 'all, throughout infinite time and space, have some general powers identical to those of all other objects' without there being some cause of this. The complexity of the universe he appealed to in his presentation of the cosmological argument, turns out in the end to be the cover for a tremendous orderliness. But if it was all a matter of coincidence, the fact that one body has a certain power does nothing to explain or make it probable that another does. The complexity of the vast number of different bodies in which 'the orderliness of identical powers and components is embodied . . . cries out for explanation in terms of some single common source with the power to produce it.'

On the basis of these considerations, together with his earlier rejection of a many-designer universe, taking h to be the hypothesis of a single omnipotent designer, e to be the orderliness of the world, and k to be the existence of a complex world, Swinburne concludes P (e / h.k) greatly exceeds P (e / k), hence P (h / e.k) is much greater than P (h / k). Moreover, we can also reasonably assert that an omnipotent creator would have created an ordered world rather than a chaotic one, so P (e / h.k) is high (= 1, according to Swinburne). Hence P (e / h.k) greatly exceeds P (e / -h.k), and therefore P (h / e.k) is much greater than P (h / k). Thus we can conclude, on Bayesian grounds, that the orderliness of the universe considerably adds to the probability of the existence of a designer for it.

Swinburne's presentation of the argument from temporal order in Bayesian terms certainly does show the strength of the argument. Indeed, one wonders why, on his premises, temporal order simply *adds* to the probability of God's existence (as he claims), rather than actually making the probability of God's existence >0.5. For Bayes's theorem states

$$P \ (h \ / \ e.k) \ = \ \frac{P \ (e \ / \ h.k)}{P \ (e \ / \ k)} \ \ x \ P \ (h \ / \ k)$$

Swinburne thinks that P (e / h.k) = 1, and P (e / k) must be in his view very low (because he thinks that a highly ordered universe such as this one is incredible without God), so let us say P (e /k) = 0.1. P (h / k) is small for Swinburne, but following his defence of the cosmological argument, in which he argued that the existence of a complex world added some probability to the postulation of an omnipotent creator who designed the world, it is presumably not negligible, so let us say it is >0.05. On these rather conservative figures P (h / e.k) comes out at >0.5!

Against this interpretation of the probabilities, however, we still have to ask ourselves the same question that, following Mackie, we asked in connection with the cosmological argument: is the unlikelihood of a disembodied infinite spirit mysteriously creating this world really less on our background knowledge than the unlikelihood of pervasive temporal order throughout the universe as a basic brute fact, not further explicable. In other words, is P (e /h.k) really greater than P (e /-h.k)? It is far from clear that a highly ordered, but otherwise inexplicable universe is actually more problematic than the mysterious operations of a unique and otherwise inexplicable disembodied spirit bringing this universe about. In other words, even accepting Swinburne's claims about the remarkableness of all-pervasive temporal order at face value would not necessarily show that theism is more probable than atheism; in particular, it does not show that, on what we know, it is likely that a disembodied spirit would (or could) bring about an ordered material world.

But, in addition to this weighty indicator of the subjective nature of probability judgments concerning the explanation of temporal order in the world, there remain considerable doubts about some of the elements of Swinburne's account of it. It may indeed be possible to show with some plausibility how the order that we at present experience in the world may actually have evolved randomly from an initially far less ordered state of the universe. In the first place, Swinburne talks confidently of the *all*-pervasiveness of temporal order, as if this is something we have or could have evidence for. He means by this talk of all-pervasiveness that physical objects 'throughout infinite time and space, have some general powers identical to those of all other objects'. One wonders how Swinburne can be so sure of this. Has he any evidence that there have been *physical objects* at all places and all times? And even if there are, do they always have the same powers? This is not the story told by many cosmologists. (Black holes and the like are hardly physical objects. Moreover, many speak of the first instants of the universe as involving immense and irreversible alterations in the nature and powers of the earliest existing things.) Even leaving these doubts aside, there is a certain naivety in thinking of the entire universe as a system with the sort of stability Swinburne seems to envisage. He appeals to our belief in induction to support his view that there is an order in nature which is not imposed or invented by men (1979, p. 137), but such an appeal cannot take us very far, for the simple reason that belief in induction just *is* belief in mind-independent order. In any case, although we do have to postulate a continuing order in the world in order to theorize scientifically about it at all, such a postulation does not in itself show that there is order or that, if there is, it is *all*-pervasive.

It is true that any world in which human beings could acquire knowledge by empirical means (through perception and measurement) must have a degree of stability in itself, and be accommodated either directly to human senses or indirectly to our artificial instruments of measurement and perception. The true relevance in this context of Hume's point that any world which we can observe must have a degree of stability is not that *any* world must have stability, but that a world lacking stability in the required respects would be a world which we could neither observe nor theorize about scientifically. So it is no coincidence that our observations and theories do reveal an order in the world. Moreover, that we, a successful species, should be perceptually attuned to our present environment is something to be expected on evolutionary grounds, though it obviously does not follow from this that we will be perceptually attuned to every environment we might find ourselves in. The presupposition of our making observations and theories at all is that there is an order in our environment, and order to which our senses are adapted. But it hardly follows from this, that the universe was or will be forever such as to enable us to theorize about it in the sense of successfully uncovering significant projectible regularities in nature. Perhaps there are places and times at which things are so out of phase either in themselves or with our perceiving and measuring that we would be unable to learn anything about what is going on at them. If there were such places we would be unable to know whether the breakdown of our theories and observations at those points reflected thoroughgoing cosmic disorder or simply a breakdown in our own observing and theorizing activities. Moreover, if either cosmic disorder or lack of accommodation between our perceptions and the world was sufficiently thoroughgoing in any part of the universe, we would be precluded from knowing anything substantial about it, apart from realizing our knowledge was breaking down. So the fact that in what we have been able to discover about the universe, we have uncovered order and regularity tells us nothing about the conditions that might obtain in places and times that are beyond our ken.

What I am trying to suggest is that however thoroughgoing our experience of order in the world might be, it could not preclude equal or greater tracts of disorder, some of which might be such as to be necessarily unknowable to us. The reason I am interested in this speculation at this point is because I want to show that Hume's 'Epicurean' account of the presence of order in the world (*Dialogues Concerning Natural Religion* §8) cannot be lightly dismissed by the theist. What Hume asks us to envisage is a world in which there is originally total chaos and disorder, in which whatever there was moved around constantly and with no appearance of order. (In reply to the objection that movement in itself requires a first mover, Hume – or, rather Philo, his mouthpiece – answers that regarding movement as originating in matter itself is no more inconceivable than seeing it imparted to matter by mind or intelligence.) So we have random agitation throughout the universe. How do we get from there to a combination of perpetual agitation in matter with 'a constancy in the forms which it produces' which is what we actually find in the world? According to Hume, any random moving of things must, over a long enough period, produce a semblance of order, must, in other words, achieve whatever stability it can, and having achieved it, continue to maintain itself at least for a time in the stable state, for that is the nature of a stable system. If there is anything in a world consisting of randomly moving entities which is potentially conducive to a more stable set-up, then, if the results of the random movements ever produce the conditions for a degree of stability (which they presumably will in time), the resulting stable systems will continue to maintain themselves at least for a time. As Hume comments:

> the continual motion of matter, therefore, in less than infinite transpositions, must produce (the) economy or order (we find), and, by its very nature, that order, when once established, supports itself for many ages if not to eternity. But wherever matter is so poised, arranged, and adjusted as to continue in perpetual motion, and yet preserve a constancy in the forms, its situation must, of necessity, have all the appearance of art and contrivance which we observe at present. (1779, p. 53)

Of course, it might be objected that this Epicurean account of world order pre-supposes that matter is initially such as to have potentially orderable qualities. Indeed it does, but I cannot see that this is an objection to the account when it is presented as an alternative to the theistic explanation of temporal order in the world. For what that explanation finds incredible is the emergence of world order out of chaos without a guiding hand. Here is an account of how it could happen. It is true that if the original particles had no attracting or combining properties (or their opposites), then no order would emerge at all, but I do not see any reason to suppose that completely monadic primary elements are a priori more likely than ones that do attract and react with each other. Once it is granted that there could be active and reactive primary elements in nature, the Epicurean account suggests a way in which random movements alone could produce a degree of stability out of an initially chaotic world.

In a sense, of course, this is what is suggested in the biological realm by evolutionary theory. Indeed, Richard Dawkins (1978, pp. pp. 13-14) sees evolution's 'survival of the fittest' as an example of a more general principle which he dubs 'survival of the stable'. In evolution what we have is precisely the development of order through eliminating those random mutations which are unstable. The trouble with all the stable existents of our experience, however, is that none of them are systems so stable as to endure forever. Their survival (and hence their stability) is circumscribed by incursions from outside, for they are not self-contained systems, but rather, elements in larger systems. And the largest system of all, the universe, is one that is tending to become, in one depressing sense, much more stable, according to the second law of thermodynamics. According to this law two physical systems in contact with each other will tend to become more alike in temperature and energy, eventually achieving a statistical equilibrium. Applied to the isolated and single system of the whole universe, this means that there will be a general levelling down or up of everything within it, until differences of energy within it are eliminated. This is sometimes spoken of in terms of an increase of disorder in the universe, for disorder is seen in terms of quantity of information within the universe. With everything becoming closer in terms of energy levels, there will be fewer differences within the universe and fewer discrete identifiable systems within it. But, however dull and lifeless a place the universe will become on this view, it will obviously be much more stable, and *in that sense* more ordered than it previously was.

We have in evolution and the second law of thermodynamics two illustrations of the way in which stability might naturally arise from instability. Of course there is a certain tension between the two examples. Evolutionary theory appears to predict an increase of complexity and differentiation, at least within the biological realm, whereas the second law assures us that increases of order of that sort are going against the general trend of material development, very much the exception rather than the rule and, in the end, to be lost in the advance of disorder in the universe as a whole. That the tension between evolution and the second law is only apparent can be explained because each growth of biological order in the development of organisms is paid for by thermodynamic losses in the larger systems to which the organisms belong. Nevertheless, one wonders whether the sorts of appeal to cosmic order made by Swinburne are entirely consistent with the implications of the second law, or with the currently fashionable ideas of the universe eventually collapsing totally in a black hole. On both these types of theory the sort of order we experience is seen as a merely transient phase in the history of the universe en route to a far more stable though far less interesting and hospitable system.

According to contemporary physics, then, *our* world order is not going to exist for eternity. In the end, most of the types of entity we recognize, together with their properties and regularities will disappear. Moreover Big Bang theorists believe that most of the substances we find at present around us were not present in the early history of the universe but formed out of the originally created hydrogen and helium which themselves began to exist only after the cooling-down following the initial battle of creation and annihilation fought out between particles of matter and anti-matter. All this suggests that considerable qualification is needed in Swinburne's appeals to an order among objects throughout infinite time and space. Still, it might be felt, in contrast to the disorder envisaged at the Big Bang and in the subsequent demise of our universe, that the order we currently experience is that much more remarkable and more in need of explanation. How could it have come about and established itself purely randomly? Swinburne himself raises just this point in considering Hume's Epicurean hypothesis, suggesting that the amount of order in the universe is highly difficult to envisage as having come about in purely random fashion (and he compares the difficulty of this with the difficulty of imagining Shakespeare's works being the result of random typing by monkeys). What Swinburne says is, of course, quite right if we are envisaging the random shaking of particles as suddenly and instantly producing with one shake a world such as this, fully formed and organized. That would indeed be like an illiterate and inhuman creature suddenly typing out reams of sentences homographically equivalent to Shakespeare's works. But this is not how the universe or life are construed as evolving. The process is seen much more in terms of initial random steps being controlled by the environments in which they are made and then providing a context for the control of future random steps. Hence there is both a direction to any evolutionary process, and an appearance of design. Biological evolution gives us a marvellous picture of such a process, showing not monkeys randomly and inexplicably typing out *Hamlet, King Lear, Macbeth* and the rest, but the means by which monkey-like creatures might have evolved randomly into a race, one of whose members was the William Shakespeare whose unpredictable interaction with his culture and his environment resulted in his plays.

The history of the universe clearly includes many events which are highly improbable on any evidence available to us. Indeed, even quite mundane events, like a chance meeting of old school friends in a rush hour in a foreign city or my winning some complicated combination bet at the races would presumably be given a very low prior probability, yet such events do happen (or so I am told). However low the prior probability of the undesigned coming-into-being of this universe, it cannot be ruled out a priori. It could just be that the universe and everything in it just exists, as it is, with no explanation at all, hence the teleological and cosmological arguments cannot be deductively valid. But they can, of course, be made to seem inductively highly plausible, because we are not accustomed in our experience to unexplained existence and uncaused order. It would be a trivial rejoinder to say at this point that this is just what we are accustomed to, because the universe is full of uncaused order and unexplained existence, because in our physics and our biology we implicitly reject this view in attempting to explain the unexplained. Moreover, it would be completely inappropriate to reject the teleological argument as Salmon does (1978, pp. 150-1) by suggesting that the material universe provides us with millions of examples of *undesigned* natural systems, for whether these systems are designed or not is just what is at issue. However, what cosmology and biology attempt to do is to show how complex natural systems can evolve from disorder as a result of purely natural happenings. The fall-out from the chaotic disorder of the Big Bang gradually cools and settles into hydrogen and helium atoms, and forms into stars and galaxies and solar systems and the other elements, all rushing apart from each other, until they begin to cave in. . . . The original living molecules begin to reproduce and to compete for sustenance, and to develop protective shells, sense organs, limbs, brains and so on, so as to improve their reproductive chances. . . . The significance of the 'law' of the survival of the fittest and the survival of the stable is not that before anyone had thought of them a teleological argument might have been deductively valid, for it never was, but rather that before they had been spelled out and their empirical implications examined, the existence of undesigned order in the universe might quite legitimately have seemed highly improbable.

In reply to the suggestion that the order we perceive in the universe might have evolved through a gradual settling-down of originally random elements, it might be said that we have no evidence of atoms of past millennia behaving differently from ours; that when we observe stars million of light years away, their component elements appear like ours. Part of the answer to this must be to point out once more that on some present day theories many commonplace atoms (such as carbon atoms and zinc atoms) did not exist at all at one time, but were themselves formed at later stages of the universe. It will then, of course, be said that the laws that govern the formation and evolution of atoms and, maybe, of electrons, neutrons, protons and other sub-atomic particles are of universal application, and that if a hydrogen atom of now has different properties from a hydrogen atom in the early minutes of the universe, this must itself be explained in terms of some law of nature which has universal application.

It can readily be conceded that any genuine law of nature has universal application and, further, that scientific explanations are ideally expressed in terms of universal laws and are not merely probabilistic or restricted to particular spatio-temporal regions. But the point at issue is whether there are any laws of nature to cover and explain evolutionary processes completely. We have seen clearly enough, in considering Darwinism, that biological explanations stop short of explaining the juggling and mutating of genes, which provide the input to evolutionary change. Might not something of the sort be the case in the evolution of the universe? And how, in the absence of any precise theories covering the early 'minutes' following the Big Bang, can we be sure that this was not the case? Of course, once a degree of stability had been achieved in the universe, it would have continued at least for a time. Such indeed is the nature of stability. Once we realize this, millennia of stability are actually to be expected, even after initial randomness (though as I have pointed out, some believe everything will eventually end up back in the melting pot). What we are asking is whether it is unlikely that the temporal order in the universe could have emerged from initial randomness. If, as is often suggested, the Big Bang was followed by an incredibly active and volatile stage, it could well be that some sort of stable system evolved very quickly from the chaos within minutes, perhaps, and so observers might be able to uncover 'laws of nature' regulating much since the first few minutes. So immense tracts of regularity, even regularities governing the development of matter as we understand it today, are not inconsistent with the Epicurean account of order in the universe, whereby order evolved from an initially random shaking out.

My Epicurean objection to Swinburne is not that I can show his account of order as ruling throughout the universe even at the very start to be wrong, or even unlikely, but, equally, he cannot show mine to be wrong or unlikely. In the first place, neither of us has access to the first few minutes of the universe. On my account, even if we had, the chaos reigning then might preclude any information-gathering about it at all and this actually points to a further inconclusiveness in basing a claim about universal order in our universal experience of order, for, as already pointed out, the constitution of our senses and our minds are such as to be able to perceive and organize experience only if there is a high degree of order in our sensory input. So if there was disorder of the sort I am postulating, there might be physical limits on its observability. More crucially, however, assuming that we could gather information about the early moments of the universe, some scientists might be ingenious enough to discern within it patterns they could project right through to the present. But although the uncovering of such regularities would show that the Epicurean account I have offered was in error, and that Swinburne was right in speaking of the all-pervasiveness of order in the universe, it is not at all clear that such a demonstration would help Swinburne's theism. For what would be being said now would be that in the immediate post-Bang state, energy behaves like this, and particles like that (and then that they continue to develop along those lines). But how could we show that these initial moves in the development of matter and energy, from which all the other order in the universe would derive, were not purely random jumps from which everything else then took its cue? Presumably what we would need to settle this question would be other instances of immediate post-Bang universes to see if matter and anti-matter generally behave like they did at the start of our universe, and that is just what is lacking. In other words, without other universes to compare this one with, we can never be in a position to decide whether the order in this one is the result of initial randomness or not. So even allowing Swinburne all-pervasiveness of inferable order throughout the universe would not rule out the possibility that everything had started in a type of randomness, nor even that this is an improbability. The very uniqueness of the universe and its early stages, assuming it had a beginning, in the end makes it impossible to decide whether the order we find in the universe, even if this were completely all-pervasive, was actually the result of an initially random start, or whether it was imposed from outside, which is what Swinburne thinks is more likely. All we really have here are competing intuitions and no means of deciding between them.

Of course, even on modern cosmological and biological theories, many individual events in the history of the universe and of life on earth must remain extremely improbable. Some have objected to evolutionary accounts of life on the grounds that the likelihood of living stuff emerging from the conditions present on the primeval earth at the 'right' time to start the sort of life we now find on the earth is so low as to be negligible. But, as I have already suggested, individual events can be extremely 'improbable' and still happen. Indeed, part of the charm of evolutionary theory is the way in which it suggests how a history of improbable chances can also be a history of an ordered and irreversible system of intricate development. Presumably that each potentially successful mutant that did survive long enough actually to breed – and so to play its irreversible role in the development of its species – also depended on a host of extremely improbable events, but in retrospect its reproduction of itself is part of the continuous line from its earlier ancestors to the present-day members of its species. So it is not an objection to evolutionary theory or to cosmology that some of the crucial events in them are, taken in isolation, extremely improbable, so long as these theories are able to suggest how, from highly improbable events, order can arise.

In comparing teleological accounts and what I have been calling evolutionary accounts of world order, we are considering competing intuitions of probability. I say intuitions here because we do not, it seems to me, have enough examples of the early history of universes or of biospheres to estimate whether atheistically understood Big Bang or Darwinian accounts of the order we experience are more likely to apply in the case of our universe and our earth than rival theistic accounts, despite their greater empirical content. What does seem to me to be clear, on the other hand, is that the considerations on which the cosmological and teleological arguments are based are not such as to provide much in the way of argumentative force. The order in the world may be as Swinburne describes it, and not explicable by any modified Epicureanism; the existence and order of the world may be utterly remarkable and improbable. Nevertheless, the postulation of a divine spirit mysteriously working to bring these things about is, on the basis of what we know, hardly less remarkable or improbable. The cosmological and teleological arguments are undoubtedly part of the world picture of many theists, but the picture must look for its argumentative support from other directions.

Section 3   God as necessary being

The ontological argument has often been regarded as notorious by believers and unbelievers alike. It seems to be a piece of sophistry, a trick whose pretensions are nevertheless difficult to expose, which makes it the more maddening. But the very idea of the thing is a scandal: to prove the existence of God from mere reflection on a definition! As well as being something fundamentally opposed to the canons of empiricism, the attempt, as it seems, to define God into existence must be the height of irreligion. How can something worthy of worship emerge genie-like from polishing a human mental construction?

I think this is profoundly to misunderstand the insight involved in the argument, which is perhaps the most religious idea of all. The idea, as we shall see, is not properly a human *construction* at all, except in the sense that it involves a negation of all thought and all intellectual discrimination. Given this it is hardly surprising that, as I shall attempt to show, as an argument it is a bad argument, and the concept involved an incoherent concept. But it is a concept which many religious people have found deeply satisfying, perhaps

143

indeed because it has a Zen-like effect of mesmerizing those who submit themselves to it – who find it so satisfying in fact, that they are inclined to find all other stopping-places for explanation shallow and unsatisfactory. (And this is why the God of the ontological argument, the *ens realissimum* or absolutely necessary being so often hides, as Kant noted (1787, pp. 509-10), beneath apparently cosmological thinking).

The religious nature of the thinking which underlies the various versions of the ontological argument becomes apparent when we reflect on the way God is conceived in the argument. Although in Anselm's famous definition, God is spoken of as that than which nothing greater (or more perfect) can be imagined, we have to ask ourselves what underlies the relevant notion of greatness or perfection. It is abundantly clear in Anselm himself, as well as in other versions of the argument, that the perfection intended in the case of God is the perfection of a different type of existence from any other thing. God is conceived as having a type of existence which is entirely unlimited by contingency or dependence of any sort, and this clearly has to be something quite different from anything we encounter in normal experience. Everything we encounter in normal experience is determined, limited, questionable in some way as to its cause or the reason for it to be as it is. It is easy to see how the idea of perfect, non-contingent existence begins to be assimilated to the notion of pure existence, uncontaminated by any determination or limitation whatever, and consequently by any concept whatever, for all concepts are products of the human mind and hence, in religious thinking, often regarded as therefore limiting the things of which they are predicated. Moreover, everything that is definitely one thing rather than another opens the question as to why it is that rather than another, and hence subject to the demands of the principle of sufficient reason. But God, the perfect pure existence, is outside such a demand, which is why he can properly be the terminus of all explanation. The line of thought runs quickly and smoothly from the idea of perfect existence, to that of non-contingent existence, to that of pure existence, and on into the realms of apophatic theology, the *via negativa* and mysticism. God is pure being, beyond any human conceptualization or dependence, and how, the thought goes, could pure being not exist, for that is its nature? And so perfect, non-contingent existence is also logically necessary existence. And how, from the other point of view, could God not be pure being? And, if God is pure being, all the individual things that exist do so as participating in the divine being, albeit in an imperfect, limited, finite way.

Although we see, even in Aquinas, God characterized as that whose essence is simply to exist, and as that which is beyond all form and determination, the roots of this line of thinking, in Western thought at least, are clearly neo-Platonic, and perhaps, following hints in such dialogues as *Phaedo*, *Phaedrus*, the *Sophist*, the *Republic* and *Timaeus*, even Platonic, for Plato talks of things that are as participating in existence (*Sophist*, 256e), and of existence itself as a form (*Sophist*, 254d). He speaks of being as self-existent, as existing before the heavens (*Timaeus*, 51-2), and of absolute being (*Sophist*, 249a), although he does think that motion and life and soul and intelligence are 'in' absolute being (or the perfectly real, as some translations have it). Then, most strangely in the *Republic*, he speaks of the good, as being beyond being (509b), but that is what is to be contemplated by intelligence and the aim of dialectic. This idea of God or the good as being beyond being is one that recurs again and again in mystical and religious attempts to express the peculiar necessity and non-contingency of God.

It would no doubt be a travesty of Plato to attribute to him a concept of God as pure being, formless and with no determination or intelligible essence. His repeated assertion is that the soul is to ascend to an intelligible region (*Republic*, 517b) and that what truth and intelligibility there is in earthly things derives from their participation in the Forms. Mysterious as all this is, it is a world away from the obscure world of the neo-Platonists and the Orthodox spirituality they nourished. All I am suggesting here is that there are some themes in Plato himself that might have pointed in the direction taken by Plotinus when he spoke of the one as

> not something, but before everything; neither is it being, for
> that which is being has the form of its being; but this is formless,
> lacking even intelligible form. For since the nature of the one
> procreates all things, it does not itself form part of them.
> (*Enneads VI*, ix, 3)

Interestingly, Plotinus himself does not claim that the One is unknowable by nature. Its unknowability by our intelligence is due to the discrimination and distinction between knower and known

145

involved in any rational apprehension, which will distort the essential unity of the One. It was left to the Greek fathers, to Dionysius the Areopagite, to St Basil and St Gregory of Nyssa, to St Gregory Nazianzen and St John Damascene, to assert the radical and essential unknowability of God. In the treatise *Concerning Mystical Theology* (1.5, P.G. III 1048 B), attributed to Dionysius, we read that God, who is

> wholly apart from all things, is above all affirmation, as the supremacy of Him who, being in His simplicity freed from all things and beyond everything, is beyond all denial,

while in *Of The Divine Names* (XIII, 3, PGIII, 981 A), also attributed to Dionysius, God is said to be neither one nor many, but that which transcends the distinction, being unknowable in what he is. St John Damascene in *De Fide Orthodoxa* (1.4, PG XCIV, 800 BA) clearly expresses the idea of God as beyond being and knowledge:

> God does not belong to the class of existing things: not that he has no existence, but that he is above all existing things, nay even above existence itself. For if all forms of knowledge have to do with what exists, assuredly that which is above knowledge must certainly be also above essence; and, conversely, that which is above essence will also be above knowledge.

This apophatic attitude is entirely characteristic of Eastern Christianity from its earliest times. In his classic work on the subject, Vladimir Lossky sums up the difference between the religious attitude of Orthodoxy with the intellectual bias of Plotinus and the neo-Platonists as follows:

> the Platonic purification was above all of an intellectual nature, intended to free the understanding from the multiplicity which is inseparable from being. For Dionysius, on the other hand, it is a refusal to accept being as such, in so far as it conceals the divine non-being; it is a renunciation of the realm of created things in order to gain access to that of the uncreated. (1957, pp. 37-8)

What is involved is an attitude of life and mind, a refusal to encumber oneself either mentally or emotionally with anything that would reduce God to the ways of created things.

What, it might be objected at this point, has 'a refusal to accept being as such' to do with the ontological argument, which appears to be entirely based on ingenious speculation on the concept of being? No doubt apophatic theologians would reject any formal presentation of anything like the ontological argument. That must certainly be conceded. But it does seem possible that those who would put God beyond being and conceptualization, and those who are attracted to the reasoning underlying the ontological argument are trying to express much the same thought: that God has a type of existence which is totally beyond what is possessed by any created thing, and that created things are less real than absolute being and have reality only 'in so far as they have their being from God' and 'remain in him', as St Augustine puts it (*Confessions* VII, 11). This placing of God beyond finite reality in a way that we can only gesture at is surely what is intended by the introduction of the notion of existence into the definition of God (and into nothing else), and even more by the application to God of the concept of necessary existence.

What I shall now do is to examine three versions of the ontological argument in some detail. What I will say, however, will also have some bearing on those religious attempts to think of God as pure being beyond all form or determination or as necessarily existing. It is true, of course, that apophatic theology must in a way be allowed to subside into its own silence, but I hope to have done enough to suggest that it is based on the feeling that God has a quite exceptional type of existence which precludes our applying any of our normal categories to him. Clearly this feeling is by no means confined to Eastern Christianity. Apart from examples from outside Christianity altogether, one finds the feeling in the German mystical tradition of Meister Eckhart and Jacob Böhme and its prolongation in Hegelianism and Paul Tillich. If, involved in such thinking, are the ideas that the God is to be thought of as being-itself and as logically necessary (and, despite pretensions to drop the use of language altogether, such ideas often do lurk in the background), then what I have to say about the ontological argument will show the mystical idea I have been referring to to be inextricably muddled.

We will begin by examining the argument which is certainly in

Ch. 2 of Anselm's *Proslogion*. This is the argument which has received most attention, and is what is often referred to as *the* ontological argument. What Anselm is attempting to show here is that the idea or concept of God is such that once you understand it, you will see that God exists. So, he takes in a literal and philosophic spirit the Psalmist's verse 'The *fool* has said in his heart: God is not' (Ps. 13.1). According to Anselm, we all believe that God is 'something than which nothing greater can be conceived', and even the fool can understand what is meant by this. So what he understands is in his mind, even if he does not appreciate that the being he is thinking of exists in reality as well as being something he is thinking of. Anselm explains the difference between existing and merely being thought of by reference to a painter who first imagines what he is going to paint and then actually paints it. However, unlike the painting before it is painted, God (as defined) cannot just be an object of thought:

> Certainly that than which a greater cannot be conceived cannot stand only in relation to the understanding. For if it stands at least in relation to the understanding it can be conceived to be also in reality, and this is something greater.

A greatest conceivable being that was only an object of thought, and which stopped short of actual existence, would actually not be the greatest conceivable being. Whatever we thought of as going to make up our imaginary greatest being, one that had all its perfections, *plus* real existence, would be yet greater.

Therefore, if 'that than which a greater cannot be conceived', only stood in relation to the understanding, then 'that than which a greater cannot be conceived' would be 'something than which a greater can be conceived. But this is certainly impossible.'

In other words, Anselm sees a contradiction in the notion of a greatest conceivable being that did not actually exist. It would not be what it essentially is: the greatest conceivable being.

> Therefore, something than which a greater cannot be conceived undoubtedly both stands in relation to the understanding and exists in reality.

The substance of this argument is the suggestion that actual existence is an essential ingredient of the concept of the greatest conceivable being. Existence therefore follows from the idea of God as the greatest conceivable being. It would be contradictory to think of God, and to think of him as not existing, in the same way as it is contradictory to think of a triangle's angles not adding up to two right angles. The reference in the last sentence is, of course, to Descartes's Fifth Meditation, where Descartes says that because existence can no more be separated from the essence of God than can its having angles equalling two right angles from the essence of a triangle, or the idea of a mountain from that of a valley, 'so there is not any less repugnance to our conceiving a God (that is, a Being supremely perfect) to whom existence is lacking (that is to say, to whom a certain perfection is lacking) than to conceive of a mountain which has no valley.'

God, then, is seen by Anselm as the greatest conceivable being, and by Descartes as the supremely perfect being. As Anselm's 'greatest' refers to perfection, rather than to size, there are close similarities between the two. Furthermore, the idea of God as perfect is one with many religious resonances. I have heard some religious fundamentalists object to this way of thinking on the grounds that it seems inappropriate to tie God down to what we as human beings consider to be a perfection or lack of perfection. This objection would have more force against Anselm, at any rate, if, in his definition of God, he was more positive than he actually is. What he actually says is that God is something than which nothing greater (or more perfect) can be conceived. There is no implication here that we can form an adequate conception of God, nor, except in the one case of existence, is there any indication of what his perfections might be. Indeed, Anselm's words are quite consistent with a considerable degree of reverential agnosticism. What he is saying is that God is *at least* as perfect as anything we can conceive, which on the face of it allows God to transcend and even go against human conceptions of perfection as much as you like.

However, Anselm's initial definition does raise two problems before we can proceed to the nub of the argument. The first problem is whether 'something than which nothing greater can be conceived' is a coherent or determinate concept at all. Are our ideas of perfection such as to allow us to rank things in order of perfection? After all, we might think that the God of traditional theism, all-wise, all-powerful and all-loving was pretty perfect in those directions, but conceive of a being, the Apollo at Olympia, say, who was more perfect in respect of bodily beauty. Yet, an embodied Apollo could presumably not be all-powerful, even if he was more beautiful and more musical than a disembodied spirit could be. A further problem here is that with perfections like bodily beauty and musicality, we can always imagine someone surpassing even the most perfect example. We cannot imagine maximal beauty or maximal musicality. Perhaps the Anselmian reply here should be to say that only those perfections which can be regarded as being possessed in an unsurpassable way are to be envisaged as applying to God, which would cut out reference to physical beauty and musicality and other qualities that do not have what Plantinga (1975, p. 91) has called intrinsic maxima. The question would then arise as to whether those properties that do have intrinsic maxima can all compatibly co-exist in one subject. If they could not, we would have a reason for denying that one thing could unequivocably be that than which nothing greater could be conceived.

There seems no reason on the face of it why a being should not be able to do everything and know everything and exist. But the question does arise as to why power, knowledge and existence should be regarded as perfections or desirable greatnesses. Perfect for what, desirable to whom, one might ask. This is simply to point to the fact that the notion of perfection always conveys an implicit reference to a respect in which the object in question is perfect. Thus great physical power might be regarded as a perfection in a reasonable man, but not in someone sadly mentally retarded. It is difficult to see how any normal property can be a perfection per se. Leaving aside questions about knowledge and power, which do not enter Anselm's argument, we can still ask in what respect existence is a perfection.

Norman Malcolm claims that the doctrine that existence is a perfection is

> remarkably queer. It makes sense and is true to say that my future house will be a better one if it is insulated than if it is not insulated; but what could it mean to say that it will be a better house if it exists than if it does not? My future child will be a better man if he is honest than if he is not; but who understands

Religious Explanations

the saying that he will be a better man if he exists than if he does not? Or who understands the saying that if God exists He is more perfect than if He does not exist? (1960, p. 43)

In order to find an answer to Malcolm's rhetorical question, and to see the background against which existence is a perfection, we need to be slightly less literal about things than Malcolm. What Anselm, in common with medieval thinkers generally, would say is that it is better to exist than not to exist. This does not seem to me to be totally nonsensical, although with some beings, one might ask better for whom. Nonetheless, it is an expression of an attitude to reality: *ens et bonum convertuntur*. Existence is good, what exists is good. Something conceivable, but lacking existence, either because it has ceased to exist or because it has never come into existence, has been deprived or lacks an important good. Surely it makes *sense* to say that of the children we might have had, as in Strauss's *Die Frau ohne Schatten*, though, to be sure, in a different way from the way in which my actual child might lack the good of being able to speak Japanese. (Some philosophers will naturally object to the implicit references being made here and elsewhere to possible but non-existent *beings*. These can, without any loss to the argument, be replaced by speaking of properties being instantiated. Thus questions about my possible children can be rephrased in terms of the instantiation or non-instantiation of properties such as 'child-of-O'Hear-born-in-1979'. Talk about God as the greatest possible being will have to be translated into talk about the instantiation or actuality of maximal greatness and Anselm's proof amounts to a claim that maximal greatness carries with it a guarantee of its own instantiation.)

The idea that existence is a good, and that to belong to the community of existing things is a blessing, and that to bring other beings into existence, as God does, and as, in a way, parents do, is an act of supreme and supererogatory generosity gives us a background against which existence might be considered a perfection, which something could have or not have. The question which remains, however, is whether this perspective is universally acceptable. There are other traditions, taking a very different view of existence, regarding it rather as a curse, a subjection to pain and sorrow, and something to be shunned. Thus the Chorus in *Oedipus at Colonus* has it that

What is best of all is not to be
But, life begun, soonest to end is best (1224-5),

and Nietzsche, in the *Birth of Tragedy* (§3) represents this as part of the primeval Dionysian wisdom, imparted to King Midas by the satyr Silenus. The similarly pessimistic strain in Indian thought, which regards existence as a burden and an illusion to be cast off, is too well-known to need any special emphasis, but it does raise the interesting question as to whether the argument of *Proslogion* §2 could ever have had any appeal to people outside traditions in which existence was naturally regarded as good. Certainly the idea that existence is a perfection is not something self-evidently true, and it is difficult to know how the argument between Anselm and Silenus could be resolved or even conducted.

Let us assume, however, that the being than whom no greater can be conceived is not an irredeemably vague or incoherent concept, and, further, that existence can satisfactorily be regarded as a perfection. What then happens to the argument? There are two classic lines of objection, the first of which says that the argument 'proves' too much, while the second claims that it can prove nothing at all. The first objection was raised by a contemporary of Anselm, a monk called Gaunilo, who claimed, in effect, that if Anselm's argument was valid, an analogous argument could be used to prove the existence of the greatest conceivable island (for the greatest conceivable island must have at least the perfection of actually existing). Presumably we could also 'prove' greatest conceivable lemons, tables, cars, and so on, by similar moves. There are at least two ways Anselm can counter Gaunilo. In the first place, he could have questioned whether the greatest conceivable island (or lemon or table or car) is in fact a coherent concept. Surely, in all of these things, there are various different perfections, which cannot necessarily co-exist. Thus, in an island we might, for different reasons, value a tropical climate and a temperate climate; in a car both speed and high performance are regarded as qualities. But in both these cases, and possibly in all such cases, you cannot instantiate all the perfections together in a high degree. So, for any possible island, car, etc., however perfect, you could always imagine another one more perfect in some respect. Moreover, as Plantinga has pointed out, the perfections we value in islands are not such as to admit of intrinsic maxima (cf. 1975, p. 91), so for any island we could imagine, we could always imagine one having yet one more dancing girl, palm tree, coconut and so on. Maybe this would go for perfections in all finite material things, and so for any finite material object x, we could never speak of the greatest conceivable x.

Anselm did not in fact counter Gaunilo in this way. What he appears to have done is to insist that the logic of *his* argument cannot be applied to islands and the like, but only to 'that than which a greater cannot be conceived', and then to spell out some of the special qualities of that being. In particular, he says that it 'exists with the undoubted ground of truth itself'; it cannot be conceived not to be; and, it cannot 'be conceived to have a beginning and an end'. What he may well be claiming here is that his greatest conceivable being is self-subsistent, necessary and independent of everything else, in a way that no island or any finite material thing could be. Even if we wrote existence into the definition of some island, this would not show it to be self-subsistent or existentially independent. These are certainly qualities God is often conceived of as having, though it has yet to be established whether having these qualities is the same as him existing with logical necessity. However, as this is the essence of the second ontological argument, it can hardly be used to show the validity of the first ontological argument. So while Anselm's reply does mark out a crucial difference in the way he conceives God and the way he conceives islands and other material things, it does not really meet Gaunilo's point as directed against the first argument.

Let us, however, grant that Gaunilo can be met by the claim that concepts of most perfect islands and the like are inherently vague, and incoherent, and move on to the most familiar line of objection to Anselm's first argument. This is based on the claim, made famous by Kant, that existence is not a predicate. The objection is that in *Proslogion* §2 Anselm treats existence as one of the predicates involved in the concept or definition of God, so, if existence is not a predicate, then there is something illegitimate about his whole procedure. Unfortunately, however, Kant's argument in favour of his claim fails to carry conviction.

What Kant says in *The Critique of Pure Reason* is that

'*Being*' is obviously not a real predicate; that is, it is not a concept of something which could be added to the concept of a thing. It is merely the positing of a thing, or of certain determinations, as existing in themselves. Logically it is merely the copula of a judgement. The proposition 'God is omnipotent' contains two concepts, each of which has its object – God and omnipotence. The small word 'is' adds no new predicate, but only serves to posit the predicate *in its relation* to the subject. If, now, we take the subject (God) with all its predicates (among which is omnipotence), and say 'God is', or 'There is a God', we attach no new predicate to the concept of God, but only posit the subject in itself with all its predicates, and indeed posit it as being an *object* that stands in relation to my *concept*. (1787, pp. 504–5)

And Kant goes on to say that as nothing is added to the concept of a possible thing by positing it as existing, 'the real contains no more than the merely possible'. As evidence of this, he asserts, remarkably, that a hundred real thalers do not contain the least coin more than a hundred possible thalers, although perhaps to pre-empt the obvious rejoinder that a hundred real thalers comprise about a hundred more coins than the merely possible ones, which contain no coins or thalers at all, he does have the grace to concede that his 'financial position' is affected very differently by real coins than by possible ones.

Kant's argument, such as it is, contains the real (and not the merely possible) confusion of assimilating the 'is' of predication to the 'is' of existence. This is clear from the way he attempts to show that in 'God is' we attach no new predicate to the subject. His reasons for saying this appear to be, first, that the 'is' in 'God is omnipotent' adds no concept to those of God and omnipotence, and, second that the 'is' in 'God is' posits God 'only as an object that stands in relation to my concept'. The first reason would be relevant only if the two occurrences of 'is' in 'God is' and 'God is omnipotent' were the same, but clearly they are not. The 'is' in 'God is omnipotent' is, as Kant rightly implies, only the 'is' of predication, and does not imply that God actually exists. (It could, for example, be part of a discussion of the attributes of God prior to settling anything about God's existence, in the same way as we might say 'Unicorns are horses with horns' and then set out to see whether there are any such things.) The 'is' in 'God is', however is precisely the assertion of God's actual existence. Kant (and this is his second point) claims that in asserting God's existence, we are doing no more than positing an object as standing in relation to our concept. One wonders what could be meant by this rebarbative phrase except that we are saying that the thing actually exists. Is saying that something exists to engage in a form of predicating? This is what still has to be settled.

To say that some word or phrase is a predicate is roughly to say that if we apply the word or phrase to some other name or concept in a sentence, we will thereby convey some further information about the thing named or concept mentioned. On this basis, existence is certainly and unequivocally a predicate. 'Unicorns are horses with horns, and what is more, they exist' is certainly to add something to what we believe about unicorns. It is to say that concept unicorn is instantiated in the real world. 'Christians believe that God is the supreme judge, and he actually exists' suggests a very different attitude on the part of the speaker to the Christian God than that taken by agnostics or atheists. It is to say that the being referred to by Christians as 'God' has a reality beyond Christian belief. So, not only are Kant's arguments to show that existence is not a predicate quite inadequate, the claim itself is false as it stands.

However, even though saying that something exists or saying that some property is instantiated must be regarded as a form of predication in some general sense, it is possible to show that the concept of existence or instantiation in the real world cannot significantly function as part of a definition; showing this will be enough to refute the argument of *Proslogion* §2 and Descartes's Fifth Meditation in which existence is introduced as a key defining property of the being than which no greater can be conceived. In order to show this, I can do no better than follow Plantinga (1967, pp. 35-7, and 1975, pp. 95-7), who is able to demonstrate clearly what Kant was perhaps struggling towards, namely, the relevant difference between existence and other properties. Plantinga's point is that while we cannot subtract a true defining property from a definition without potentially altering the class of objects to which the definition refers, this would not be the case if we subtracted the concept of existence from a definition which included the property of existence. Adding or subtracting the concept of existence to or from a definition, then, makes no material difference to the definition. He shows this by considering two concepts, bachelor and superbachelor. A bachelor is defined as an unmarried male over the age of twenty-five. A thing is a bachelor if and only if it has these properties. This concept clearly applies contingently, if at all; in other words, what the definition says is that *if* anything has these properties, it is a bachelor, but it does not say that there necessarily are any such things. So 'There are bachelors' is true, but not necessarily true. Now, in an attempt to circumvent the contingency of 'there are bachelors', we might invent a new concept, that of a superbachelor, which is defined as an object which is an unmarried male over the age of twenty-five *and which exists*. Superbachelorhood would, in effect, be defined as bachelorhood plus actuality of bachelorhood. Just as it is a necessary truth that bachelors are unmarried, by definition, so it would appear that it is a necessary truth that superbachelors exist or that superbachelorhood is instantiated by definition. Have we then, Gaunilo-like, defined a special type of bachelor into existence?

To think that we have is to misunderstand the nature of a definition. In saying that bachelors are necessarily unmarried, what we mean is just that it is necessarily true that *if* anything is a bachelor, it is unmarried. Definitions, in other words, are disguised hypotheticals, of the form, it is necessarily true that for all x, if anything is an x, then it is F, G, H, etc. So the necessity attaching to the superbachelor's possession of existence or to superbachelorhood's actualization is simply that it is necessarily true that *if* anything is a superbachelor, then it is unmarried, male, over twenty-five and existing, or that *if* superbachelorhood is instantiated, then so equally are the properties of bachelorhood and actuality of bachelorhood. But, clearly, this does not mean that there are any superbachelors or that superbachelorhood is instantiated. Moreover, worse for the idea of a superbachelor, it is obvious that nothing can be a superbachelor without being a bachelor and vice versa, nor can you have bachelorhood without superbachelorhood. For all superbachelors are bachelors, as being a bachelor and equally there can be no bachelorhood without anything that is a bachelor is also a superbachelor, because anything that is a bachelor is unmarried, male, over twenty-five *and existing*. Similarly, any case of bachelorhood is a case of superbachelorhood, for any case of bachelorhood is a case of bachelorhood and of actuality of bachelorhood. So 'there are some superbachelors' and 'there are some bachelors' have just the same truth conditions, and 'x is a bachelor' and 'x is a superbachelor' have the same satisfaction conditions, and it is in this sense that adding existence or actuality to or subtracting it from a definition neither increases nor decreases it. So we can conclude that even though Kant was wrong in asserting that existence is not a predicate, it is true that existence cannot significantly be used as a defining predicate, as Anselm appears to be doing in *Proslogion* §2. Finally, it is worth emphasizing that importing existence into a definition does not make it necessary that the thing thus defined exists. For, as we saw, 'there are some superbachelors' entails 'there are some bachelors', because any superbachelor is a bachelor. But 'there are some bachelors' is clearly a contingent truth, so 'there are some superbachelors' is too. And the same goes for bachelorhood and superbachelorhood.

Adding the concept of existence to the concept of the most perfect conceivable being, then, adds nothing material to the concept, nor does it make it necessarily true that there is such a being. And the same must be said for the analogous move in respect of properties. Adding actuality of maximal perfection to the properties involved in the definition of maximal perfection cannot guarantee that maximal perfection is actualized, any more than it does in the case of superbachelorhood. It is important to note that our Plantinga-inspired refutation of the argument of *Proslogion* §2 does not depend on denying that existence is a predicate, nor is it committed to any particular formalization of the concept of existence. Thus, it is not committed to the Fregean view that existence is a property properly predicable only of descriptions and not of names, so nothing should be taken to follow from what has been said about the logical status of the word 'God' in the assertion 'God exists'. On the other hand, what has been said does something to show how the predication of existence, which cannot form part of a definition, is rather different from the predication of other properties, such as blueness or squareness, which can. To that extent, what has been said provides some informal support for the basic distinction made in Fregean Logic between existential assertions and other types of assertion (one reflection of which consists in the fact that the argument of *Proslogion* §2 cannot be formalized straightforwardly in modern predicate logic, in which the existential quantifier is quite clearly different from straightforward predicates).

The refutation of the argument of *Proslogion* §2 which has just been advanced can be summed up by saying that existence cannot constitute a defining characteristic of anything, on the grounds that anything that actually falls under a definition or description will, ipso facto, have existence. Jonathan Barnes (1972, pp. 45-50) has argued that this principle is unsound, and hence cannot serve as a counter-argument to the ontological argument. He considers a number of cases where it appears that non-existent individuals can quite legitimately be seen as falling under various descriptions. Thus,

(1)   Socrates is a model for all aspiring philosophers,

and

(2)   Hamlet is one of Shakespeare's most problematic creations.

While these examples suggest that care is needed in stating the principle that anything falling under a definition will have existence, they do not seem to me to show that it is false.

(1) shows that definitions can certainly be satisfied by non-living persons, and other beings that have ceased to exist, and, possibly, by beings that do not yet exist. In saying that only existing things can satisfy definitions, what is intended is that only things which have existence *at some time* can satisfy a definition. It is not necessary that they have existence at the same time as the statement about them is made. While naturally saying that something has existence at a specific time can informatively be added to a definition, it is not the case that saying that it has existence at some unspecified time is an informative addition to a definition, and this is all that Plantinga's argument requires to show the coincidence of concepts like bachelor and superbachelor. Although, as we shall see shortly, eternal life is an important strand in Anselm's concept of God, in *Proslogion* §2 the logical necessity of 'God exists' is taken to follow from the addition of mere (or temporally unspecific) existence to God's nature. Further, I will show that it is possible (and necessary) to prise apart God's mere existence from his eternity, in such a way that the logical necessity of his existence would not follow from his eternity alone. His actual existence becomes logically necessary only by (illegitimately, as I am arguing) importing 'mere' existence into the definition.

Barnes's (2) is perhaps a more worrying challenge, raising as it does the whole problem of talk of fictional and imaginary individuals. The apparent strength of (2) as a counter-example to what is being said here is that, unlike

   (3)   Hamlet is a bachelor,

it does not require qualification by prefacing it with 'In the play . . .' or anything of that sort. It appears to be straight-forwardly true. On the other hand, (3) is false, because whatever else Hamlet is, he is not a living person, and so, in an unqualified sense, Hamlet is not a bachelor. It is part of the meaning of 'bachelor' that a bachelor is (or was) a living person, and has (or had) existence as a living person. On the other hand it is not part of the meaning of 'Shakespeare's most problematic creation' that anything satisfying it has existence as a living person, though surely anything satisfying it must have existence as an identifiable part of one of Shakespeare's works. So if anything is one of Shakespeare's most problematic creations, it is an existing Shakespearean pro-blematic creation, and that is as true and as trivially uninformative as saying that if anything is a bachelor, it is an existing bachelor. The *type* of existence that satisfies the description in question is something implicit in the description itself, which is why adding the notion of existence to the description is redundant. What I am saying is that Hamlet does have existence as a Shakespearean creation and this is why Hamlet potentially makes (2) true. If Hamlet did not have the type of existence appropriate to Shakespearean creations, then, even if he were a living person he could not do this. Of course, saying that he was also a real person would be to say something additional. It would be to say that Shakespeare's character was based on a person, but adding that he was based on an existing person, would not, strictly, add anything to *that* (although it might be said to clarify the fact that one really meant a person) because only an existing person is a person (as opposed to a Shakespearean creation).

    In the cases of bachelors and perfect beings, on the other hand, it is equally clear from the definitions themselves that they would not be satisfied by fictional or imaginary entities, and there is nothing added to the definition by saying that they could be satisfied only by beings having existence in the real world, for part of what is involved in being a living person or all-powerful is that one is alive or all-powerful in the real world.

159

Hence, I conclude that Barnes has not shown that the principle that anything that falls under a definition will, ipso facto, have existence is false. It will have existence, and just that type of existence involved in satisfying the definition. Normally, of course, this means full-blooded existence in the real world, but for the reasons advanced here I do not see that the fact that we are sometimes inclined to speak of things which have existence as fictional or imaginary creations counts as a refutation of the general principle that to speak of something as an F is no different from speaking of it as an F that has or had or will have existence, the F - term itself indicating the type of existence in question. In so far as the argument of *Proslogion* §2 appears to introduce existence as an idle defining predicate, then, it must be rejected.

From an argument which depends on a misunderstanding of the logic of existence, we must now turn to the form of the ontological argument which has a much closer connection with the religious ideas referred to earlier. This is an argument, the seeds of which are arguably to be found in Anselm's *Proslogion* §3 and in certain passages in his reply to Gaunilo which attempts to show not that God exists by definition, but rather that God has a special and ontologically superior type of existence. Reflecting on this is supposed to lead us to the conclusion that unless the concept of God is in some way contradictory, he exists necessarily. To put this as succinctly as possible, the argument would show that if God is possible, then he exists.

In *Proslogion* §3, we read that God 'so truly is that it is impossible to think of him as not existing', in contrast to 'whatever else there is' which 'can be conceived not to be'. Anselm goes on to apostrophize God as follows:

> Therefore, you alone, of all things, exist in the truest and
> greatest way, for nothing else so truly exists and therefore
> everything else has less being.

We are some way here from the apparently trivial addition of existence to a definition; not too far, in fact, from the Platonic doctrine of degrees of being. What appears to be in question here is an idea of God as having a perfection of existence beyond anything else. What is at issue is a type of existence, not existence per se. This impression is reinforced by what Anselm says in reply to Gaunilo's criticisms, in which he speaks of God as something that could not be conceived of as having a beginning or an end, whereas anything else that exists (such as an island) could be thought of as having a beginning or end. One's intuition sides with Anselm here. For any particle of matter, even if it has in fact existed for ever and will never cease to exist, we could always imagine being destroyed. Even if the universe as a whole is actually an unending process, we could perhaps imagine it coming to an end. And even if the idea of any actually existing bit of matter being annihilated totally, without any trace or transformation into something else, is difficult to accept, we could surely readily accept that everything in the world that is actually existing might even have been and some quite different universe exist in its stead, or even none at all. We can always ask why this universe, rather than some other. God, on the other hand, is thought of as having a type of existence to which no such questions can attach. As Anselm puts it:

> even if there is nothing existing which can be 'understood' not to be, nevertheless *everything* can be conceived not to be, except that which is supremely. In fact all those things – and only those things – can be conceived not to be which have a beginning, or an end, or a combination of parts, and . . . which do not exist everywhere and in their totality and always.

The idea is that just as any part of something changing and complex could be imagined not to exist and indeed does not exist at certain times and places, so we could imagine every part of a changing, complex thing as existing at no time and nowhere. Further, the parts of a complex object could be split up and dispersed, so that the whole ceased to be. Anselm continues:

> But that alone cannot be conceived not to be in which conceiving discovers neither beginnings nor end nor combination of parts, and which finds it existing always and everywhere in its totality. (*Opera Omnia*, I, pp. 133–4)

So the inconceivability of God's non-existence comes from his eternity, his simplicity and his omnipresence.

The suggestion in Anselm that God's special type of existence could actually form the basis of an argument from his possibility to his actuality may have been partially recognized by Anselm himself. He wrote, again in reply to Gaunilo, that, if that than which a greater cannot be conceived

> can at least be conceived to be it necessarily follows that it exists. For 'that than which a greater cannot be conceived' cannot be conceived to be except as without a beginning. However, whatever can be conceived to be and actually is not can be conceived to be through a beginning. Therefore, it is not the case that 'that than which a greater cannot be conceived' can be conceived to exist and yet does not exist. Therefore, if it can be conceived to be, it necessarily is. (*Opera Omnia*, pp. 130-1)

Here the point is that anything that could be conceived of as having a beginning in time could be conceived as beginning at some other time, so it is contingent that it exists when it does. Hence, what has perfect, non-contingent existence cannot have a beginning. Whether or not there really is a distinct modal argument in Anselm (and this is highly contentious, cf. Barnes, 1972, pp. 18-26), these hints and suggestions in his writings have been developed and expanded into a full-blooded argument in a very similar way, apparently independently, by both Norman Malcolm (1960) and Charles Hartshorne (1962, 1968). Both authors attempt to show that God is such that, if he exists, he exists necessarily, by which they mean that he is not the sort of thing that can merely *happen* to come into existence. Malcolm, who rejects the first version of the ontological argument on the grounds that *existence* is not a perfection, defends the second version on the grounds that it is treating God as having necessary existence, which he contends, is a perfection. He explains necessary existence by reference to two particular attributes of God, his eternity and his causal or ontological independence. We have already seen that Anselm takes God's eternity to rule out his coming to be if he does not exist now. It is undoubtedly true that if God does not exist now, it is logically impossible that he should start to exist, for anything that started to exist now would, by definition, not be eternal. Moreover, if he started to exist, his existence would presumably come about either by the causal activity of something else, or by chance, and either of these circumstances would be incompatible with God's ontological self-sufficiency, his power of existing through and from himself or subsistent existence. As Malcolm puts it, God cannot *come* into existence

> for if He did, He would either have been *caused* to come into existence or have *happened* to come into existence, and in either case He would be a limited being, which by our conception of Him He is not. Since He cannot come into existence, if He does not exist, His existence is impossible. (1960, p. 49)

Similar considerations would rule out our thinking of God as capable of ceasing to exist, for this would again suggest that he owed his continued existence either to other causal agencies or to the absence of the chance event which would amount to his non-existence. Malcolm is, of course, following medieval precedent in understanding God's eternity to imply more than endless duration. He reads it as ruling out as *senseless* questions about God's ceasing to exist, if he exists. Hartshorne stresses a slightly different aspect of God's ontological independence, suggesting that if God (like our universe) could be conceived not to exist, this would be tantamount to saying that he was not fully independent:

> Were God to exist, yet his non-existence to be conceivable, he would either exist by sheer chance or luck, or else owing to some other cause. Either way, he would not be the best conceivable being, and hence would not be worthy of worship as God. He must then exist without conceivable alternative. (1968, p. 326)

So we have to regard God's existence as something necessary, if it is a fact at all. It could not be a merely contingent fact.

Both Hartshorne and Malcolm are agreed, then, in ruling out merely contingent existence for God, and they take this to follow from God's perfection as involving eternity (in the strong sense) and ontological independence. Now, according to Malcolm, if God exists, he exists necessarily and if he does not exist, his existence is logically impossible. Hence, given that either God exists or he does not exist, his existence is, in Malcolm's words,

> either impossible or necessary. It can be the former only if the concept of such a being is self-contradictory or in some way logically absurd. Assuming that this is not so, it follows that He necessarily exists. (1960, p. 50)

And, we might add, whatever necessarily exists, exists; so, God exists.

Malcolm's argument to the effect that God's existence is either impossible or necessary has an air of speciousness about it, which is worth bringing out, because even if, as we will, we question his reading of the second disjunct, it would be possible to prove God's existence on the basis of the rejection of God's logical impossibility alone, if we allow Malcolm his claim that if God does not exist, his existence would be logically impossible. What he shows in his analysis of Anselm is that it is impossible (necessarily not the case that) if God does not exist for him to come into existence. Is he entitled to conclude from this that if God does not in fact exist, in the actual world, he necessarily does not exist, in the sense that he exists in no possible world? At the very least, there appears to be an illegitimate transposition of modal operators from outside the hypothetical to the inside, from the justifiable premise 'Necessarily (if God does not exist now, then he can exist at no time)' to the conclusion, that if God does not exist now, then necessarily he can exist at no time. Arguing like that, we could show the logical impossibility of anything I do not in fact do in my life, because while it is true that 'Necessarily (If I do not do ø when I am alive, then at no time can I do ø)', it is not true if I do not do ø while alive, I necessarily do not do ø. Of course, in general, one is not entitled to move from schemata of the form 'Necessarily (-A⊃-B)' and '-A' to schemata of the form 'Necessarily -B', but this appears to be what Malcolm is doing. Indeed, if Malcolm had shown that if God does not exist, then his existence is logically impossible, he could, as I shall underline later, actually move straight from his arguably correct belief that God's existence is *not* logically impossible (falsity of consequent) to the conclusion that God does exist (falsity of antecedent). So it is important to point out the suspect nature of Malcolm's reasoning at this point.

However, it is possible to present much less questionable arguments on the basis of Anselmian considerations, and this Hartshorne has done in at least two forms, in which he exploits the apparatus of modern modal logic. In addition to apparatus of the propositional calculus, in order to symbolize his arguments, Hartshorne employs the modal operator for necessity, 'L'. (He does not actually use the operator for possibility, 'M', as in modal logic 'Mp' ('possibly p') can be written as '-L-p' ('not necessarily not

-p'). In the arguments which follow, the proposition symbolized by 'p' is always the proposition 'There is a perfect being', or, perhaps better, 'Divine perfection is instantiated.' Then, following Anselm's insight as to the impossibility of God existing merely contingently, we can argue as follows:

(4)	p→Lp	(Anselm's principle: perfection could not exist contingently)
(5)	Lp v -Lp	(Law of excluded middle)
(6)	-Lp→L-Lp	(Form of Becker's postulate: modal status is always necessary)
(7)	Lp v L-Lp	(5,6)
(8)	L-Lp→L-p	(4: the necessary falsity of the consequent implies the necessary falsity of the antecedent)
(9)	Lp v L-p	(7,8)
(10)	-L-p	(Intuitive assumption: divine perfection is not logically impossible)
(11)	Lp	(9, 10)
(12)	Lp→p	(Modal axiom)
(13)	p	(11, 12)

(cf. Hartshorne, 1962, pp. 50-1)

To those not familiar with modal logic, a comment should first be made about step 6. Modal status refers to the way a proposition is characterized with respect to necessity, possibility and impossibility taking these notions in their logical senses. Thus, to say that a proposition is logically necessary is to say that it is true not only in the world as it is, with the physical laws and conditions actually obtaining, but in any world (or state of affairs) that could be coherently described, even in a world as different as you like from ours. In other words, it is true in all possible worlds, to use Leibniz's definition of logical necessity. To say that a proposition is logically impossible is to say that there is no possible or describable world in which it is true, while to say that one is logically possible is to say that there are describable worlds in which it is true. Now, the idea that modal status is itself necessary is one that accords well with thinking of modality in terms of possible worlds. If a proposition is logically necessary (=true in all possible worlds), then it is surely logically necessary (= true in all possible worlds) that it is true in all possible worlds. Moreover, if a proposition is possible (= true in some possible world), it seems reasonable to think of its being logically necessary, or true in all possible worlds, that it is true in some possible world. What Becker's postulate is getting at is the sense that modal status is something that does not depend on contingent features of the world, or our knowledge, so whatever modal status a proposition has, it will have it in all possible worlds. It should be noted that Becker's postulate cannot be refuted by examples such as 'Goldbach's conjecture may be a necessary truth, but we cannot at present assert that it must be.' As Kneale, from whom this example is taken, points out (1962, pp. 565-6), there are three different usages of modal words in this sentence, of which only 'necessary truth' refers directly to the modal status of Goldbach's conjecture; the phrases 'may be' and 'must be' are here being used to express relations to human knowledge, while 'cannot' brings in either moral or linguistic propriety. What is needed to refute Becker's postulate are counter-examples showing that a proposition is contingent or necessary in the strictly logical sense, but in that same sense only contingently contingent or necessary: that is that some proposition was true in all possible worlds or in some possible worlds only in some possible worlds. It seems clear that Goldbach's conjecture, if true, is true in all possible worlds, and that it is true in all possible worlds that this is so, even if we cannot show this or assert it with propriety.

There are, of course, many different formalizations of the logic of modality, and not all of them include anything like Becker's postulate or make any attempt to deal with the sense that modal status might be necessary. In many of them, 'Lp' will not be equivalent to 'LLp', so in them, Hartshorne's proof could not be formulated, because step 6 of that proof would not be acceptable. However, in one of the most familiar systems of modal logic, S5, step 6 would be valid.[4]

So let us for the moment grant that S5 is acceptable, and that the necessity and the absence of necessity of propositions is itself something that is true in all possible worlds (and not subject to the vagaries of particular worlds). Then there are three controversial steps in Hartshorne's proof, and 4, 8 and 10. We have already, in effect, said something about 10, which simply says that divine perfection is not self-contradictory. We can surely grant Hart-shorne this, and so we are simply left with 4 and 8. The inference in 8 is correct, provided that 'p→Lp' in 4 is read as 'p entails Lp', which is Hartshorne's intention. On 4, Anselm is said by Hartshorne (and by Malcolm) to have established that *if* God exists, then his existence is logically necessary. If this is correct, then we have before us a pretty convincing proof of the existence of God.

Before examining 4 any further, we can look at a simpler proof of Hartshorne's also using Anselm's principle, though it appeals directly to a theorem in S5. (p and the other symbols are to be read as before.)

(14) -L-p   (i.e. God is possible)
(15) L(-p v Lp) (Anselm's principle: it is necessary either
                   that God does not exist, or he
                   exists necessarily)
(16) L-p v LLp   (Equivalent to 15, by a theorem of S5, T29
                   in Hughes and Cresswell (1972, p.
                   51)
(17) L-p v Lp   (In S5, LLp ≡ Lp)
(18) Lp   (14, 17)
(19) p   (Private correspondence of Hartshorne,
                   reproduced in Hubbeling, 1981).

In this proof, the assumption 1 and 2 correspond to 7 and 1 respectively of the longer proof and the rest is simple to show in S5. However, one wonders why, if S5 is being used, Hartshorne needs to appeal to such a complicated proof at all, because in S5, Anselm's principle, together with the assumption that God is possible, would actually lead on its own to a Hartshorne-style proof of God's existence, as the formula (N) '-L-Lp→p' is actually a theorem in S5, though not in S4. (For details, see Chellas (1980), p. 18.) The suggestion that what is possibly necessary actually obtains might at first sight seem rather surprising, but thinking of what is meant by possibly necessary in terms of possible worlds can make it actually seem quite acceptable intuitively. For what '-L-Lp' says is that in some possible world 'p' obtains in all possible worlds. If this is so, then 'p' does obtain not only in all possible worlds, but also in this world, the actual world. (Not surprisingly, '-L-Lp→Lp' is also a theorem of S5.) As Hartshorne reads 'Lp', '-L-Lp' amounts to saying that it is possible that it is necessarily true that perfection exists. According to Hartshorne, non-contingently existing perfection, if it exists, exists in all possible worlds. So the antecedent of (N) appears to be saying that in some possible world, divine perfection obtains in *all* possible worlds. Hence, if divine perfection is possible at all (= 'p' is true in some possible world), it obtains in all, hence it obtains, simpliciter. This indeed is just what Malcolm claims for God, when he says that God's existence is either impossible or necessary. So, if it is possible (i.e. not impossible), it is necessary, and obtains. And it is not hard to see why Hartshorne at least should think this idea does indeed reflect some deep religious convictions about the superior, non-contingent type of being enjoyed by God.

It would be nice to relate all this to some philosophical reflections on the respective acceptability of various systems of modal logic which express differing intuitions about the necessity of modal status. Certainly Hartshorne would want to say that divine necessity is itself strongly or necessarily necessary, and this might seem to indicate the appropriateness of using a logic such as S5 for capturing this sense of necessity. Moreover, (N) does seem in accord with Hartshorne's approach – he refers to it frequently in his *Logic of Perfection* – which might again suggest taking S5, rather than some weaker system regarding the necessity of modal status, as the system for divine necessity. However, nice as it would be to pursue this line of thought, there are two reasons why we cannot. The first is the technical reason that (N) is not a theorem only in S5. It is also a theorem or an axiom of a number of systems of modal logic, specifically the Brouwersche systems, which do not include any axioms to the effect that necessity or possibility are themselves necessary (cf. Hughes and Cresswell, 1972, pp. 57-8; Chellas, 1980, pp. 131-9). Even more strikingly, however, we can prove God's existence, employing the considerations about the non-contingence of perfection invoked by Hartshorne, without using any system of modal logic at all, but simply appealing to modus tollens:

(20) $-p \to L-p$ (Variant of Anselm's principle: if God does not exist, he necessarily does not exist)

(21) $-L-p$ (God's existence is not logically impossible)

(22) p (By modus tollens)

So the considerations underlying Hartshorne's arguments do not really rely on modal logic at all. But, even more fundamentally, the second reason why we cannot draw any conclusions about modal logic from any of this is that Hartshorne's formalizations of Anselm's principle, and Malcolm's interpretation of it as well, are completely misguided. To see this, we will have to contrast the semantics of 'Lp' with the considerations which lead Hartshorne and Malcolm to think that God's existence can correctly be described as logically necessary.

'Lp', as has been said, expresses the idea that 'p' is logically necessary, or true in all possible worlds, or if one jibs at talk of possible worlds on the grounds that it sounds like talk of 'something like distant planets, like our own surroundings, but somehow existing in a different dimension' and also as throwing up imponderable puzzles relating to the identification of individuals across possible worlds, one can read 'Lp' as meaning that 'p' is true in 'all possible states (or histories) of the world' or in 'all counter-factual situations' (cf. Kripke, 1980, p. 15). Clearly, if 'Lp' is true, then 'p' is true; and this move, and the interpretation of 'Lp' just given, are explicit in Hartshorne's two proofs. It is also under this interpretation that (N) is regarded as a theorem or an axiom of various systems of modal logic. Finally, in Malcolm's version of the ontological argument, in his crucial disjunction to the effect that God's existence is either impossible or necessary, the second disjunct must be read as 'it is logically necessary that God exists', for otherwise nothing would follow in the way Malcolm intends about God's actual existence from the rejection Malcolm makes of the first disjunct.

In all the arguments under consideration, then, God's existence is being treated as logically necessary, in the sense just elaborated. It is in this sense, and, I shall argue, only in this sense that God's actual existence follows from his necessary existence. The sense in which Anselm and his interpreters speak of God's existence as necessary is, however, subtly different, and leads to no conclusions about his actual existence. For what is claimed for God is that he is eternal and causally or logically independent. His existence is such that its only source is God's own nature. As Anselm puts it:

> The supreme Substance, then, does not exist through any
> efficient agent, and does not derive existence from any matter,

and was not aided in being brought into existence by any external causes. Nevertheless, it by no means exists through nothing, or derives existence from nothing; through itself and from itself, it is whatever it is (*Monologion* §6, quoted by Hick, 1968, p. 346).

It is because of this that it makes no sense to think of God happening or being caused to exist, if he did not exist, or of happening or being caused to go out of existence, if he does exist. This is all that is shown by Anselm and, as we have seen, it is in these terms Malcolm explains what he means when he speaks of God having necessary existence. In order to see why God's actual existence does not follow from his Malcolmian necessary existence, we need only reflect on the fact that there would be no contradiction in claiming that an eternal and ontologically independent being was possible but not actual. In possible words terms, such a being (or the set of properties going to make up such a being) could be found in one possible world and yet be absent from others. Whether such a being is to be found in the actual world remains to be decided, perhaps by reflecting on such things as the cosmological argument. Here we have a curious result: the cosmological argument appears to be after the existence of a causally unconditioned being, yet mere causal non-contingency is not enough for some of its proponents (such as Richard Taylor), who then mix it up with the idea of logical necessity, as the only fitting end to causal explanations. On the other hand, Anselm and his followers, in seeking to show the logical necessity of God's existence, actually base their claim on considerations that would establish only God's causal independence. Of course, one can readily agree that a being worthy of worship would be causally independent. But it is unclear that there has to be anything causally independent. We can describe possible worlds with no such being, but only series of conditional beings. Perhaps this one is such; our reflections on the cosmological argument have suggested it might be. Even if one wanted to say that there must be or must have been something about the universe which does not depend on anything else for its existence, some sort of original matter would fit the bill. And original matter would not only lack many properties of the divine; it would also be quite clearly logically contingent in the sense that there are describable worlds consisting of or starting from some quite different sort of stuff altogether.

What, though, of Hartshorne? As will be evident from the quotation from him given above (p. 163), Hartshorne conflates the ideas of ontological independence and logical necessity. He says that if God's non-existence were conceivable, then, if he existed, he would exist either by chance or due to some other cause. Clearly, inconceivability (logical necessity) is being construed here in terms of causal independence. But these notions in fact do not go hand in hand. Later in the same paragraph, Hartshorne sums up his position by saying that 'God's existence can only be unconditioned', meaning by that that God's existence is not to be thought of as subject to conditions which might or might not be fulfilled.

It is necessary to distinguish two possible ways in which God's existence might be unconditioned. It might be not subject to any other causal factors, or to the vagaries of chance. In this sense, God's existence could not be subject to any contingent causal or chance factors, because it would not be brought about by anything else, contingent or otherwise. But a being that is unconditioned in the sense of being causally independent is not, by virtue of that fact, logically necessary, as already indicated. There might be an original stuff in the universe, eternal and not caused by anything else, causal or random. But it would not thereby be logically necessary. It might not have existed at all. Would such a substance exist by 'sheer chance or luck', as Hartshorne puts it? The answer to this must be that it would not be a matter of chance or luck in the same way that a random genetic mutation is chance or luck, because, unlike the genetic case, there would be no causal background with respect to which the primary substance might or might not be a matter of chance. But, if chance or luck existence is existence with no causal background whatsoever, then the primary substance would be chance existence. But, by the same token, for all the talk of ontological independence, so would God, for God, even if he is conceived as *logically* necessary, has no *causally* sufficient explanation of his existence.

Of course, Hartshorne wants to affirm a necessity for God which would not attach to a contingent prime matter, and this is why he has to make God's existence logically necessary, because being causally or ontologically independent does not make a being logically non-contingent. Logical necessity of existence is thus the second sense of divine unconditioned existence. Subsistent existence

– existence through and from oneself – is just another attempt to conflate causal and logical necessity. For how could a being cause itself? One has an image of a fire that is constantly renewing itself and sustaining itself in existence, but it is an image that is not only at odds with the second law of thermodynamics: it does nothing to explain the cause of the process as a whole. Such a process would still be causally (and logically) contingent; the fire would not *exist* through and from itself, even if it could, contrary to physical law, maintain itself in existence.

Hartshorne himself says that to reject, as we are doing here, the idea that something could be the ground of all possibility, *including its own*, is simply to restate the positivist position and to misunderstand the idea of perfection (cf. 1962, p. 97). I think that there may indeed be an unresolvable incompatibility here, between those who can and those who cannot make sense of the idea of something being its own ground. Those who can make sense of the idea, however, owe the rest of us some further account, as what they are doing appears to be plain contradictory.

Pending some further clarification of the idea of a being that is its own ground, we have to conclude that causal or ontological independence is not sufficient for logically necessary existence, nor, despite what Hartshorne says, is logically necessary existence necessary for not existing by virtue of some other cause or luck, for the putative prime matter of the universe would be due neither to other causal factors, nor to luck in the sense in which this is different from caused existence, without being logically necessary. Yet it appeared that causal independence was the feature that distinguished the second version of the ontological argument from the first. What has to be added to his causal independence to give God logically necessary existence? To answer this question we need at the same time to spell out just what logically necessary existence is. It is, in Hartshorne's own terms, the inconceivability of non-existence. The God who has to exist is not in fact the God who has an eternal, ontologically superior type of existence to everything on earth; he is the God whose essence it is to exist, the God, in other words, of the first version of the argument. God's necessary existence turns out not to be a special type of eternal, non-caused existence which need not have anything logically necessary about it, but simply the making of the proposition 'God exists' into a necessary truth. And what, we might wonder, in the absence of any further demonstration of its necessity, could possibly make *that* into a necessary truth, other than making it true by definition, or follow from a definition?

My argument here is not a simple restatement of the old empiricist principle that no existential proposition can logically be necessary. 'There exists a prime number between 9 and 13' is logically necessary, as Swinburne has pointed out (1977, p. 264). Moreover, it could be added, numbers and other abstract objects are eternal, non-composite and causally independent. What, then makes the refusal to admit logically necessary existence justifiable in God's case, but not in the case of abstract objects? My answer to this question can be given in terms of possible words. While it is obviously the case that in no possible world is there no prime number between 9 and 13, and that it would be incoherent to assert the opposite, it is by no means clear that there are possible worlds in which there is no eternal, ontologically independent creator, which is what God is claimed to be. Our reflections on the cosmological and teleological arguments suggested that even this world is not clearly grounded in such a being. At best, it is a matter of probability that there is such a being in *this* world. We can surely describe other worlds, a static Parmenidean block universe or a chaotic, ever-changing world, for example, or worlds where the gods died, in which it was far less likely that there was an eternal, ontologically independent creator, and in which there would be no incoherence in thinking that there was no such being. Certainly, the attributes of eternity, ontological independence and simplicity do not in themselves imply existence. Hartshorne claims that the inconceivability of God's non-existence arises from his nature. My counter to Hartshorne is to say that nothing he or Anselm or Malcolm have said about God's nature makes God's non-existence inconceivable, which is why I am suggesting that he is left, in effect, surreptitiously writing existence into the definition of 'God'

What has emerged from our analysis of the arguments of Malcolm and Hartshorne is that there is nothing to necessary existence or logically necessary existence over and above the assertion that God exists by definition, except the causal independence that God is taken to have. But causal independence would do nothing to guarantee him existence in all possible worlds, as we have seen. At some points, indeed, Hartshorne seems to come very close to collapsing his modal argument into the first version of argument. In answer to the question as to what necessary existence could be a property of without illegitimately assuming that God exists, he says

> the definition, the idea of deity, is what is assumed to be there; and the necessity is that this definition, this idea, alone among ideas of an individual being, cannot fail to be realized in existence. . . . (1968, p. 327)

This reference to an individual being is important. Sometimes Hartshorne writes of God as the actuality of all actuality and the possibility of all possibility, and concludes from this that talk of the possible non-existence of God would be contradictory (cf. 1962, pp. 38–41). It would indeed be contradictory to say that what is actual, and described in terms of its being actual, does not exist, but it does not follow from this that anything that is actual *has* to be actual, or, despite Hartshorne, that it might not have existed, nor, crucially does it follow that there is any *one* being that encompasses all actuality and possibility. (Whether such a notion is even intelligible will be examined in the next section.) Hartshorne writes elsewhere that 'any language adequate to formulate the meaning of "perfect" in the theistic sense will make "perfection exists" analytic or L-true' (1962, p. 55). Of course, he goes on to suggest that there is something special about the case of God or the metaphysically perfect being, so as to block similar moves in the case of perfect islands and the rest.

This something special is summed up in his ten marks of contingency, which, as will appear, would indeed rule out non-contingent islands and the rest. However, from our point of view, what is significant about Hartshorne's account of contingency is that only one of the ten aspects of contingency has anything to do with logical necessity of existence. The ten marks of a contingent being are

(1) by existing, it prevents some other things from existing
(2) that it depends causally for its existence on some other individuals
(3) it could be known to exist, but it could also conceivably be known not to exist
(4) it depends for some of its qualities on *some* other existing things

(5)   it is itself a cause required for the existence of some but not all other things

(6)   it includes in its actuality, the actuality of *some* other things as its parts or constituents

(7)   it has quantitative and qualitative limits

(8)   it has, or could be conceived to have, a beginning at some time and an ending at some time

(9)   it can be defined or identified only empirically, and not by universal concepts alone

(10) it is good for some purposes only

(cf. Hartshorne, 1962, pp. 74-5)

Marks 1,2,4,5,6,7,8 and 10 clearly apply to anything material and finite. The point of mark 9 is apparently to rule out talk of merely possible individuals; an individual, with the exception of God, has, according to Hartshorne, to be identified empirically and cannot be specified in purely general terms. Of marks 1,2,4,5,6,7,8,9 and 10, marks 6 and 8 come directly from Anselm. Marks 1,2,4 and 5 can be regarded as expansions of the notion of causal dependence, and together with mark 6 suggest that a contingent being is causally 'closer' to some other contingent beings than to other contingent beings, which is itself a symptom of contingency. (Why should it be more closely related to some things than to others?) It is not strictly relevant to present purposes, but it should be noted that in expounding his positive idea of non-contingency, Hartshorne rejects the classical theistic view that God is causally and onto-logically separate from everything else. He wants to say that the actuality of all finite things is constituted by their being included in divine actuality, and that God derives some of his qualities from each of the other things in the universe. But despite disagreement over what amounts to a type of dependence and potentiality in God, Hartshorne and the classical theist are in agreement in thinking that contingency is in part constituted by being more closely related to *some* things than to others. Marks 7 and 10 have already been referred to in our discussion of the vagueness of unqualified talk of perfection in the case of finite things, the spirit of which Hartshorne would apparently go along with (cf. his 1962, p. 84). Mark 9 would seem reasonable enough for anyone of an empirical frame of mind who does not wish to have to quantify over merely possible individuals. God, it is claimed, lacks all these marks. But what is abundantly clear is that the absence of marks 1 and 2, and 4 to 10 in a being do nothing to make it logically necessary that it exists, or clearly absurd to deny its existence. As we have seen in examining the cosmological argument, it is not self-contradictory to deny that there is one eternal, non-contingent being on which everything else depends. For logical necessity of existence, we have to go to mark 3. But the opposite of mark 3 – that the possessor of mark 3 could not conceivably be known not to exist – would appear to obtain only in the case in which existence was part of a thing's nature, but this is just what does not follow from causal independence or simplicity or eternity in the case of God. It seems that for all Hartshorne's profound reflection on God's non-contingent nature, he has not in the end succeeded in formulating a distinct version of the ontological argument.

As far as making God's existence depend on definitions or meaning postulates, we can pose the following simple dilemma. Either his existence is part of the definition or meaning postulate or it is not. If it is, then the definition falls foul of our objections to the first argument, while one can simply question the applicability to the real world of the language in which the meaning postulate appears. If his existence is not part of the definition, and 'necessary existence' does not include existence, but refers to some other aspects of God's nature, then it will always remain an open question as to whether the definition is instantiated by any actually existing being. Referring in this context to a meaning postulate once more only raises the question as to whether the language in which the postulate is found is to be regarded as a language applying to the real world or not, again, a matter for a posteriori investigation.

The temptation to think that there is a divine being that must exist is a strong one. It alone appears to promise an end to our search for causal explanations. But the concept appears to rest either on the absurdity of a self-causing thing or on a confused understanding of the way the concept of existence functions. The Hartshorne-Malcolm attempt to renew the ontological argument brings out the depth of Anselm's thinking, and shows how his concept of God did not involve a merely trivial play with the notion of existence; but it also shows, no doubt unintentionally, how in his thinking genuinely religious ideas about God's causal independence are inextricably intertwined with dubious ideas about the logical necessity of his existence. I hope that the analysis here has done something to separate the two strands.

There remains a further refurbishment of the ontological argument to consider. It is that given by Plantinga (1974, pp. 196–221, 1975, pp. 98–112) and it draws on strands from both the arguments so far considered. Plantinga agrees with the spirit of the Kantian objection to the first argument, to the effect that one cannot define things into existence, because existence is not a defining property in the required sense. (Indeed, in our formulation of this objection, we drew heavily on Plantinga.) However, Plantinga does not think that merely adding existence to a contingently applicable concept is what Anselm is up to. He proposes instead that we follow the lead of Hartshorne and Malcolm and consider the property of necessary existence. This he reads as existence in all possible worlds. He points out that existence in all possible worlds does not in itself constitute greatness. Something that existed only in some possible worlds (such as Napoleon) might well be greater than something that existed in all possible worlds (such as the number seven). Moreover, something that existed in all possible worlds might have a lot of perfection in some possible worlds, but a pretty meagre amount in the actual world. Further, Plantinga has problems in speaking of possible beings which are not actual. In order to get around these problems, he frames his version of the ontological argument in terms of the property of maximal greatness. Maximal greatness is defined for the purposes of this argument as the property of having maximal excellence in every possible world, where maximal excellence is being omniscient, omnipotent and morally perfect. So a being cannot have the property of maximal greatness if it does not exist in every possible world, or if it is not omniscient, omnipotent and morally perfect in every possible world.

The argument now comes out as follows:

(23) There is a possible world in which maximal greatness is instantiated

(24) Necessarily a being is maximally great only if it has maximal excellence in every possible world

(25) Whatever has maximal excellence is omnipotent, omniscient and morally perfect

(26) Maximal excellence is instantiated in every possible world
(27) An omnipotent, omniscient and morally perfect being exists in this (the actual) world.

Step 23 is what is entailed in saying that maximal greatness is possible. Steps 24 and 25 are true by definition. 26 follows from 23 and 24. 27 follows from 25 and 26, together with the principle that what exists in every possible world exists in this world.

Clearly, the most crucial step in the argument is the first, that is the acceptance that maximal greatness is possible. The rest appears to follow smoothly, given the definition of maximal greatness. Plantinga himself, however, points out that we can introduce a number of other concepts, such as near-maximality and non-maximality, the mere possibility of which is tantamount to denying the possibility of maximal greatness (1974, pp. 218-9). Near-maximality is enjoyed by a being if and only if it does not exist in every possible world, but has a degree of greatness not exceeded by that of any being in any world. Non-maximality is the property of being such that there is no maximally great being. If either of these, or any similar concept were logically possible, then maximal greatness is impossible. If near-maximality were possible, then in some possible world there is a being who does *not* exist in every world, yet whose greatness cannot be exceeded in the worlds in which it does exist. So the possibility of near-maximality would leave no room for maximal greatness which requires a different being, one who exists in every world, who is all-powerful, all-knowing and all-good in every world – and you clearly cannot have two all powerful beings co-existing in the same world or worlds. Non-maximality is possible only if in some possible world there is no maximally excellent being, while, as we have seen the possibility of maximal greatness is equivalent to there being a maximally excellent being in every world.

The question immediately arises, therefore, as to the grounds on which we might decide the relative possibilities of these various incompatible properties. Plantinga himself appears unable to give any compelling reason in favour of one being possible, rather than another, and admits as much (cf. 1974, p. 220). I cannot see any way out of the impasse either, once we have reached this point. (It is interesting to note that there, as with his treatments of other minds and the teleological argument, Plantinga thinks that a position can be rational, and argued for rationally, while resting on an unsupported premise. There is indeed a curious air of fideism about Plantinga's thought.)

However, what can be done is to raise some doubts as to whether we should have been allowed to get to the point in question at all. What is going on with all these concepts (maximal greatness, near-maximality, no-maximality) is a surreptitious settling of questions of actual existence by apparently purely conceptual or definitional means. The passage from 23 to 27 makes this clear. If we assert that maximal greatness is possible, we are also asserting that there is, in the real world, an omnipotent, omniscient, morally perfect being. If we assert that non-maximality is possible, we are denying that there is a maximally great being in this world. If we assert that near-maximality is possible, we are at least denying that there is any maximally great being in the real world, even though there could still be a maximally excellent one. An initial reaction here is to say that one cannot settle such questions of existence simply by considering definitions; and that in considering whether these 'definitions' are logically possible, one is actually deciding on questions of contingent fact. It is true that in defining a triangle in a given way, one is committed to denying the existence of triangles with angles of more than 180°. But *this* existential claim rests on the contradictoriness of its subject. It is a matter of fact, but not of contingent fact. On the other hand, there is no obvious contradiction in saying that there is no omnipotent, omniscient, morally perfect being. In so far as this is denied by the mere possibility of maximal greatness, it appears that what we have here is in fact a statement of contingent fact (there is a God), ingeniously masquerading as part of a definition. To bring this out, let us consider the concept of maximal unicornhood. We can define maximal unicornhood as the property of being a unicorn in all possible worlds; then something would be a maximal unicorn if and only if it was a unicorn in all possible worlds. Is maximal unicornhood possible? One's immediate reaction might be to say that there is no reason why it should not be, but one should be careful, for if there are no unicorns in this world, then it is not possible, for part of what is involved in saying that maximal unicornhood is possible is saying that there is a unicorn in this world. In other words, in the case of maximal unicornhood, impossibility follows from the merely contingent fact that there are no unicorns in the real world. Decisions about the possibility and impossibility of maximal unicornhood will have to involve reference to contingent facts about the actual world. Similarly before satisfying ourselves that maximal greatness, as defined by Plantinga, is possible, we will have to ensure, among other things, that there *is* an omnipotent, omniscient, morally perfect being in this world. The reason why both Plantinga and I are uncertain as to whether maximal greatness or non-maximality are possible can be attributed to the fact that before knowing whether these concepts are possible, one has to establish certain questions of facts, for part of what is entailed by saying that they are possible is that certain apparently logically contingent things, such as the existence of a maximally great being, are or are not the case in this, the actual world.

In addition to appearing to settle contingent existential questions by definitional means, Plantinga's introduction of properties like maximal greatness, non-maximality and near-maximality actually subverts the intuition underlying the analysis of logical possibility and logical necessity in terms of possible worlds. For in this analysis, any non-contradictory concept or logical possibility is said to obtain in some possible world. Thus, if the existence of God is possible, then there is a possible world in which there is a God, while if the non-existence of God is possible, there is a possible world in which there is no God. But the second of these possible worlds is excluded by the possibility of maximal greatness; that is, if there is a possible world in which there is a maximally great being, then there is no possible world in which there is no God. On the other hand, if there is a possible world in which there is a non-maximal being, then there is no possible world in which there is a maximally great being. So what appear, on the face of it, to be genuine logical possibilities (God's non-existence, maximal greatness, non-maximality) are ruled out once other logical possibilities are admitted. However, in a penetrating analysis of Plantinga's argument, Mackie (1982, pp. 55-63) has suggested that the concepts whose mere possibility rules out as impossible other apparent possibilities – maximal greatness, no-maximality, near-maximality – are all what he calls 'world-indexed properties', that is to say, they are properties in which a being is said to possess in a given possible world not only the properties it has in that world, but also the properties it has in other worlds. So, a maximally great being in world W1 possesses maximal excellence in W1, certainly, but also, and in W1, it possesses maximal excellence-in-W2, maximal excellence-in-W3, etc., and it is because of the properties it is said in W1 to have in W2, W3, etc., that its existence in W1 alone rules out what appear from other points of view to be open possibilities in other worlds such as W2, W3, etc. At the same time, and for similar reasons, if no-maximality is realized in W3, say, then maximal greatness cannot be realized in W1. Plantinga's ontological argument, then, shows that a possible worlds analysis of logical possibility cannot survive the introduction of world-indexed properties, for once these are allowed, we can no longer say that *every* logical possibility is realized in some possible world, for some of these properties, if realized in any possible world, will mean that other possibilities (of both world-indexed and non-world-indexed properties) can be realized in no possible world. Once world-indexed properties are banned from the possible worlds scene, of course, Plantinga's argument would not even get going. Mackie's demonstration of the effect the introduction of such properties has on the possible world analysis of logical possibility has the virtue of showing that such a ban would not be a purely ad hoc manoeuvre to disallow Plantinga his argument.

From another angle, it is possible to show that Plantinga's use of the concept of maximal greatness is tantamount to just another formulation of Anselm's original argument. For, as defined by Plantinga, maximal greatness is the property of being maximally excellent in all possible worlds. A being that is maximally great, then, is maximally excellent not just in all possible worlds in which it exists, where it is an open question as to whether it exists in specific worlds, but in all possible worlds, for it is part of its definition that it exists in all. Hence it is necessarily maximally excellent and necessarily existing. In fact, what is being proposed by the definitions of maximal greatness (and maximal unicorn-hood, for that matter) is that a certain property is instantiated in every possible world; in other words, where F is to stand for maximal excellence, that $(\exists x) Fx$ is true in all possible worlds, or logically necessary (i.e. $L (\exists x) Fx$). In speaking of the *possibility* of maximal greatness, we are back to speaking of the possibility of a necessary truth, and following our consideration of Hartshorne's argument and S5 it should occasion no surprise to see that here too from

-L-L (∃x) Fx

we have informally deduced both

(∃x) Fx

and

L (∃x) Fx

The necessity of the maximal excellence of the maximally great being can quite legitimately follow from the definition, in the same way that the necessity of the properties of a triangle follows from the definition of the triangle. But where can the necessity of its existence come from? We have seen at sufficient length that, unlike the triangle case, it cannot derive from a definition, for existence cannot function in the required way as a defining predicate. Nor is the necessity canvassed by Hartshorne and Malcolm sufficient to establish existence in all possible worlds. Plantinga's version of the ontological argument is indeed ingenious, but it is unclear once it is unravelled that it takes us any further than the other versions we have examined. What is needed, and what is absent from it, is a clear account of where the logical necessity of 'There exists maximal excellence' is supposed to come from.

Our survey of three main versions of the ontological argument has shown that they all involve the claim that 'God exists' is a necessary truth. We have found no justification for this claim, beyond the questionable suggestion that divine existence could be part of a defining description and the conflation of non-contingency and logical necessity of existence. I said at the beginning of this section that the underlying motivation for the ontological argument involved a negation of human thought and intellectual discrimination. It does so because in the argument existence is treated as if it were a form, a quality pertaining to God's nature. God's existence is treated as one of his defining properties. But as we have seen, the importation of existence into a definition in this way is necessarily redundant. The idea in the arguments is that existence is itself something that characterizes God's nature, but it is not fully realized that that is to say nothing about *how* God is or what he is. And this is where the whole process begins to subside into incoherent gesturing. Formless existence is itself regarded as a something, yet a something it would be impudent to attempt to delimit by the application of any descriptive predicates. Necessity of existence is, as I said earlier, transformed into pure, formless existence. We are now in a position to see why: necessity of existence involves treating existence as a defining predicate, yet adding existence adds no further form or describable quality to an object, for other qualities already ensure that they will be satisfied only by something existing in the appropriate way. The situation becomes even worse when existence alone is taken to be God's chief defining property; thus we are told (and by no advocate of the ontological argument), that God's essence is simply to exist. But a being that just existed, and whose essence was existence, would be a nothing, a non-existent, because it makes sense only to speak of something with some describable properties as existing. This tendency to treat existence itself as an all-encompassing something, a sort of ground from which all particular things derive, is undoubtedly deeply embedded in religious thinking. Existence, however, is not a something, not a process, or a ground or anything else, and this is why I say that the ontological argument and all thought which, consciously or not, depends on conceiving existence as a something in its own right, instantiable apart from all particular determinations of things, is incoherent.

I am well aware that Thomists, alerted by my oblique reference to Aquinas, will accuse me of unforgivable crudity in the preceding paragraph. They will say that not only is God's nature or essence to exist (or as in Burrell, 1979, p. 42, 'to be God is to be to-be'), but that if he is to be the source of all being, he cannot himself be *a* being or a particular thing at all. (If he were just a larger particular thing, he too would require a cause.) So it is not the case that God, the ground of existence, is *a* thing. Hence Aquinas in speaking of God's essence as his existence does not treat God's existence as the sort of property or attribute which would be used to pick out particular finite objects. What, though, could be meant by denying that God is a something? What the Thomist surely owes us an account of is just how we can meaningfully speak of a God who is 'subsistent existence itself, in no way determined' (*Summa Theologiae* la.11,4), which is close to saying he is not a something, but not a nothing either. The problem is, of course, that if we start predicating attributes of God (such as omnipotent, omniscient, morally good, and so on), we seem to be implying that God is at least determined in so far as he is regarded as having those attributes apply to him. So, not surprisingly, we find Aquinas at one point denying in effect that we can in any clear way predicate attributes to God or separate God's attributes from his existence (cf. *Summa Theologiae* la. 13,5). As one commentator, Brian Davies, puts it:

> When, for example, we call creatures 'wise' we are saying that they possess a certain attribute. And when we say this we have to allow that the attribute in question is distinct from other attributes and even from the fact of there being anything to possess it. In the case of God, however, we cannot distinguish his attributes from each other; nor can we distinguish them from his very existence. (1982, p. 11)

I would defend the crudity of my previous paragraph on the grounds that attempts to avoid such crudity appear to lead us to a not-thing whose attributes are indistinguishable from each other and from that to which they are attributed and that such an idea is hardly distinguishable from the idea of an incoherent nothing. It is clearly not for nothing that Aquinas himself says that we cannot know what God is, but only what he is not (*Summa Theologiae*, 1.3. Intro.), and also that while God is necessary in himself (*per se nota*) he is not necessary relative to us (*nota quoad nos*) (*Summa Theologiae*, la. 2.1).

Dummett glosses the latter distinction by saying it may be possible 'that a statement may not be capable of being known a priori by us, and yet have a meaning such that its truth conditions could not but be fulfilled' (1973, p. 118); examples of such statements might be Fermat's Last Theorem for which no-one has found a proof, and for which one may never be found, or, according to the essentialism made fashionable by Kripke and Putnam, before people knew enough chemistry, the statement 'Water is H_2O.' But the difference between these cases and 'God exists' is that we are given by the proponents of their necessity some idea of the grounds on which their necessity is said to rest: respectively, on the nature of mathematical truth in general and because of the microstructure of the stuff we refer to as water, which is said to be an essential property of the stuff. On what does the necessity of God's existence rest? None of the answers we have examined – God's perfection, his maximal greatness, his independence and timelessness, his purity of existence – show that his existence is necessary in the sense that the truth conditions of 'God exists' could not but be fulfilled. Without some indication of the grounds on which this might be so, the non-believer is surely entitled to continue to regard Aquinas's distinction between what is necessary in itself and what is necessary relative to us as of little help in unravelling the perplexities involved in the notions of divine existence and necessity.

Section 4 God as world process

The ontological argument and the idea of God as being-itself are incoherent. Saying this, however, does not refute the often associated belief that God is somehow the source of all wordly processes, in the sense that all wordly processes derive from God and are part of his unfolding of his nature. Often in nature one has the feeling that what is before one is an expression of something more profound, more fundamental, that we and what we see before us are part of some larger whole, of some great process of which we and our environment are simply passing phases. One then awakes and realizes that such thoughts are nonsensical as applied to nature, that what is beneath our feet is in no universal sense more basic or fundamental than anything else, and that the physical process of which our world and experience might be a part is not only so vast as to make our lives almost totally insignificant but, more important, something that could be regarded as in no sense conscious or capable of expressing its nature in the same sort of way a creative artist might do. Nevertheless, it may be possible to think of God and world processes in a more religious and less literally physical way. In order to see whether this might be so, we will now examine some aspects of process theology as this has been developed in the writings of Hartshorne.

Roughly speaking, the term process theology may be used to refer to any theological account of God which pictures God as undergoing real change and development. In this rough sense, process theology did not originate with Hartshorne, nor is it confined to him. Its ancestry can be traced in Theravada Buddhism, and in Western thinkers as diverse as Heraclitus, Faustus Socinus, Hegel, Schelling, Bergson and, of course, Whitehead. Obviously, process thinking permeates much Indian thought, which views the world and God itself, if God is truly separable from the world, as a unified process. It would also find kinship with European idealist thought, in which the world and all its history and experience are conceived of as moments in the self-discovery of the Absolute. Those from within the Christian tradition who are attracted to process thinking claim that the idea of a God who changes is more compatible with the historical and personal dimensions of the Biblical God, particularly that of the Old Testament. Richard Swinburne (1977, pp. 214-5) and Jurgen Moltmann may be mentioned as representatives of this trend in contemporary Christian thinking.

The issues involved in considering Hartshorne's views are of two sorts, though, as we shall see, they overlap. There is first the 'internal' question as to whether Hartshorne's God is religiously satisfactory, and second, the 'external' question as to whether there is any reason for thinking that there is a God progressively creating or developing himself in and through the world process. As regards the religious question, Hartshorne's central deviation from ortho-dox classical theism is his claim that for God time is a matter of real experience, just as it is for us, with a past that is past and a future which is open and undecided. Moreover, God's own future is partially dependent on the choices of other free creative beings in the universe, namely men. Although God will always react to what we do with perfect love, what he reacts to in this way is not chosen by him, nor is it known to him before we do it. Hartshorne thus sees God very much in terms of a human person, making his choices as he goes along, and reacting to what we and others do without foreknowledge of what we do. This view stands in stark contrast to the classical view in which God is unchanging and unaffected by what we do. On the classical view, God is perfect in himself, and admits of no potentiality or change. This, of course, leads to difficulties in considering God's relationship to time and his creation which do not arise for the process view.

If God is changeless then it is, at first sight, difficult to see how he can be all-knowing, for knowledge of temporal events changes in its character with the passing of time. Thus, we cannot now say that God knows that Socrates is sitting down, though we might once have been able to say that. A way out of this difficulty might be to regard God's knowledge as timeless, and, where appropriate, as involving an implicit time reference. Thus God's knowledge of Socrates' sitting is not to be seen as knowledge of a tensed utterance

('Socrates sits', where 'sits' is the present of sit), but as knowledge of the tenseless 'Socrates sits (timelessly) at such and such a time on such and such a day.' On this view, God's knowledge would be constituted by knowledge of timeless propositions: God would appear to survey the whole of time from a point outside time, and so his knowledge would not change with the passing of time. Similarly, we could regard God's creative action, not itself as successive, even though the historical events he brings about are, from our point of view, successive. God would have timelessly willed Adam to be followed by Eve, to be followed by Cain, to be followed by Abel and so on. His willing Adam to precede Eve, to precede Cain, to precede Abel does not entail that he had to will Adam, *then* will Eve, *then* will Cain and *then* will Abel.

Placing God outside time in this way may enable us to continue speaking of his knowledge and his will as changeless. What he knows and what he wills, he knows and wills in a non-tensed way, in a single, unchanging act of will and moment of perception, or vision, to use Aquinas's expression. I do not want to claim that this picture is necessarily incoherent, but, equally, it would be wrong to think that it is without difficulty. In the first place, one might ask whether, on this view, God could have any conception of the reality of time. If all things were equally present to him, the passing of time could hardly have the same significance for him as it does for us, nor could he ever experience the irrevocable passing of things. It seems hard to reconcile God's timelessness with God having any sense of what it means for us to experience time, even if we are not forced to conclude that for God time is but an illusion of finite human perception. Why we might be forced to conclude this is because, as Swinburne (1977, pp. 220-1) has pointed out, if all moments of our time are equally present to God, then there is something they are all simultaneous with (God's timeless perception), from which it is difficult not to conclude that they are not *really* all simultaneous with each other. The drawback of concluding that our perception of time is an illusion in this way is that even if it is an illusion in some metaphysical sense, the experiences we have of events succeeding one another are themselves successive. As Geach has pointed out (1969, p. 92) even an illusion of successiveness 'is already a real succession of experiences'; our experiences are uncombinable and necessarily non-simultaneous. Hence there is something logically incoherent about denying the reality of time. Time relations characterize our experiences at least.

Perhaps, as I say, speaking of God as timeless does not mean that time is unreal, or that he can have no knowledge of what time means for us, although anyone who wants to maintain both divine timelessness and the reality of human temporality may have some difficulty in making God's knowledge of time appear existentially convincing, though this is presumably a problem with God's knowledge of any embodied states. But a greater problem for the classical theist, insistent on maintaining the changelessness of God, is to explain how a God that knows all things timelessly can have full knowledge of free human actions. The initial problem here is that God knows what I am going to do, presumably even before the world came into being. How then can my choice be free, if its outcome is already present in the mind of God? One way out of this problem is to say that while it is necessarily true that if God (or anyone else) knows that something will be the case, it will be the case, it does not follow from someone's knowing that something will be the case that what is going to occur is itself fated or necessary. To conclude that it is is to illegitimately transpose the modal operator from the outside of a condition to the inside (as in the case of the fatalist's claim that if a future tense proposition has a truth-value *now*, what it refers to is unalterable and fixed now).

This reply solves part of the problem of God's foreknowledge of my free actions, but only part. For while the stock anti-fatalist moves may help us to see in a formal sense how the truth of a knowledge claim does not in itself mean that what is known is necessary or determined or fated, we may still want to ask for the justification of the knowledge claim. And, in pressing the question here, we may well begin to doubt the extent to which a future action of mine can be both free and infallibly known by God. The crucial point about knowledge here is that knowledge, to be knowledge, requires the existence of some grounds. Now, my knowledge of a past or present event may have perceptual or testimonial grounds, and this may be enough to secure knowledge, without any implication that what I know was causally fixed, predetermined or fated. Thus, I know that I am now sitting at a table writing, because I perceive the relevant facts, and there is no further implication that those facts are themselves determined in any way. My present perception is quite enough to ground knowledge in this and similar cases. Likewise, testimonial evidence can ground knowledge claims about the past, without any implication that the past events were determined in any way. But what of my knowledge that tomorrow such and such will happen? There is no question of my perceiving or having testimonial evidence for something that has not yet happened, and might not happen. If I can have knowledge of the future at all, it can only be based on evidence to the effect that what will happen is already somehow determined by present states of affairs. Knowing the present states of affairs in question and the relevant determining laws, I may be able justifiably to claim knowledge now of some future event. Thus, I might claim to know that Jones will be late for our meeting tomorrow, because of my knowledge of Jones's incorrigible unpunctuality. Knowledge, if I have knowledge here at all, must in part be based on my knowledge of Jones's present character and dispositions, which I believe will determine his future behaviour in this respect. *If* this belief is correct (and, I am arguing, only if it is correct can I now be said to have knowledge rather than probable opinion here), then Jones can hardly be said to have been free, when he turns up late tomorrow, in the sense of having been able to have chosen otherwise, all things being as they were at the time. Yet it is just this sense of freedom that classical theists characteristically insist on when they speak of human free choice.

It will, of course, be said that God's foreknowledge of my future actions it not based on the same sort of causal evidence as my knowledge of Jones's future unpunctuality. Is it then based on something more like a divine perception of the future? Here we are back with the problematic picture of God surveying every moment in time in one immediate grasp. But, we might ask, how can my future action be surveyed *now*, even out of our time, if it does not yet exist at least in some other world? If it can be surveyed by God now, then it does exist now, even if not in our time. But, if it does exist already, how can I be free with regard to it? If, on the other hand, it does not exist now, then God cannot survey it now, and hence he does not know it now. But if he does not know it now, then he does not know all future events now, and so he can be all-knowing only in the sense that he comes to know everything when it is able to be known and not in the sense that he knows everything at all times. While this may well give a perfectly reasonable interpretation of divine omniscience, it does so only at the cost of requiring change in God, for, on this view, he comes to know free

189

actions as and when they occur, given that they are not causally determined from the beginning of creation and are not perceivable before they have happened.

It might be objected that in the previous paragraph I have misconstrued divine timelessness, by speaking of God knowing of things *before* they have happened. While conceding that I do not fully understand the idea of a timeless person, I would simply pose the following question at this point. Does God's omniscience entail that it is true now that he knows what I will freely do tomorrow? If it is now true, then, on the basis of the considerations adduced earlier, what I will do tomorrow must in some sense already exist or be determined, and hence not be free. If it is not true that God knows now what I will freely do tomorrow, then, given that he will at some time know it, then there must be addition to his knowledge and hence change in God. Neither option appears acceptable to a classical theist, and the onus is on him to explain how invoking divine timelessness can help him out of the dilemma. It is surely not enough to claim, as Geach does (1969, p. 98), that in the created world propositions about what God knows and wills in the world are not unchangeably true, while still claiming that, as far as God is concerned, God's will and knowledge are unchangeable, when, in the case of human free action, God's will and knowledge appear to depend on what we, as free agents, freely and unpredictably decide to do in time. Geach's claim here is an application of Aquinas's general thesis that 'being related to God is a reality in creatures, but being related to creatures is not a reality in God' (*Summa Theologiae*, 1.13.7), to which Hartshorne obviously strongly objects for religious reasons; and which on the face of it, for logical reasons, is an extremely puzzling claim: if A is related to B, how can B not be related to A? Aquinas answers this question by saying that when we move from the left to the right of a pillar, no change is implied in the pillar, but only in us, so clearly what he intends by the non-relationship doctrine is to deny that any change in us involves a real change in God. While, as Geach has insisted, we have no adequate way of distinguishing real from unreal changes, so as to distinguish cases where I grow taller (real change), and so my father ceases to be bigger than me (no real change in him), it is hard to see how God does not really change as a result of coming to know about actions that free agents unpredictably do in time. If it is said that he knows them outside time, I can make sense of this only on the assumption that it is in some sense already true what I will do tomorrow, and this seems to have disastrous consequences for the view that what I do freely, I do unpredictably.

It is, then, extremely hard to reconcile the view that God's knowledge and will are unchangeable with the view that human beings act freely and unpredictably. (As we shall see in the next chapter, the view that human beings act freely and unpredictably is even harder to reconcile with the Thomistic view that God *causes* our free actions.) Process thought is, in part, an attempt to come to terms with human creativity, and it does this at the expense of denying unchangeability in God. In a wider context, it is also an attempt to describe a more intimate relationship between God and the world than appears possible on traditional theistic lines. For there, God is held in no way to depend on, be changed by or be affected by the world or what happens in it. This is the doctrine of God as pure act, having no potentiality or need, and it does, of course raise in an acute way the question as to why God created the world at all, even more, the question as to why, having created it, he felt inclined to redeem it as the Bible has it. Hartshorne himself quotes Berdyaev to the effect that the static conception of God as pure act, having no potentiality and completely self-sufficient is a philosophical, Aristotelian conception, and not a Biblical conception. Moreover, classical theism makes it hard to see how the experiences of finite beings can have any value in and for themselves if they add nothing to divine reality, whereas if they are an integral part of the divine unfolding, 'the immediate facts of present action pass into permanent significance for the Universe', as Whitehead put it (1951, p. 698).

Against the classical theists' belief in divine omniscience, Hartshorne is insistent that unless God himself is unaware of the future history of the world,

> the world process would be the idle duplicate of something in eternity. A God who eternally knew all that the fulfilment of his purpose would bring could have no need of that fulfilment or of purpose. Complete knowledge is complete possession: it is just because a man does not know in detail what 'knowing his friends better' would be like that he has the purpose to come to know them better. As Bergson and Peirce were among the first to see, even a world purpose must be indeterminate as to details.

> For one thing, an absolute and inexorable purpose, supposing
> this meant anything, would deny individuality, self-activity,
> hence reality, to the lesser individuals, the creatures.
> (1962, pp. 205-6)

We see in Hartshorne the characteristic American assertion of the
intrinsic significance of every moment of experience, combined
with a form of Absolute Idealist metaphysics. For he holds that the
way each worldly experience contributes to the divine plan is not in
the same way that someone might observe the behaviour of others
from an external point of view, but rather by being included in
God's experience. Hartshorne speaks of God as the universal
Individual, who 'includes all actuality' with 'unique effectiveness
and adequacy' (1962, p. 10), and of God as being enriched by what
goes on in the world, indeed even as actually existing 'only in what
is particular, in actual "states"' (1962, p. 92).

In answer to objections relating to the perfection of a being who
existed through the world, and who depended on free and chance
happenings in the world, Hartshorne distinguishes between an
individual than which no greater is conceivable and one who, in no
conceivable state of existence, could be greater. He asserts that
while God is the greatest conceivable individual, he continually
surpasses the state he is in at any given time. According to
Hartshorne, this admission of potentiality and perfectibility in God
actually makes God more perfect than he is under the classical
conception where God has no unactualized power to be. The ability
to develop and to become and to react is seen as in itself better than
the simple and changeless plenitude of existence ascribed to God by
the classical theist.

Hartshorne makes an important distinction between, on the one
hand, the abstract necessity of God's existence as the perfect being,
and as co-extensive with all actuality (which necessity is, of course,
unchanging), and, on the other, his concrete actual states, which
are contingent and transient. This distinction, which is sometimes
called the divine dipolarity by process thinkers, means that divine
perfection can (and indeed must be) realized through an arbitrary
selection by God from among the countless possible states that he
could actualize. Hartshorne does not think that the perfect being
exists independently of his actual states (any more than you or I
exist independently of our actual states), but he does think that in

speaking of God in an abstract way as the perfect or necessarily existing individual, he can give some account of God's traditional attributes of eternity and changelessness, while still seeing God's actual states as the moment-by-moment states in which God is perfect.

In Hartshorne's view, God's actuality comprehends all actuality, and his potentiality comprehends all potentiality. He writes

> if x is red, then the perfect must possess all the value and actuality of x and its redness. And if x could be, but is not red, then the perfect individual is potentially in possession of this being-red of x. (1962, p. 97)

An apparent problem with this view is that if perfection involves experiencing everything that is, then the perfect being will experience evil. However, Hartshorne's view is that experiencing or perceiving evil is not thereby to be evil, and that perceiving it fully in its wickedness will actually make being wicked impossible.

> But it is otherwise with suffering. How does one perceive a particular, concrete suffering in its concrete particularity? I see no way but to sympathetically share it. And hence for me the old heresy of a suffering deity is no heresy. (1962, p. 44)

And Hartshorne goes on to state that his view of perfection does not entail an absence of perfection either in God or in the world. In his view, supreme power – the object of religious worship – is not a monopoly of power, unilaterally determining all things, but 'an ideal form of give and take' a two-sided relationship between God and his creatures, with God in a sense depending on them as well as they on him.

We have now to compare Hartshorne's giving-and-taking God with the changeless God of classical theism. In addition to the religious reasons favouring a God of process, following Hartshorne himself, we can quote no less an authority than Hume in Hartshorne's favour. In the Fourth Part of the *Dialogues Concerning Natural Religion*, Hume has Cleanthes arguing that a belief in Deity whose ways are incomprehensible to us is mysticism, and, as such, epistemically indistinguishable from atheism, for it amounts to a postulation of a cause that is unknown and unintelligible. Cleanthes goes on

those who maintain the perfect simplicity of the Supreme
Being . . . are complete mystics, and chargeable with all the
consequences which I have drawn from their opinion. They are,
in a word, atheists, without knowing it. For though it be
allowed that the Deity possesses attributes of which we have no
comprehension, yet ought we never to ascribe to him any
attributes which are absolutely incompatible with that intelligent
nature essential to him. A mind whose acts and sentiments and
ideas are not distinct and successive, one that is wholly simple
and totally immutable, is a mind which has no thought, no
reason, no will, no sentiment, no love, no hatred; or, in a word,
is no mind at all. It is an abuse of terms to give it that
appellation, and we may as well speak of limited extension
without figure, or of number without composition.
(1779, p. 32)

In other words, Hume is suggesting that a changeless person would
be no person at all. Certainly it is hard to see how attempting to
reconcile divine changelessness with human freedom produces
anything but a retreat into mystery.

On the other hand, Hartshorne's God has certain drawbacks
from a religious point of view, which derive from his changeable-
ness and his possession of potentiality. It is not without reason that
Aquinas wishes that term of his first way to be an unmoved mover.
A mover that could itself move and be moved is one that admits of
a degree of dependence and which clearly requires explanation as to
why it moves or is moved as it does. The denial of change in God is
intended to block questions of this sort, although Hartshorne
might reply to this that we can still ask questions about the reason
why a changeless God had his will fixed as it is. Perhaps more
seriously for Hartshorne's view is the Thomist claim that if God is
the cause of the existence of all things, then he cannot change and
must be timeless. The existence of Hartshorne's changing God
raises the question of something beyond it or at least of its
dependence on other things: such a God would only be a particular
being among other beings, and there will be no guarantee that
something or other might not bring about its non-existence (cf.
Davies, 1982, pp. 81–2).

A changing God, a God that admits of potentiality is certainly
not the completely independent stop to all further causal question-

ing intended by the cosmological argument. But does it follow from this that a changing God would be merely a being among beings, and subject to possible extinction by something else as Davies claims? I think that it is easy to show that this is to misunderstand Hartshorne, but that doing this will detract seriously from the probability that there is such a being as Hartshorne describes. It is a central aspect of Hartshorne's conception of God that 'all actuality is included in His actuality, and all possibility in His potential actuality.' (1962, pp. 40-1) Despite some unclarity here, it would seem to follow from this at least that so long as there is anything at all– any actuality – there would be a God. On this view, God is certainly not *a* being among other beings. To speak metaphorically, God is more like the soul of whatever is, or, as Hartshorne has himself said, the world is the body of God (1953, p. 142), the universe the living garment of deity (1962, p. 215).

However, thinking of God as the metaphorical soul of whatever is, or as comprehending all actuality would on their own afford theism too easy a victory, for, on these terms, one could hardly assert the existence of anything and deny the existence of God. But equally, asserting the existence of God would be saying very little over and above saying that the world existed. Clearly this is not what Hartshorne intends. As we noted in the previous section, Hartshorne does speak of God as an individual being, and as we have seen here, he is a being who suffers, chooses and reacts with love to whatever happens in the world. So the plausibility of Hartshorne's God is the question of the plausibility of a being living in and through the world process, the moments of which constitute the experience of that being.

One might begin by asking whether it is intelligible to think of the world as a process at all. Hartshorne himself makes a great deal of claims to the effect that whatever happens anywhere in the universe is communicated with the speed of light in all directions, that the entire universe acts upon each particle to constitute its inertia, that the same basic modes of action pervade the whole universe, that one cannot leave the universe, and so on (cf. 1962, pp. 204-5). But, even if these observations show that it is correct to think of the universe as a physical system, they do nothing to show that it is a conscious organism, or that there is one individual shining through and experiencing the whole thing.

At a very basic level, it must be said that the universe can hardly be regarded as a sentient being. It is hardly necessary to point to the absence of a nervous system or brain in the universe, or to the obvious dissimilarities between the cosmos and a living thing. Further, from our own experience of matter on this planet, we know that living matter is comparatively rare and late, and there is no reason to suppose that what is to all appearance dead and inert and unfeeling could somehow be providing experiential input for some cosmic super-organism. Of course, one could hardly refute the claim that it might be, but this is in part at least because one is quite unclear what is being claimed here. Is it being claimed, for example, that when someone explodes some dynamite in a rock, either the rock or the universe as a whole feels it and suffers? Certainly the rock itself does not exhibit pain behaviour, c-fibre stimulation or any of the other things which form the basis of our pain attributions, and it is equally unclear how any of these things would have any application in the case of the universe as a whole. This lack of any basis on which to attribute sensation or experience to inert matter, or to the universe as a whole, is the fundamental weakness of all pan-psychic theorizing, and leaves the pan-psychist in the position of saying in effect that although dynamited rock and the whole universe do not feel pain in the same way as human beings or animals do, they nevertheless feel it in their own way. While one can point to certain aspects of the cosmos which are shared by living things – its inter-relatedness, its waxing and waning, and so on – what is crucially lacking is the presence in the cosmos of any of the criteria for the ascription of sensation, will, motivation, belief and the other things that comprise our conception of the psychological.

The claim that the cosmos itself is a feeling entity is so under-determined as to be practically empty. We are left quite unclear as to just what is meant by such claims, over and above a gesturing at certain aspects of the cosmos, which in individual physical systems would not be taken to imply sentience in any way analogous to talk of a man or an animal having feelings. However, more puzzling than the thought that the world might be the living body or garment of the deity is the thought that all the experiences of all those beings in the universe which are undoubtedly living and feeling are *also* experiences of God, or the world soul or whatever. The problem here is to attach a sense to the idea that my

196

experiences are also the experiences of some other being, or perhaps even that my individuality is an illusion, hiding the truth that my experiences are, properly speaking, the experiences of God. One obvious problem with such suggestions is that experiences are identified in the first instance through their being the experiences of some individual being. This peeling-away of experience from the individual, and treating of experiences as themselves individual substances, possessible indifferently by one or more beings, is no doubt part of the Cartesian soil in which European idealism historically flourished. But it overlooks the fact that our identification of particular experiences operates by reference to the person having the experience. So neither God nor anyone else could have the experience I am now having, because whatever they had, it would be an experience of theirs, and not mine, not *this* experience. All this is undoubtedly truistic – a fact of grammar, as Wittgenstein insists – but it does mean that it is impossible to say in any straightforward way that God can have my experiences.

Hartshorne could reply at this point that his talk of all things contributing what they are and have to the one is not intended to run against the rules of language or to deny that experiences are always experiences of individuals rather than things in their own right. What he means is not that God *has* my experiences; after all, how could he, given the difference between my cognitive perspective and God's, and the way in which one's memory and knowledge qualitatively permeate the experiences one has? What he means is that God shares all the experiences of all the beings in the world through some sort of sympathy or insight into them, and that God develops through his interaction with the world. While this position would defuse some of the difficulties involved in thinking of the world as God's body, and the experiences of individuals as, at the same time, the experiences of God, it still leaves a major problem with all these conceptions unsolved.

The problem is this. Hartshorne's talk of a suffering deity can at first sight seem religiously attractive. A God who participates in the suffering of the world in some way looks more sympathetic to our predicament than one who is changeless and, literally, unfeeling. Hartshorne's God might appear more able to care than the God of classical theism, and, from the Christian point of view, Christ's suffering will now appear as a vivid illustration of the essential nature of God, rather than as some inexplicable gratuity on God's part. But all this is only at first sight. For Hartshorne's picture is of God increasing his own perfection in and through the suffering of the world. This conception is no part of classical theism, and for good reason. For how could a perfect being use the pain of creatures to achieve his own fulfilment? How could a perfect being include in his own existence an atrocity like Babi Yar or even an everyday occurrence like a cat tearing a bird to pieces, to say nothing of the apparently pointless waste and suffering that goes on in nature? Would a being that acted in such a way be worthy of worship? Hartshorne might reply that God, though perfect and striving always towards greater perfection, is not powerful enough in his striving to minimize the pain and suffering in the world, without loss of ultimate perfection, but at this point we begin to fall into one of the classic dilemmas for theism. The more God is like one of us, needs his creatures and is unable to prevent evil and suffering either in the short or long term, the less he seems worthy of worship – he might be worthy of sympathy rather more. On the other hand, if God is all-powerful, it seems monstrous that he should use the suffering of others to perfect himself. If he can stop it at all, why does he not stop it now? The proper response to such a being would hardly be one of worship.

The objections of the previous paragraph are predicated of Hartshorne's God on the basis that this God is using the sufferings of his creatures to perfect himself. As we shall see in the next chapter there may be no objection of a moral or religious sort to a God who creates for their own good, creatures with a potentiality for suffering and wickedness, although, I shall argue, the positive justifications adduced by traditional theism for God's having created this world are not convincing. Strangely, perhaps, Hartshorne himself adds little to the traditional 'free will' defence in discussing the suffering and evil in the world. He maintains that God is powerless to prevent suffering both because of the existence of free, active decision-makers in the world and because of a general indeterminacy in nature. The first of these factors is considered generally desirable. Whether having free creatures necessitates the evil and suffering there is in the world will be considered in the next chapter. The second factor is not so clearly desirable, nor is it clear just why it makes evil and suffering occur. Aside from that, whether a process God who was himself a struggling being, prone to wickedness and suffering would actually be a being worthy of worship is highly questionable because it would imply that, however admirable the being was in other ways, it was itself subject to all sorts of weaknesses and limitations and, for that reason, not worthy of worship. This is presumably why Hartshorne does not take such a line, although it would perhaps be more consistent with some aspects of process thinking.

We have a world process in some sense, but not in any sense that would entitle us to see it as a conscious process. We could no doubt maintain that there is a God behind the world process, and responding to it. But, to maintain this view rationally, we would have to be able to find reasons other than the mere existence of the world process itself. God, as a perfect individual, conscious and creative, cannot be defined into existence by simply saying that he is co-extensive with all that is actual. So we would return to these other proofs for the existence of God, which we have considered and rejected. In addition, the process view that God fulfils himself in and through the world poses, in a peculiarly acute form, the problem of evil, to which we will turn after a brief consideration of one other way in which the world might be seen as a divine process.

Hartshorne, it will be clear, stresses freedom and creativity both in God and in creatures. One of our main objections to Hartshorne's account, then, is that this perspective appears to make God indefensibly reliant for his own development on the evil and suffering in the world. But what if the world process were not the result of God's free creative activity, but were in some sense a necessary emanation from the divine source? We need first to ask what sort of concept of God would result from seeing creation as stemming necessarily from his nature. In the first place, as pointed out earlier, saying this could not be equivalent to saying that the world was *logically* necessary. Ideas of logical necessity are based on what can and cannot be conceived, and we could certainly imagine the world being different in various respects, so whatever necessity the world has, it could not be logical necessity. What we would be saying by saying that the world flowed necessarily from God's nature would be to say that, for whatever reason, God himself had no power to do otherwise. God would, in fact, be being conceived as subject to the same sort of necessity as other natural processes. This idea would in effect reduce the personality of God to

199

vanishing point. Freedom, power and genuine creativity would obviously be gone from him, while his knowledge and will would be at most epiphenomena, observing and acquiescing in what had to be. One wonders in what sense such a being would be God at all, or in what sense such a God would explain why things were as they are. As we have seen, a large part of the motivation for belief in God is to see an explanation of the world and its laws in terms of God's choice. But a God that *had* to create or express himself in exactly the ways he does provides no explanation of the way things are. The question would immediately be raised as to why God was forced to act in this sort of way. Further, a God who had to create in the way he does would be a person in only the most minimal sense, at most a suggestion that natural processes are as a whole, in some unexplained way, self-conscious As already suggested, there is little reason for thinking that this is so, and there would be even less motivation for worshipping such a self-conscious universe. Why should we be moved to give thanks to such a being, or to seek to gain its love, given that he has done nothing freely and would not be able to respond freely to our attitude to him? One's attitude to such a being would be hardly distinguishable from nature mysticism, a sort of self-submersion in nature. But compelling as nature mysticism can be psychologically, it is an attitude of mind that prescinds from any attempt at explanation, for the explanation of natural processes is to be sought not in mysticism, but in science. In worshipping a God who has to create as he does, and in nature mysticism, one is really doing neither more nor less than worshipping the laws of nature and submitting oneself to their inevitability.

NOTES

1   As we shall see in Section 3 of this chapter, in later works Plantinga offers a different argument for the existence of God, based on a concept of divine excellence. One important feature of the later argument parallels the present one, however: in both cases, Plantinga thinks that the basic premise is not itself defensible, although in neither case does he think that this renders the consequent argument irrational. However, in this section, I will restrict my attentions to what is said in *God and Other Minds*, and take at face value Plantinga's statements to the effect that the teleological argument is the best available.
2   We shall see shortly that P (e / h.k) is actually rather lower than Swinburne

thinks, possibly even lower than P (e / -h.k), which would be extremely damaging to his case.

3 Darwin himself did not believe this. He thought that acquired characteristics could be genetically transmitted. However, for the sake of simplicity in speaking of 'Darwinism' in what follows. I intend to be understood as referring to Darwin's original evolutionary views as supplemented (and strengthened) by modern genetics.

4 It is worth noting that in S4, for example, it would not be. S4 and S5 are distinguished precisely in terms of their respective attitudes to Becker's postulate. S4 has it that only logical *necessity* is itself necessary; it is only in S5 that *all* modal status is logically necessary, and that what is possible is necessarily possible. On S4 and S5, cf. Hughes and Cresswell, 1972, Ch. 3.

5

Suffering and Evil

So far, we have considered arguments in favour of religious belief, cases where religion has been invoked to provide an account of why certain things happen, or why they are as they are. We now turn to a more complicated matter, because while experiences of suffering and evil have led many people to embrace religion, for many others similar experiences provide strong grounds for the rejection of religion. And certainly from the point of view of the rationality of religion, suffering and evil do seem to be a problem for the religious to explain, rather than a support for their faith. For, on the face of it, it is difficult to see how a good God could allow so much apparently gratuitous suffering in the world and could have created beings (men) capable of such depths of self-deception and wickedness. We shall examine arguments purporting to show that the existence of suffering and evil in the world is difficult or even impossible to reconcile with the existence of a good and omnipotent creator, as well as approaches to evil and suffering from Eastern religions, but before doing so, some general points about the place of evil and suffering in life are worth making.

I shall use the term hedonism to apply to any theory of life which holds, explicitly or implicitly, that a life without pain, or loss, or sin is more desirable than a life that includes experiences of these sorts. I say explicitly or implicitly here so as to include under the umbrella of hedonism those religious views which regard the negative aspects of human life as merely stages in a journey towards a hedonistic existence in the next life, as simply an ultimately dispensable means to a more desirable type of existence. Much Christian preaching seems to me to look at the pain of this life in this way as simply an unpleasant test ground to enable us to attain a

state of untroubled bliss. On the other hand, many critics of theism
write as if a life without suffering or loss or sin would somehow be
better than the life we have. What I want to suggest is that such a
life would not only not be a human life at all, but it would
necessarily lack most if not all of those facets of human life which
are admirable to us.

I have already remarked in Ch. 3 on the sense of a shared
mortality, which provided a basis for the reconciliation of Achilles
and Priam. It is as co-sufferers that men can begin to manifest the
moral attitudes of sympathy and generosity to one another.
Equally, as Nietzsche shows in *The Birth of Tragedy* (§9), Greek
'cheerfulness' was the sublime and dignified affirmation it was
because it was but a bright image projected on the dark wall of the
Dionysian suffering of man and nature. Even the Catholic liturgy
for Easter speaks of Adam's fall as *certe necessarium peccatum*,
meaning that without the fall there would have been no incarna-
tion; but another and more potent interpretation of the necessity of
sin is that self-knowledge and hence, true virtue, can be achieved
only through a full realization of one's potential weakness. On this
view, actual sin is no dispensable stage on the way to virtue; it is an
essential aspect of one's conquest of self-deception. Again, what act
of true courage is not a conquest of fear and a rejection of suffering,
what act of true generosity is not a loss of something precious to
oneself, what great work of art is not born out of struggle? As
Nietzsche so often stressed, in rejecting the suffering endured by
the great artists, you reject their work too. The question
rhetorically posed by H.J. McCloskey, as to whether I, as a moral
agent,

> should choose for other people a world in which there are
> intense moral struggles and the possibility of magnificent
> triumphs and the certainty of many defeats, or a world in which
> there are less intense struggles, less magnificent triumphs and
> fewer defeats, or a world in which there are no struggles, no
> triumphs and no defeats (1960, p. 113).

admits of no clear-cut or straightforward answer once one begins
to set the cost of a hedonic life against the sense that an admirable
human life is very much a matter of sustaining rationality, balance
and beauty in the face of despair, decay and loss.

Our weaknesses and the negative side of human life, then, are the soil in which virtues grow, and in which joyful affirmations of life can be heroic rather than mindless and unfeeling. We can, of course, push the negative aspects of life aside, and fail to see the way in which the two sides of life are mutually sustaining; a life led without this realization will tend to be an unintegrated series of distractions and dissipations, punctuated by moments of numbing sorrow which we do not know how to cope with. What I am trying to suggest here is what has been expressed incomparably by Rilke throughout his *Duino Elegies*, and especially in the tenth. No-one who understands Rilke could continue to regard hedonism as an ideal from which one could mount an attack on religion; equally no religious believer could think of a hedonistic paradise as an ideal form of existence for human beings, let alone one which would 'justify' our sufferings here below.

When Rilke reproaches himself and us for being 'wasters of sorrows' and for staring away 'into sad endurance' beyond our sorrows, he is asking us to recall the way in which

> they are nothing else
> than our winter foliage, our sombre evergreen, *one*
> of the seasons of our interior year – not only
> season – they're also place, settlement, camp, soil, dwelling.

Our culture, which Rilke contrasts unfavourably with those of Ancient Egypt and classical Greece, however, resembles a fairground, full of booths of happiness, amusement, titillation and curiosity for most of the time; death and loss we push out of sight, except for the occasional pompous and empty ceremony, a factitious

> market of comfort
> with the church alongside, bought ready for use: as clean
> and disenchanted and shut as the Post
> on a Sunday!

In Rilke's view a complete life is one in which lamentation and jubilation are seen as two sides of the same coin, in which each attitude takes its sense from the presence and the recognition of the other.

I am claiming that suffering and wickedness are central and essential aspects of human life, and that most of what we find admirable in human life involves in some part an acceptance of suffering and the conquest of evil. (I am not, of course, saying that we should not strive to eliminate suffering as far as we can; but rather that we should, at the same time, strive to come to terms with its inevitability.) Arcadian fantasies are in themselves a tribute to our ability to surmount despair, but they should not be regarded as political blueprints nor used as moves in philosophical argument, because used in these ways they simply serve to divert attention from both the horror and the attendant greatness inherent in human existence. To an extent, what I am saying here agrees with Ninian Smart's view that whatever else it would be, a totally rational and pleasant life, without suffering and wickedness, would not be a human life, and so a God could not have created *human* beings who were not prone to our physical and moral weaknesses (cf. Smart, 1961). But unlike Smart, who uses this point in defending divine goodness, I am not speaking from a perspective outside of human life attempting in any way to *justify* its special mixture of positivity and negativity. I am speaking from inside human life, and underlining the way in which those human achievements (and not merely moral ones) which are precious to us, are precious precisely as responses to our weakness and our mortality, and to the apparently gratuitous suffering that surrounds us.

The difficulty with assessing traditional religious 'solutions' to the problem of evil is that both those who propose them and those who attack them tend to do so by attempting to adopt a position external to our life, and our perspective on life. They ask themselves in effect whether or not a God who is all–powerful and all–good would or should have made the world and human beings as they are. Each side will stress one side of the problem at the expense of other considerations: the religious believer the way in which evil and suffering are a necessary condition of human achievement, his opponent the cost involved in this condition of achievement; the atheist then goes on to say that from an absolute point of view the cost is too high, while the believer asserts the contrary. The inconclusiveness of the ensuing argument derives from the fact that each in his own way attempts to assess the value of the world as it is from an external and absolute point of view, as if there was some objective scale of cosmic valuation of these things. The theist appeals to the goods made possible by the existence of suffering and wickedness and claims that these outweigh the harm, while the atheist stresses the negativity of suffering and wickedness. But in doing so, the atheist tends to appeal implicitly to a vision of a hedonic existence which is not recognizably human, while the theist sees suffering and wickedness as means to an end or stages to be overcome and to be justified because of the way they will be overcome, rather than as integral aspects of life as it is and a necessary part of any human achievement. In fact, neither protagonist in the dispute fully appreciates Rilke's insight into the duality of human existence and the way in which

> losing also in *ours*; and even forgetting gathers
> a shape in the permanent realm of mutation.
> (For Hans Carossa)

In order to bring these points out more concretely, I will now examine some of the traditional attempts to maintain or deny the absolute goodness and power of God in the face of the manifest evil and suffering in the world.

As usually presented, the problem of evil is seen in terms of reconciling three propositions, all of which the traditional theist wishes to assert:

(1) God is all-powerful.
(2) God is all-good
(3) Considerable amounts of evil and suffering exist in the world.

The opponent of theism might begin by asserting that these three propositions cannot be consistently held together, that the truth of 3 stands in some sort of contradiction to the conjunction of 1 and 2. An all-powerful, all-good God just would not have made a world which included evil and suffering. Now, while this may be the atheist's belief – and one which is as instinctive for many an atheist and unbeliever as cosmological thinking is for the theist – it is not in itself enough to convict the theist of inconsistency in holding 1, 2 and 3 together, for nothing has yet been done to show that 1 and 2 together entail the falsity of 3. Argument is needed to show that the existence of an all-powerful, all-good God would necessarily rule out any possibility of a world such as ours. The theist rightly asks for proof of why this should be so. After all, we are all prepared to undergo, and even to cause others to undergo, some suffering in order to achieve a great good, if the suffering is a necessary means to that good. Further, a morally good God might even permit a certain amount of moral evil in his creation if he is not immediately or directly responsible for it, but if it is a by-product of his having given some of his creatures creative freedom, itself a good and a means to many other goods, which could not be achieved if he had peopled his creation with automata. Perhaps the good to be achieved through this world as it is will justify all the evil and suffering in it. Even if it is hard to see how this could be, we surely cannot rule the possibility out on logical grounds. It is clearly going to be difficult for the atheist to show that an all-powerful, all-good God *could* not have created a world such as this one, which included physical ills and free beings who did evil things. Strictly speaking, indeed, all that the theist needs in order to avoid the charge of inconsistency, is to maintain that it is possible that an all-powerful, all-good God has a good enough reason for creating this world with all its evil and suffering. The onus is now on the atheist to show that God could not have had such a reason, and this is going to be difficult to do, given that God's intentions and plans are not, on any theistic view, totally transparent to human beings. Indeed, God's transcendence of human insight in this respect provides the basis of one famous solution to the whole problem, exemplified not only in some Old Testament prophets (notably Isaiah), but most of all and centrally in the Islamic tradition, in which Allah, not man is taken to be the best of judges, and in which human goodness is taken to consist first and foremost in submission to the will of Allah, and faith in the justice, mercy and goodness of Allah. There is, of course, a danger inherent in this approach which arises from seeing God, rather than men as the standard of goodness, and that is that if divine 'goodness' is too far removed from what would be agreed to be good in a human being, it becomes unclear just what might be meant by calling God good. Nevertheless, in order to show that God's power and goodness are not inconsistent with the presence of suffering and evil in the world, all that the theist has to maintain is that there could exist an explanation of why God acts as he does which would not do violence to a properly informed sense of goodness. He does not have to hold any extravagant view of God's *goodness* being quite different from ours. Any mystery could be held to reside in the complexity and difficulty of the explanation rather than in the sense in which God is good.

However, pointing out that it is difficult to show positively that God's power and goodness are logically inconsistent with the evil and suffering that exist in the world is not at all the same as denying that the evil and suffering in the world make it unreasonable to believe that God is both all-good and all-powerful. Like the cosmological and teleological arguments, the problem of evil, it might be urged, is best seen in terms of the degree to which it makes belief in God more or less probable. Granted that it is difficult to show a logical incompatibility between 3 and the conjunction of 1 and 2, does the truth of 3 make the conjunction of 1 and 2 highly improbable? What this question asks, in effect, is whether, without denying the logical possibility of a solution, it is not extremely hard for us to see how a good and all-powerful God could create or allow the amount of evil and suffering there manifestly is in the world.

It must be conceded by the theist that the answer to the question is that initially it is hard for us to see how such a God could allow the amount of evil and suffering that there is in the world, for even if it is accepted that all the evils human beings do and all the sufferings they respond to are justifiable in terms of the spiritual development of human beings, there will still be a vast amount of suffering in the animal world which we have no direct knowledge of and which inevitably seems to us to be quite gratuitous. Furthermore, much of the unpreventable suffering which we do have knowledge of – of children and animals – is extremely hard to see the point of even from a theistic perspective, as it appears to have no potential positive value at all for those undergoing the suffering, because they are not in any position to show courage or endurance, or to see their suffering in the way a saint might see his. Many compassionate believers see this type of apparently gratui-tous suffering as a severe test of their faith. (Even if their faith leads them to suppose that in the future all will be made well, it will still be a test of faith to accept that the present, apparently gratuitous, suffering of the child or animal is a necessary means to its future bliss. In default of a convincing explanation of this point many will, at the sight of an innocent child's unpreventable suffering, be inclined, like Ivan Karamazov, to return God the ticket to life, and to resent the thought that at the resurrection one will doubtless oneself be praising God for healing all earthly wounds, for there are some wounds that to all present appearance are too pointless and horrible to be compensatable in the future.) Indeed, John Hick, who is very sensitive to considerations of this sort, is compelled to suggest that the apparently gratuitous suffering in the world is part of God's way of creating an 'epistemic distance' between men and himself, so that their faith in him will be freely given (cf. his 1966, p. 335). Leaving aside to the next chapter the question of why it might be thought a virtue for men to have to go beyond their intelligence in assenting to the existence of God, one could hardly respect a God who appears so to use the suffering of one creature as a means of eliciting a desired response from another. Moreover, the very fact that the suffering of the innocent animal or child is seen as a condition of faith is tantamount to admitting that the answer to our original question is that it is hard for us initially to see how the truth of proposition 3 does not significantly reduce the probability of the conjunction of 1 and 2.

In order to reply to his opponent, the theist needs to suggest that the discussion so far has appeared to go against him because it has assumed that humanly unpreventable physical suffering of the sort where there is no question of any personal development on the part of the sufferer is an unmitigated horror, and one we could not easily accept being used by a God even for the best of motives. But why, it could be said, should we place so strong an emphasis on physical suffering? Even in some human moral systems physical suffering is not the paramount moral consideration, but tolerable if the means to a sufficiently good end. In fact, this is very much the attitude taken by Aquinas to physical suffering (*malum poenae*) which he sees as a natural consequence of God having created, for the symmetry and balance of the whole, a world which includes corruptible beings and even some with actual defects. He also states that it would show in God a lack of respect for the completeness of nature were he to prevent defectible things in it 'falling away'; the sort of falling away he has in mind as being inherent in the balance of nature is the lion killing the ass (cf. *Summa Theologiae*, la. 48.2). But the ultimate aim of this world – soul-making – is of such a good as to justify the suffering that is inherent in it, particularly as we can be assured that, unlike the ship's pilot who fails to take all reasonable precautions for the ship's safety, 'God does not fail in providing everything for salvation' (*Summa Theologiae*, 1a 49,2).

What Aquinas is in effect claiming here is that only a limited human perspective would place the sort of emphasis on physical suffering that we find in Ivan Karamazov. His solution thus has some affinity with the suggestion of some Indian thinkers, which we will consider shortly, that illusion is actually the source of suffering. Aquinas is not, to be sure, saying that suffering is an illusion, but he is saying that it is an illusion that suffering is an unmitigatable evil, and that religious enlightenment can show us that this is so. Like Dante, on his journey through the other world, the religious person can begin to understand that it is divine love that moves everything in the universe and that the desire and the will of the believer can themselves be

> turned like a wheel, all at one speed
> By the love which moves the sun and the other stars.

From such a perspective, the believer can indeed be said to know that the suffering of the innocent cannot be in vain, for it is always under the control of the love of God.

It is at this point that the dispute begins to become undecidable. The atheist says that he cannot understand the notion of a divine love which appears so to use the suffering of the innocent. The theist accuses the atheist of taking too narrow a view, and over-emphasizing the disvalue of present suffering. The atheist says that the presence of apparently gratuitous suffering means that the world cannot be moved by the love of God; the theist replies that he has strong reasons from his religious experience for thinking that the world is moved by the love of God, and that these reasons are strong enough to show him that the apparently gratuitous sufferings we see around us are only apparently gratuitous. Although in this book we have not found this appeal to religious experience convincing in itself, it is hard to accuse the theist of irrationality in appealing to his experience at this point. The problem of evil should not be taken as the crucial test for religious belief, because to do that would suggest that one is in possession of some objective way of balancing physical suffering against goods of various sorts, whereas it is just the evaluation of the evil of physical suffering that is at issue, and this is why discussions between theists and atheists on this matter almost inevitably have an air of futility about them. Moreover, as I have already suggested, the suffering we find in man and in nature is so much a part of human experience and so integral a part of the fabric of our life that even if there is a sense in which we can call much of it gratuitous (i.e. *we* can see no point to it), a world without it would be a world in which life would be unimaginably different. Unless we are prepared to say that a world with no suffering and with all the loss of depth and potential for achievement that this would entail would be a better world, then we are in no position to assert categorically that a good and all-powerful God could not have made the world as it is. Some will no doubt object that this world could have provided the basis for all the achievements there have been in it with considerably less gratuitous suffering than there actually is in it. Unfortunately, I am unable to discover the basis on which such judgments are made. What I am certain of, however, is that many of the most noble, dignified and sympathetic of men's responses to the suffering and tragedy in existence are responses precisely to the apparent gratuity of it all. A more difficult objection might be to point to the lack of any achievement of many of the sufferers. Would a good God have made people's achievements dependent in the way I have indicated on the suffering of those who never have the chance to fulfil themselves? It is here that the religious believer will have to appeal to his faith that God is ultimately good, and to assert that God will not in the end allow any suffering to be useless, but, if his faith is strong enough, this need not be an irrational position. He can combine what we have said about the comparative worthlessness of a life without struggle with his certainty that love moves the world, to conclude that it is not totally improbable that all struggle and suffering are in some sense part of the redemption of the world.

Unpreventable physical suffering, then, only provides a conclusive counter-objection to religion for the man who is prepared to say that there can be no satisfactory reason for it in terms of other goods, to which it is a necessary means. But saying that is actually to prejudge the issue in his own favour, for one of the differences between a religious and a non-religious perspective is precisely in their respective evaluation of physical suffering. On the other hand, as I shall underline later in this chapter, the religious case becomes weaker to the extent that the good which present suffering is a

211

means to is presented as being a future physical bliss for those who suffer now. What I said earlier about the centrality of suffering in our life and our world was meant to suggest the difficulty in conceiving a worthwhile life without negative aspects. It was in no sense intended to suggest that a future life of eternal bliss could somehow make up for what is unpleasant now. Not only would such a calculation fully merit the scorn of Ivan Karamazov, but my main aim so far in this chapter has been (heretically from the point of view of the orthodox Christian) to question the worth of a completely blissful existence. What the religious believer needs to do is to urge that there is or could be a perspective from which what appears to us to be useless and pointless suffering is actually a means to an otherwise unattainable end, so that not even an omnipotent God could achieve the end in any other way, and if he needs to invoke his trust in God's goodness at this point, this need not be completely irrational. Of course, the religious believer will be implying in this approach to the problem that there are, in God's view, and ultimately in ours too, goods greater than the absence of pain and suffering, but this has already been granted in order to attempt a solution at all.

I have so far concentrated on the existence of what I have called unpreventable suffering in the world, particularly in the case of children and animals who have no chance to turn it to any good themselves, because this seems at first sight to be the most difficult problem for the religious believer concerned to hold each of 1, 2 and 3. But suffering of this sort is by no means the only negative aspect of the world. We must now say something about human wickedness and all the suffering attributable to that. In fact, as Mackie (1955) has pointed out, there is an intimate connection between the religious defence of the existence of unpreventable pain and suffering in the world and what the religious person will say about human wickedness, for if pain, death and other physical deprivations in the world provide the basis for human achievements of an admirable sort, they also provide the context for many of the less admirable characteristics of human beings. After all, in an Arcadian plenty, there would be no need for crime or oppression; without death or disease, there would be little cause for despair or self-pity; if we could get just what we wanted, there would be no need to indulge in self-deceptive fantasy. What Mackie calls second-order goods, that is, admirable responses to the first-order evils of pain and misery, must also be balanced by all the second-order evils (cruelty, exploitation, resentment, self-pity and the like), which are also made possible by first-order evils.

At this point, the theist is likely to appeal to what is generally known as the free-will defence. The point of the free-will defence is to say that God is not actually responsible for what human beings do, because he has endowed them with free will, which means that they themselves choose and are responsible for what they do, including, therefore, the wicked deeds they do. A contrast is thus drawn between something like people suffering because of an earthquake or a disease, for which God is directly responsible, at least to the extent that people could not mitigate the suffering, and something like the Jews suffering in Auschwitz. The former type of suffering is directly attributable to God. It is a by-product of his having created the type of universe he has, and justifiable to the extent that it is a necessary means to a proportionately greater good end. Auschwitz, on the other hand, being the product of moral wickedness and an evil will is not justifiable at all. But saying that does not mean that God does unjustifiable things, because Auschwitz is not something God did. It is true that he permitted it to happen. Being omnipotent, he could have intervened to strike down the Nazis, but he did not do this because an evil like the Nazi movement was the outcome of God having given men free will. If he were to intervene in such cases, this would be a limitation on human freedom and actually undermine God's entire plan which is for men to come to realize God's love for them in perfect freedom. Critics of the free will defence sometimes claim that God should intervene occasionally to stop the worst wickednesses; perhaps what is being suggested is that he should have allowed one of the early assassination plots against Hitler to have succeeded. But there is a certain disingenuousness about this suggestion. If men were never able to do the worst of which they are capable (and how, in any case, can wickedness be quantified?), then they would never realize the extent and possibility of their wickedness, and hence of their freedom. If, on the other hand, they did realize what they were capable of unimpeded, but saw that they were generally prevented from doing the worst, then they would quickly realize that their freedom was being interfered with, and that they were not really free after all.

The point of the free will defence, then, is to attribute cases of

213

moral wickedness in the world (as opposed to cases of morally justifiable suffering) to men exercising their free will. The presence of genuine freedom in the world – and with it the creativity and the quality of second-order goods it makes possible – is regarded as a most desirable feature of a world, and hence something a good and all-powerful creator will want to bring about. However, having free beings in a world might mean that they use their freedom to do wicked as well as admirable things. But this would not be the creator's intention, and nor would it be a necessary consequence of his having created free beings. In so far as it happened it would be due not to him, but to the beings he created.

Clearly the free will defence is working with a sense of freedom which is opposed to determinism, for if men were determined to do what they freely do (as is suggested in Hume's famous account of free action), then God will be as responsible for Hitler's wickedness as he is for the weather. The free will defence is thus consistent with those theologies which regard men as not pre-destined by God as to their eternal future, but which see men as working their destinies out for themselves, and not as automata doing what they are determined to do. However, this still leaves an awkward question for the free will defence, for as Mackie has argued powerfully, the choice God was faced with in creating men was not a choice between making automata and free beings who sometimes and spectacularly go wrong. Could he not have made men

> such that they always freely choose the good? If there is no logical impossibility in a man's freely choosing the good on one, or on several occasions, there cannot be a logical impossibility in his freely choosing the good on every occasion. . . . [God's] failure to avail himself of this possibility is inconsistent with his being both omnipotent and wholly good. (1955, p. 209)

Mackie's argument at this point is unfortunately based on the spurious principle that what can sometimes happen can always happen. As Wittgenstein has pointed out (1958, p. 110), we cannot infer, for example, from the fact that some false moves are made in some games, that it is therefore possible for every move in every game to be false, or from the fact that orders are sometimes disobeyed to the possibility of orders always being disobeyed. If it is true that all men could freely choose the good on every occasion, it cannot be because of any simple move from ($\exists$x) Fx to -L-(x)Fx.

Nevertheless, Mackie does bring something more substantial forward in support of his claim. The argument is that even if we are non-determinists about human action, the human freedom we value even in the non-deterministic sense of freedom, cannot mean complete randomness or indeterminacy. The acts men freely do must have some connection with their nature, their characters and dispositions, or we would hardly think of the actions as being theirs, or them being responsible for them. But, if this is so, then God is responsible for men's evil acts, for he created them with strong dispositions for evil. For God to avoid this responsibility, Mackie points out that the sense of freedom involved must be randomness or indeterminacy, and this, as we have seen, cannot be a good in action, or indeed in anything else, let alone a good enough good to justify God in having allowed Auschwitz and all the other horrors men have perpetrated. So it would simply not be good for God to have made men so as to act randomly. But if they do not act randomly, but in line with their characters (even if non-deterministically in line with them), then God is to blame for not having given them better characters, less prone to succumb to weakness and temptations.

Plantinga criticizes Mackie on the grounds that in his attack on the free will defence, Mackie confuses two states of affairs, one of which is logically possible and the other of which is not (cf. Plantinga 1956, §2, 1974, Ch. 9, and 1975, pp. 32-55). For while it is logically possible for God to create free human beings who *in fact* always choose the good, it is not possible for him to create free human beings who always choose the good, and are made by God so that they will always choose the good, for God making them like this will be to restrict their freedom at just the point where it is important (the point between doing moral good and moral harm). What Mackie appears to be blaming God for is for not having *caused* men always to do the good. The first state of affairs (free agents always choosing the good) is a logically possible one, but it is not logically possible for God to ensure that it comes about, for that would be logically inconsistent with the freedom of the agents; if they are really free, it must be up to them, not up to God, to decide whether they do the good. The fact that God cannot make them decide to do the good is no slur on his omnipotence, because what

215

is at issue is the logical impossibility of people freely doing what they are caused by God to do. So although human agents always freely doing the good is a logically possible state of affairs, it is not logically possible for God to bring it about. (The idea that an omnipotent God can bring about any logically possible state of affairs is referred to by Plantinga as 'Leibniz' lapse'.)

However, Mackie (as Plantinga concedes) does have a way of meeting this objection. He can say that God making men such that they always freely choose the good is not to be understood to mean that God is disposing or in any way forcing them to choose the good. Mackie can agree with Plantinga that this would be inconsistently to curtail their freedom. Rather, following in the footsteps of proponents of God's *scientia media*, we are to appeal to God's omniscience at this point and imagine him eternally examining all the possible worlds and possible people he might create. Out of all the possible people that pass before his mind, he sees that some are just like those who exist in the actual world, except that they happen always freely to choose what is right. Now couldn't God have decided to create our virtuous counterparts rather than our wicked selves? If he did, then the people he did create would not have their freedom interfered with in any way by God -- their basic dispositions would be the same as ours – yet they would always make good choices, and make them apparently freely.

Assuming, for a moment, that it makes sense to think of an examination of the possible life histories of as yet non-existent beings (by an omniscient deity), Plantinga argues in effect (1965b §2) that while there are possible worlds in which we (or our counterparts) always freely did what is right and that God might foresee the possibility of such worlds, it does not follow that God could be certain of actualizing one of these worlds. Basically, the reason for this is that what we or our counterparts freely do in a world is not up to God, but up to us. In making a world actual, it will still be indeterminate what free agents will do. So it is not the case that, without interfering with our freedom, God could actualize a world in such a way that it would be certain from the start all the free agents in it did only good actions. It is indeed possible that in any world actualizable by God some of the free agents created by God (or even all, in Plantinga's view) do at least one bad action. If this is so, then it is just false that even an all-knowing, all-powerful, all-good Creator could actualize a world of free beings who always freely choose the good. And the only basis we have on which to decide whether it is more probable that some (or all) the free beings in an actual world will do some wrong actions (i.e. our own experience of this world) ought to convince us that its probability is rather high. So the free will defence can survive Mackie's arguments in their revised form, as Mackie partially grants (cf. Mackie, 1982, p. 175).

Of course, it follows from our defence of the free will defence that an omniscient God is dependent for some of his knowledge on the free decisions of his creatures, and that God cannot actualize a world containing free beings knowing in advance how those beings will make their choices (which is why, from God's point of view, it would be a matter of luck if the world he did actualize contained no moral evil). In a way, and against Molina and other advocates of *scientia media*, this is tantamount to saying that even though God might see all possible worlds in his mind, including all the possible free decisions of free agents and all the possible outcomes of these decisions, in actualizing one of the possible worlds which contains free agents, God will not know which one he has actualized until after the agents in it have made all their free decisions. Classical theists may object to this dependence of God on his creatures for his knowledge, but, as we suggested in considering process thought, it is hard to see what other relationship God could be in to genuinely free creatures. Omniscience, on this view, would not entail that God always knew everything, including free actions before they were performed, but rather that he knows everything as and when it becomes knowable. So he knows all our free actions, but only when we have made our choices, and not before. This need not be regarded as a limitation on omniscience, for there is surely something logically inconsistent in the idea of knowing the outcome of an indeterminate state of affairs (such as a free decision) before it could be known, which is what the timeless view of omniscience seems to require.

It will be remembered that the main point of the free will defence was to distinguish between God's direct responsibility for physical pain and suffering and his merely permissive role with regard to human wickedness. God's goodness is such that it would be impugned if he were directly responsible for wicked acts. However, there is one point in Mackie's attack on the free will defence which has been pushed into the background in our consideration of Plantinga, but which threatens to blur the distinction so important to the free will defender. It is that even if God does not actually make the immoral decisions himself, he still made us with all our tendencies to wickedness. He must have known, not perhaps that we were going to sin, but certainly that there was a very good chance that many (or all of us) would. Is this really consistent with God's goodness? (Mackie regards this question as administering the *coup de grâce* to the free will defence, 1982, p. 176). At this point, the religious believer will have to argue that it is, presumably because of the good that is made possible by men having a strong disposition to evil, and indeed, that if the disposition were not strong, then the good involved in transcending it would be correspondingly attenuated. . . . But it seems to me that saying this greatly weakens the distinction the free will defender is so insistent on. For the stronger the evil traits in men are, the more likely it is that there will be some moral lapses, and the more God's role is one of active causal participation in the evil that does occur, and the less one of passive spectating.

A point worth making here is that the distinction between God causing some things and his merely permitting human free actions is one that would be rejected by Aquinas, who, unlike process theologians, believed that God had full foreknowledge of all our actions. But Aquinas held that, in addition to knowing what free agents would do, God is causally operative in their willing and in their actions. As he puts it in the *Summa contra Gentiles* (III, 67.3):

> God not only gave being to things when they first began, but is also, as the conserving cause of their being, the cause of their being as long as they last. . . . He not only gave things their operative powers when they were first created, but is always the cause of these in things . . . ,

and, addressing himself directly to the question of whether a sinful act comes from God, he says in the *Summa Theologiae* (1a, 2aer.79.2) 'the act of sin not only belongs to the realm of being but is also an act, and from both these points of view it somehow comes from God.' So, in Aquinas's view, human free acts, including sinful acts, are 'somehow' caused by God. God is supposed to be able to cause free actions in a transcendent manner, so as not to interfere with the agent's freedom. How this is, I do not pretend to understand, and explaining it was a major pre-occupation of scholastic theologians for several centuries, and was an important aspect of the famous controversy between the Dominicans and the Jesuits in the sixteenth and early seventeenth century, over God's foreknowledge of free actions, in which the Jesuits in effect denied that God did physically pre-determine the free acts of individuals.

Brian Davies has spoken of Aquinas's 'commendable consistency' in seeing the human act of sinning as coming from God (cf. his 1982, p. 22). In fact, this commendable consistency needs some qualification for, as so often, Aquinas actually wants to have the best of both worlds. Although, as we have seen, he does say that the sinful act is caused by God, he does not regard its sinfulness (which he analyses as a turning-away from God) as deriving from God, because that would mean, *per impossible*, that God was causing something to turn away from himself (cf. *De Malo*, 33.1). In company with Augustine, Aquinas regards the evil in an evil act as a nothing, a privation of good, and hence as requiring no positive cause. This is understood by commentators (e.g. Burrell, 1979, pp. 99-102) to refer to the fact that when we act wrongly, we act senselessly and without reason. Malice, it is said, is based on a pretence on our part to be what we are not, while a good action is one which makes us attuned to the divine activity within us (cf. Burrell, 1979, p. 167). Whatever the merits of the psychological insights underlying the *privatio boni* analysis of evil, it must be said that God cannot be so easily excused. For even if evil is simply a privation, it still has to be explained where our tendency to opt for it (and so deceive ourselves regarding our divine end) comes from. Surely, on the theistic view, from God. So God ultimately causes our evil acts and their evil quality by making us disposed to act badly. So let us conclude that whatever Aquinas did say in detail about evil and however successful he was in reconciling human freedom and divine causality, against the free will defender, Aquinas is right in making God responsible for evil actions, even if not for the right reasons. The right theistic reason for making God responsible for evil is that he has created us with evil dispositions; saying that really makes the distinction between the suffering caused by an earthquake and that caused by some act of human barbarism far less easy to draw. For even if (contrary to classical theism, but in line with the criticisms made here of Mackie) we do not attribute to God precise foreknowledge of human free actions, we must attribute to him the knowledge that human wickedness, and hence its effects, are highly probable, given that we are as he has made us. The distinction in God's foreknowledge between the suffering caused by physical causes and that caused by human wrongdoing can only be that between precise certain knowledge of individual events and probable belief that events of certain types will occur, and, as such, hardly enough to talk of causing on the one hand and merely permitting on the other, given that God is responsible for the basic set-up in both cases.

Actually, given that the theist is prepared to countenance a good God using the physical suffering of innocent and spiritually immature beings to achieve his end of soul-making, one wonders why he should not simply dispense with the free will defence and be equally prepared to have God use wickedness. What I said at the start of this chapter about life having two sides, and the negative side being the condition of the positive should surely encompass moral wickedness as much as physical death, suffering and decay, however heterodox the suggestion might seem to a pious Christian, though, if it does, he could be reminded, once more, that the Easter liturgy apostrophizes Adam's sin as

> O certe necessarium Adae peccatum, quod
>   Christi morte deletum est!
> O felix culpa, quae talem ac tantum
>   meruit habere Redemptorem!

> (Oh, Adam's surely necessary sin,
>   blotted out by Christ's death!
> Oh, happy fault, which deserved
>   such and so great a Redeemer!)

I suggested earlier that we, being the creatures we are, can hardly achieve self-knowledge or any sort of true virtue or beauty without experiencing the wickedness of ourselves and others.

What I have been trying to show so far in this chapter is that hedonically inspired attacks on religion fail to the extent that they imply that a world without suffering and wickedness would be a better world. It would no doubt be a more hedonic world, but whether it would be a better world we are in no position to say, given that a hedonic existence could not have any of those features of triumph over hardship and evil which we regard as being so large a part of a genuinely good life. Moreover, life in a world without suffering and among a people without elements of wickedness would not be a recognizably human life. The critic of religion who wishes to blame God for our world and our life must, in consistency, be saying that a morally good creator would have created a race quite unlike human beings, and a race whose attributes we are quite unable to evaluate, for, taking suffering, hardship and evil away from them, there will be little about their lives or achievements that we can positively value. Although a critic of religion might be prepared to opt for a world as unlike ours as a hedonic one would be, it is not at all clear that his choice is objectively correct *sub specie aeternitatis*, or the one a morally good all-powerful creator would have had to have made. To the extent that there is uncertainty here about the very grounds on which a decision could be made, the argument against religion from evil and suffering fails; it has not been demonstrated that the existence of evil and suffering in our world makes the existence of all-powerful, all-good God impossible or even improbable.

On the other hand, religions purport to do more with evil and suffering than simply co-exist with them. As mentioned at the start of the chapter, they also attempt to give some sort of account or explanation of them. It is clearly one thing to say that being as we are, we cannot imagine a worthwhile existence without suffering and evil, and quite another thing to say why we are as we are and why our values are so linked to overcoming the negative features of our life. Religious attempts to explain this are markedly unsuccessful. The view of Christianity (and also of Islam, in effect) we have already touched on several times. In these religions, this life is seen very largely as a preparation for another life, a life united with God in paradise. The negative aspects of this life are presented largely as being hurdles to be overcome, and which, when overcome, will be discarded. The future life will be one without hardship, and one in which our wills will no longer be prone to evil. The problem with this sort of account is not only that the future life proposed is difficult to see as a worthwhile life. It also appears to regard our sorrow and suffering as merely temporary means to a better existence, to be overcome once and for all and having no real

221

continuing value of their own. One whole side of our existence –
our winter foliage – appears to be absent from the next life, which
resembles nothing more than an endless retirement from which all
hardship and challenge is removed. The Christian and Islamic
accounts of life's difficulties suggest too much that they are just
tests we have to undergo and then move on from, in the end
escaping from the routine of examination and trial altogether. But
if trials are ultimately dispensable in this way, one wonders why
God or Allah wants us to undergo them at all, unless (as sometimes
appears) it is to flatter his own ego, and to have us choose him and
value him freely, rather than turn our wills to him from the start.
Too often, in Christianity in particular, soul-making is interpreted
as making our souls for God, and too infrequently is it seen in
terms of souls making something out of themselves. The idea of an
eternal bliss in paradise is consistent with our making a once-and-
for-all decision for God, rather than with our achieving some sort
of spiritual level, which we then struggle to move on from, and so
on continually. But, I have suggested, it is the second rather than
the first that constitutes a worthwhile form of life, and in the
context of which alone would justify a creator in making us prone
to evil and liable to suffering. In this respect, process thought, with
its developing creator and developing creation is a morally and
even religiously more satisfactory idea than the sort of theism
which sees this life and its limitations as merely a prelude to an
existence without negativity, and, hence, without struggle and
achievement.

Mention of process thought in this context leads one naturally to
think of the great Indian religious traditions, Hinduism, Buddhism
and Jainism; because in Indian thought there is a pervasive sense of
the suffering of individuals being part of a great process in which an
original single divine essence continually moves through material
and sentient experience and back to its original state of unity. The
lives of individual men and their sufferings are given both a cosmic
significance and a promise of resolution through the doctrines of
karma, reincarnation and eventual liberation, which are fundamental in Indian religion, even in early Buddhism, in a modified
form, despite the fact that, as we shall see, it did not admit either
individual souls or a universal spirit. The basic idea behind the law
of karma is that what explains the differences between individual
men, both the differences of their birth and talents and the

differences of happiness and success in their lives, is what happened to them and what they did in previous existences. They work out now the rewards and penalties owing to them from the virtues and vices of their previous existences. And what they do in their present lives will be rewarded or paid for in future lives. In other words, individuals are seen as locked into a cycle of birth and rebirth which stretches backwards and forwards through countless existences, all of which are causally related in terms of moral achievement, suffering and happiness.

It will naturally be objected that the idea of a law relating moral qualities to physical events like an individual's stature or intelligence or success in life is absurd, and a relic of pre-scientific thinking in which it is said there was no clear distinction made between laws of nature and moral laws, and in which bad actions were considered bad just because they produced bad consequences in the physical world. Whatever the truth of such accounts of 'pre-scientific' thinking, it is certainly hard for us to envisage how the moral value of an act could be connected by law to the empirical world; nevertheless it could be pointed out that just the same sort of thinking is involved in the Christian (Augustinian) view that the Fall of the angels and of Adam upset the harmony of the world (and in Wagner's *Ring*, for that matter). The tendency to relate evil action and the physical world is no doubt deep-rooted in the human psyche.

Apart from problems with the so-called law of karma, the notion of reincarnation itself poses its own peculiar difficulties. Although, unlike many Western philosophers, I do regard psychological rather than bodily continuity as the key element in the concept of a self, and the reason why we do regard personal identity as important (though, like Derek Parfit (1971), I would regard the notion of a self as independent of and, in some circumstances, separable from questions of personal identity). The trouble with the notion of reincarnation, however, is that I and the vast majority of ordinary people have no psychological continuity between my present and any supposed past or future self. The claim made by some Indian thinkers, that specially gifted religious people do have such psychological continuity, which the rest of us are denied, looks too much like special pleading here. A psychological continuity that is attained only in extraordinary circumstances lacks just that immediacy and inevitability that is so strong in our idea of a self. At any rate, as an ordinary person, if I were told that I had been through such and such experiences in the past and that I would have certain experiences in the future, without a sense that my present experience and the past or future experiences were or would be psychologically connected, my feelings of sympathy and responsibility towards my past and future selves would certainly be no more and probably rather less intimate than my feelings of sympathy and responsibility for my parents or my dependents. The element of connectedness that makes me care in so different a way about what happens or happened to *me* are absent in these other cases. Of course, this does not stop me from caring for or feeling responsible for my close friends and family, but this is possible because of my personal knowledge of them. Even that, however, would be absent from cases where I am supposed to have past or future existences, and my relationship to them would have to be something altogether more remote and theoretical. In the light of this, it is hard to see why I should now have any more worry or responsibilty over what are called my future lives than I do over the fate of people in parts of the world remote from me, whose fate may in some sense be regarded as connected to my actions, through my voting, lobbying or charity. In short, the idea of reincarnation fails in any urgent way to engage one's moral sensibility regarding the future more urgently than do other considerations about the fate of one's children or the viability of the planet, precisely because of the lack of any psychological continuity or even acquaintance running between one's present and one's past or future selves. So even if a sense could be given to the notion at all, it is hard to see how it should provide the moral stimulus it is clearly supposed to provide in the context of the doctrine of the law of karma.

Whatever their own inherent difficulties, the law of karma, and the belief in past and future lives, function in Indian thought so as to provide an account of why people undergo present sufferings and why wrongdoing is apparently allowed to flourish. However, they can do this only because of the way the two notions are embedded in a wider perspective. Logically, the law of karma only pushes the question of our present suffering further back. We can interpret what happens to us now in terms of the misdeeds or sufferings of our past lives, but what of our past lives? How did evil and the possibility of suffering enter our past lives, or get into the world picture at all? One has to tread carefully in talking about *the* Indian view here because many Indian thinkers say that in the end these things just are mysterious and inexplicable. Moreover even within Hinduism there are many conflicting views. Indian religious thought is not dogmatic in the way Christianity tends to be. The flexibility is such that there appear to be major disagreements even within Hinduism on such fundamental issues as the existence or non-existence of a creator, the permanence or impermanence of the individual human soul, the value of wordly existence and the reality or illusoriness of phenomena. Nevertheless, underlying the disagreements there appears – to Western eyes at least – to be a considerable identity of spirit even when what is said is not offered as any explanation. Not only are the doctrines of karma and reincarnation fundamental. (Those schools which regard the individual self as insubstantial and impermanent still hold on to the concept of reincarnation, interpreting it in terms of related successions of psychic bundles.) But, with the exceptions of the ritualistic Mimamsa tradition and the dualistic 'devotionalistic' traditions (notably Vaishnavism), we find in most Hindu and Hindu-derived thought the idea that the world and all the sentient beings within it are part of a great cosmic process, from a state of unity through the manifold diversity of worldly forms and back through a dissolution of these forms to unity once more, before another creation and another dissolution, and so on and so on. Even the atomistic schools see the eternal atoms as existing in originally uncombined states, and the eternal selves as achieving bliss when they shed all their empirical qualities. At least from an ethical and religious point of view, it is comparatively unimportant whether the original and final unities are seen in terms of a divine impulse which is pure being or as absolute nothingness. (Indeed, as we have already remarked, there is no discernible difference between pure being, however divine, and nothingness.) The individual person is to regard the ultimate aim of life as being the overcoming of the divisions which separate him or her from the one, and so to escape the restless and relentless cycle of birth and rebirth. What this means in practice, is to attain a mode of life in which a person's desires are seen for what they are, namely manifestations of the tendencies which separate the individual from the unity that should be sought – and in which the sufferings of our various existences are seen ultimately as simply part of the inevitable limitations of finite existence, to be overcome in the end by the knowledge that this is so and that dualism in one's being can be overcome, together with the acceptance that such understanding brings an acceptance which is itself part of the overcoming of dualism.

In order to flesh out this somewhat abstract account, I will now show briefly how the individual is seen in the light of the world process in classical Hindu thought, and then, in Buddhism.

In the Hindu tradition we are told that there is a continual swinging back and forth from no manifest universe to a material universe and back again. The material universes themselves exemplify various degrees of perfection and degeneracy, a period of perfection being balanced by one of imperfection, just as the states of full manifest existence are balanced by periods when all that is is reabsorbed into a state of mere potentiality (or Prakriti). However, from this state in which matter is purely potential, a new material expression of the eternal unlimited ground of existence will break out. This pure ground of existence, the source of all individual beings and possibilities, is known as Brahman (or Ishvara), although Brahman in its active form as world-maker and world-controller is known as Brahma. Brahman manifests itself in countless forms and species, from stones to gods. Human beings occupy a key position in Hindu cosmology, because they alone can consciously seek liberation, that is, in the words of Pratima Bowes,

> integration with the non-dual essence of existence beyond the peculiarities of name and form. This the Gods, being steeped in pleasure, or animals, being non-self-conscious, cannot do. Nevertheless, he (man) occurs in a continuous series of manifestations of essentially the same life principle (this being in the ultimate analysis an expression of Brahman in the world of multiplicity). (1978, p. 54)

So Brahman is the power and essence of the whole universe, and men are the only beings within the universe who can consciously seek a return to the state of undivided unity which preceded the diversification implicit in this material creation.

Brahman is regarded as something which is neither personal nor impersonal, but beyond such categories, identical with everything that is and yet beyond all that is ('this-all', yet 'not this and not that'). At the same time, Brahman can be seen as the supreme Self ('that thou art') with whom man's own self is to be united. Hindu thought distinguishes between two selves, the jivatman or empirical self, which is subject to the laws governing the material world, and the Paramatman, the supreme self, the part of men which in some special sense is Brahman, and as such eternal and beyond one's individual personality, with its complex of desires and individual particularities. From this perspective the overcoming of duality and experience of union with Brahman can be seen as allowing the identity of Paramatman and Brahman to dominate one's existence, and not one's desires or the self-image of the jivatman. The jivatman, indeed, can be a powerful source of illusion about oneself and how things really are. Failure to recognize that Brahman is everything and that integration with Brahman is where true bliss is to be found, rather than in the losing of one's essential self in the diversity of the world and one's desires, is often spoken of in Hindu writings as a form of ignorance and illusion, and even empirical knowledge is deprecated to the extent that it implies concentration on divisions and differences where there should be the experience of unity. By contrast, 'to an exalted yogin, there is neither birth nor death, nor going (to other worlds) nor returning (to this one); there is no stain on purity or knowledge but everything shines as absolute consciousness.' (*Varaha Upanisad*, 3.5)

Union with Brahman, then, is what man, and through man, all nature is aiming at. However, this goal can be seen in two radically different ways, and to these ways correspond two radically different tendencies in Hindu thought. To take the later, and to Western eyes more familiar first; for Sankara and his followers, the idea that in order to attain 'being, consciousness and bliss' of Brahman, we should aim to overcome the duality between ourselves and Brahman, together with the concept of Brahman as the one fundamental reality beneath the diversity of experience, leads to the conclusion that the world itself is at root an illusion, and fundamentally valueless. The earlier Hindu writers had used the term maya to refer to potentiality in Brahman for bringing multiplicity out of unity. Sankara, however, speaks of maya as an illusory force projecting in our minds appearances that do not belong to reality. Our aim in life should be to seek liberation (or moksa) from the power of maya, and so attain being, consciousness

227

and bliss. Sankara clearly exploits the pessimistic and negative aspects of the doctrine of Brahman, treating individual existence as a painful falling-away from oneness. In a sense this provides an answer to the problem of suffering and evil, closely allied (as we shall see) to much Buddhist thought, and the attitude underlying it has been dominant in Hindu culture for several centuries. But, as critics of Sankara, notably Ramanuja, a leading exponent of the Vaishnava school, were quick to point out, if Brahman is truly everything, where do maya and its power to create illusions come from? Moreover, it is clear that Sankara takes a somewhat one-sided view of the traditional Hindu texts (as can interestingly be seen by the fact that Ramanuja presents his rival dualistic system as a commentary on the Brahma Sutra – the same text on which Sankara bases his philosophy). For the deep pessimism of Sankara is not the prevalent attitude of the Vedas or the Upanisads. There it is often stressed that Brahman being everything must imply that everything created is good and real and a genuine revelation of Brahman. There is a way of enjoyment, as well as a way of renunciation, a fact underlined by the traditional Hindu stages of life, in which power, sexuality, enjoyment and wealth all have their place, and ascetism is only the final stage of all. Creation itself is seen in the Vaishnava tradition as lila,

> a spontaneous self-projection of the divine, out of sheer joy and fullness of being, into multiplicity in order to savour itself in manifold ways – and this creative activity is called sportive because, like a sport, it is its own purpose and indulged in for the pleasure of the activity itself and not for an extrinsic purpose. (Bowes, 1978, p. 225)

Bowes sees the Vaishnava doctrine of lila as an elaboration of the Upanisadic teaching that 'the created realm is an expression of Brahman's essence' and not produced out of nothing. From the ancient Upanisadic point of view, it is possible to see the over-coming of duality in terms of relating to and identifying with Brahman in everything, in contrast to the Sankaran view of it con-sisting in a withdrawal from creation into one's non-personal Self.

However, Ramanuja and the Vaishnavists actually depart somewhat from ancient Hindu tradition, as well as from Sankara, in holding that human selves are only similar to and not identical to

Brahman. Even in liberation (or moksa), according to Ramanuja, our souls remain distinct from Brahman's undifferentiated unity, and find bliss in a union with Brahman that stops short of identity. In fact, in his dualistic conception of God and the world as separate entities, God or Brahman is seen very much in terms of a creator, not unlike the God of the great monotheisms. As such, Ramanuja's interpretation of Indian belief is subject to the problem we encountered in considering Christianity: why does a creator who is fundamentally good make men in a state which is admitted to be less than perfect and which will be eventually transcended? So even if Ramanuja were able to give a satisfactory account of the identity texts in the Hindu scriptures ('Thou that art', and so on), his dualism would do little to solve the problems raised by evil and suffering in the Indian context, because what he is doing in effect is to introduce into that context the difficulties attendant on theistic doctrines of imperfect creation and redemption from it.

Moreover, apart from the problems involved in Ramanuja's dualistic account of creation, Sankara surely does have a point in his favour against his less pessimistic Indian critics.

Even in the more positive strains in Hinduism, it is assumed that the ultimate bliss of overcoming dualism and attaining integration with Brahman (however that is conceived) is a thousand times more blissful than any pleasure in ordinary life. Moreover, ordinary life, if not all pain and suffering, is certainly not all pleasure. Looked at like this, it is clearly tempting to conclude that moksa is liberation from the illusory existence of the material world. And why, in any case, if the world is the expression of Brahman, is it so ambivalent regarding suffering and why, in the view of the non-dualistic interpretations of the Hindu texts, are we called on to transcend its finitude in the dissolution of our finite personalities? Bowes, who is a strong critic of the negative emphasis of Hinduism since Sankara, says that

> the Infinite and Absolute Being manifests itself in the realms of
> finitude and relativity through different names and forms in
> order to enjoy itself as multiplicity and diversity. (1978, p. 213)

But this sounds very much as if Brahman is using the suffering of the finite creatures in the universe in order to enjoy itself, which, as I said of a similar implication of process theology, is to make

Brahman appear highly immoral. It is no answer to say here that Brahman is no person, for only something like a person can savour or enjoy itself in the way Bowes suggests. It may be true, as Bowes goes on to say, that suffering is inherent in finite existence, because finite things are bound to change and decay, and to conflict with other finite things. She says that men, who are self-conscious, can find ultimate bliss in identifying with the infinite, but that they have to do this in order to transcend the limits and sufferings inherent in their worldly existence simply serves to make yet more urgent the question of the worth of the finite existence we all have to undergo, and the reason why Brahman should want to express itself in this way at all. To attempt to explain or justify all this in terms of the sport of Brahman is to give no explanation at all, for it simply makes us wonder why Brahman had to disport in this way, and if it can be no justification for a man's inflicting suffering on a world that he found it amusing, it can be even less of a justification for Brahman, which we are constantly told exists in a state of being, consciousness and bliss. As is clear however, many Indian thinkers would object to all questions and discussions of this sort, which seem to envisage Brahman as a person or a sort of person, and subject to moral evaluation like a person. Certainly Brahman's attributelessness gives substance to this objection, although it must be said that in so far as Brahman is characterized as consciousness, it is hard to see how we can avoid attributing some sort of personality to Brahman. If, however, we do refuse to personalize Brahman in any way, the resulting agnosticism and shelving of questions concerning the world process simply underline the explanatory emptiness of a religion that is based on a concept of pure being – a point which we have already made in connection with Aquinas, and which will be taken up again in the next chapter. This explanatory emptiness is perhaps most difficult to accept in the area of the evil and suffering in the world, for it is here, above all, that people look to something substantive from religion.

The Buddha, it is well known, had no truck with such ultimate questions and even less with the answers people gave to them, although he did appear to reject the idea of a creator on the grounds that a creator was inconsistent with the suffering in the universe. The Buddha's message was 'I lay down simply suffering and the stopping of suffering'. Of his Four Noble Truths, the first is just the proposition that life is permeated with suffering, or, more fully, that so much of what goes to make up what we call a man – birth and rebirth, ageing and dying, sorrow, pain, grief, despair, the presence of the unloved and the absence of the beloved, and the frustration of one's desires – are, one and all, suffering. The origin of suffering, according to the second Noble Truth, is craving and desire, which in the case of man arises from the complex of psychological traits and environmental circumstances which we (strongly) think of as constituting a unified, permanent self. (For the Buddha, there is no eternal self, either in an individual or in the universe.) The third Noble Truth teaches that the cessation of craving and attachment is possible through the emptying-out and freeing of one's mind, and the means to this, according to the fourth Noble Truth is the Noble Eightfold Path, a series of righteousness in various aspects of conduct through which the follower of the Buddha progresses. The state in which craving is overcome is Nirvana, which, according to the Buddha, is

> a condition wherein is neither earth nor water nor fire, nor air; wherein is neither the sphere of infinite space, nor of infinite consciousness nor of nothingness nor of neither-perception-nor-non-perception; where there is neither this world nor a world beyond nor both together nor moon and sun. Thence, I declare, is no coming to thence is no falling; there is no arising. It is not something fixed, it moves not on. It is not based on anything. That indeed is the end of suffering. (*Udana*, 8.1)

This thoroughly negative approach to enlightenment is quite characteristic of the Buddha and entirely consistent with his refusal to attend to metaphysical questions when there was the huge and pressing task to relieve suffering now. Of course, it is easy to object that he has not shown that life is predominantly suffering, and that in his teaching he has focused on the negative aspects of life. Presumably the reply to this would be that it is just the failure to recognize that attachment even to the good things of life which is a major cause of our suffering. Recognizing that the good things of life are themselves potential causes of suffering, we can then begin to see the wisdom of the non-attachment which he is preaching.

The Buddha, as has been said, rejected metaphysical speculation, and also any concept of an essential or underlying self. Nevertheless, he clearly does preach a doctrine of liberation from those finite attachments and desires which are so powerful precisely because we mistakenly see them as constituting a self. Liberation can be, thus, seen in terms of disowning this pseudo-self, and liberation from its tyrannous complex of desires and impulses. Looked at in this way, there are close affinities between Buddhism and the Samkhya tradition in Indian thought, which also sees human life as full of suffering because men accept (falsely) that the empirical mind-body complex is their true self. As Bowes puts it, for Samkhya, if man

> can disown this, then it would cease to have power over him, thereby losing the capacity to generate suffering. The unconditioned spirit is not subject to suffering, or need be if man can identify himself with his essential being, rather than with what is only contingent. (1978, p. 185)

The difference between this and the teaching of the Buddha lies in the reference to an essential being and an unconditioned spirit. But, despite the Buddha's own distaste for essential and substantial selves, his doctrine surely does implicitly make use of such notions. For *what* is it that is liberated and *into* what? Into what is what released through the Noble Eightfold Path? And what in any case is the reason for the cycle of suffering (birth and rebirth)?

So, it would not be totally unfair to say that the Buddha himself solves the problem of suffering only in the existential sense that he teaches men how to accept their suffering and to overcome them, but by seeking release from the world. There is no justification, no God, no problem; only a situation to come to terms with and, almost stoically, to rise above. So, for the Buddha, if we take his atheism and his scepticism at face value, there is no more a problem of evil, in the sense of a quest for its justification, than there is for the humanist, who also sees it simply as something to come to terms with.

But, of course, the Buddha's teaching was situated in a Hindu context, and dependent on the Hindu notions of birth and rebirth, and implicitly on the Hindu view of the world process, so it is not surprising that schools of Buddhists arose who disobeyed their master's precepts of agnostic suspension of reason. The Madhyamika and Yogacara schools both came to see the world and worldly phenomena as, in one way or another, products of an Absolute Mind; Nirvana was seen by these schools not as a state, but as a substance. As with European idealism, there is a sense that the Absolute is the inner essence of the observable world. The goal of the believer is to shed the illusory perceptions which lead him to see the empirical world as real, and to identify himself in contemplation with the Absolute. The same problems obviously arise here as arose with Hindu ideas of the Absolute engaging in creative activity, only perhaps more acutely, given the generally pessimistic attitude of Buddhists to the created world. Why does the Absolute have to engage in a continual succession of creations, given that created worlds are webs of illusion and pain, the aim of which are to return to the original state of undifferentiated being, consciousness and bliss?

Although I shall, in the next chapter, give a more positive appraisal of the a-theological aspects of Buddhism, it cannot be said that Hindu and Buddhist speculative thinking offers a theodicy (or religious explanation of evil and suffering) any more satisfactory than that of the monotheistic theodicies of Christianity and Islam. (The Buddha himself and the intellectually more austere Indian thinkers, who simply accept evil and suffering as part of the world mystery, are naturally exempt from *this* criticism, except to the extent that questions regarding the reasons for the way things arise naturally from the perspectives of Hinduism and even, to an extent of Buddhism.) We are given no convincing reason for Brahman or the Absolute engaging in the creative process at all. Indeed, what reason there is might argue more against the Brahman going in for creating at all, given that, despite its dualistic moments, the natural logic of Hindu thought, in contrast to that of Hartshorne, is to regard created existence as certainly inferior to the unity in which all difference is overcome, if not actually a state of total illusion and pervaded by suffering. The fact that we might regard the undifferentiated unity of Brahman – its being, consciousness and bliss – as tantamount to nothing at all, metaphorically as the night in which all cows are black, to use Hegel's vivid metaphor, is hardly to the point, for the Hindu framework is one in which liberation is liberation from distinctions and into the pure, Brahmanic state. In discussing Hartshorne, we have examined some of the problems inherent in seeing the world as a divine process. These same difficulties – lack of sentience in most of the universe, lack of the required sort of unity, lack of intelligibility in the suggestion that all our experiences are also experiences of some

233

divine Absolute – all apply to a greater or lesser extent in non-dualist Indian thought, but the characteristic Indian suggestion that the original unity is preferable to Brahman's created world is a problem specific to Indian cosmology, and one which suggests an insoluble dilemma. If Brahman has to create, then Brahman is limited and not fully independent. If, on the other hand, Brahman does not have to create, from a Hindu point of view, what is the purpose of creation, with all its struggles, its suffering and wickedness?

What I have argued in this chapter is that the reason for the failure of both the types of theodicy we have examined is not that we have any clear proof that a more Arcadian world than our own would necessarily be a better one. Indeed, I have argued that offering such a proof could be a symptom of a certain shallowness of mind; at any rate, the evaluations involved seem to me to be fraught with undecidable problems and unjustifiable assumptions. My criticisms of the theodicies we have examined arise from the fact that both types of system appeal to a higher viewpoint from which we will see evil and suffering in their true and justifiable light, but that both the higher viewpoints in question are ones from which creation itself (and hence the evil and suffering which we can agree are necessarily a part of the world we know and value) appears unjustifiable. The traditional monotheistic account sees this life as simply a prelude to something quite different; in this light the suffering and evil we live through appear as mere pitfalls put in our way by God so that we can show our love for him more adequately. But this makes God seem like an ignoble and possessive parent, to put it mildly, especially given that those that fall into the traps he has put along the way will be condemned to hell. What is wrong with traditional monotheism here is not that evil and suffering and their conquest are not part of a worthwhile life. It is the interpretation that is put on evil and suffering. Similarly, the process thought of Hinduism and Buddhism correctly emphasizes that evil and suffering are necessarily part of a finite life. But in so far as these systems postulate an Absolute of some sort underlying and completing the process, they disvalue the process entirely. The Absolute itself, in its self-immersion and unity, serves only to cast doubt on the painful and illusion-ridden cycle of birth and rebirth which we are then told to strive to escape.

6

Religion and the Rational Man

In the first chapter of this book, I attempted to sketch some of the attractive aspects of a religious life, and to show how religion could provide a framework for human life, how it could endow life with significance and how it could provide a community and a tradition within which evaluation of action is mediated through the social and religious roles that are assigned to an individual. This is perhaps seen most systematically in the case of the stages of life a Hindu ideally progresses through, with initial emphasis on worldly pursuits giving way bit by bit to the final stage of forest-dwelling asceticism, but all religions in one way or another perform this sort of function for their adherents. An essential part of the way this function is performed in religions is through the claim all religions make to be embodying a wisdom, usually and characteristically ancient and even arcane, a wisdom that is beyond the grasp of those who are not prepared to submit to its discipline. This is the strength of religion, and one that can be recognized even by those hostile to religion. In considering the views of Alasdair MacIntyre as expressed in *After Virtue*, we have seen that the liberal individualist does have problems with the establishment of values to live by, and that the idea of a *de novo* creation of value is an absurdity. Long-lived religions are the ideal means of fostering and transmitting pre-ordained values, in the way they situate men in a universal context, as well as in a temporal community; in the way they link individuals to their past and their ancestors; in the way they provide a history and a rationale for the virtues and values that are accepted; and in the way that they make of each man's life a quest and a destiny.

It is clear that only a conservative and authoritarian institution could perform these functions, for the condition of their fulfilment

235

is the acceptance on the part of all concerned of the good of life, a goal which is seen as rooted in the history of the community, which is not revisable or criticizable from below, and which is not based on individual whim, caprice or contract. Nothing could be further from the religious view of life than the liberal view that a man's nature and destiny is in the end of his own choosing and making, or the Millian idea that we should engage in experiments in living. This point is further underlined by the role played in many religions by the notion of a calling or vocation within a religious order, and of a grace which commands a man and seeks him out. Such notions run entirely counter to the anti-authoritarian, anti-hierarchical views which characterize so much current received wisdom, but they are not the less productive of fruitful, worthwhile and fulfilled lives for all that.

It is, of course, easy to scoff at the authoritarian aspects of religion, and many contemporary religious believers indeed would seek to do away with them. In the face of such shallowness, I repeat my conviction that it is here, if anywhere, that the strength of religion lies. Its strength comes precisely from its ability to suggest to men a supernatural 'common pursuit' and to embody, in the words of Roger Scruton, a set of 'obligations and allegiances which cannot be seen as the result of contractual choice' (1980, p. 171). In this way the significance of a life is grounded in something apparently more substantial than human choice, and this attempt at such grounding clearly responds to something deep in human nature. The liberal individualist, inside our outside religion, who dislikes religion's hierarchies, books, dogmas, traditions and authorities, needs to realize that these are the true sources of the strength of religion, socially and personally, and the means by which a religion can give to individuals a perspective from which their lives and work become more than the commodities they are treated as in technological societies, manipulable and expendable, apparently at whim. In the case of historically well-established religions, the stress on ancient texts and revelations undoubtedly serves in the minds of believers as a bulwark against what they see as the spiritual emptiness of modern life, and the contemporary tendency to treat individuals as mere ciphers.

We have to see the present-day decline of organized and institutional religion primarily in the context of social and economic change. People in general never accepted religious faith on intellectual grounds, so there is no reason to suppose that lack of religious faith in the world in general has much to do with the type of argument advanced in Chs 2 – 5 here either. Commentators nowadays often remark on the distance there is between the faith of contemporary theologians and that of ordinary believers, as if this is something particularly surprising or scandalous today. But this is no new phenomenon. Intellectual believers have always had to make accommodations with the intelligent secular thought of their time, in such a way as to radically alter the nature of what is believed. What has Thomas Aquinas's agnosticism to do with the faith of the medieval peasant or king or pope? The intellectual theologian has always in a sense patronized the ordinary faithful by using their words with an entirely different meaning, though not more so than those non-believers, such as Burke and Disraeli, who see clearly how religion might be part of the social fabric, and who advocate its public establishment *pro bono publico*, so to speak. If this role for religion is no longer possible in society as a whole it is largely because we now no longer live in the type of society implied in the Burke-Disraeli conception – a close-knit extended family, in which everyone sees him or herself in terms of his or her role in the social organism; the reasons for this are undoubtedly partly due to our organization of our lives, involving as it does the alienation of most individuals from their work and from the forces of production, and the relegation of their creativity into socially unvalued 'leisure' time, a state of affairs in which the actual meaning of our freedom is often simply the freedom to choose to consume from the range of goods hawked and advertised to us by an ever-decreasing number of state monopolies and multinational organisations. It is no doubt because the social and economic conditions for a genuinely common culture, in which men share sets of goals in life identified and concretized through public symbols, are absent that those present-day attempts to appeal to what might in other times have been the symbols of a common culture are characteristically not merely threadbare (solemn wreath-rubbish, and the rest), but can actually be socially divisive, as when those symbols are either manipulated in the interests of the economically dominant classes (as they are on public occasions), or used, more or less instinctively, by deprived hooligans in order to focus their resentment on other deprived groups in society. In these circumstances, there is little chance for a nationally established religion being much more than a facade, but this is not to say that people will not still seek and find in non-established religions or in dissenting parts of established religions some sort of framework for countering the alienating effects of present-day social and economic conditions.

Critics of religion should not under-estimate its potential value to its adherents in giving them in the fullest possible sense a meaning in life. This is no doubt why its adherents cling to it so resolutely, repel attacks on it so vigorously, and frequently see themselves bound to it by ties of loyalty – to their community, to their tradition and to their God – which enable them to circumvent or ignore the most telling criticisms of its doctrines or practices. Despite the decline in organized religion, the appeal of religion may, to some people, be particularly strong today as a counter to the social conditions I have been describing, in which intimations of a common culture are so lacking. Indeed, some adherents of some religions may see our present technological age and its ills as stemming precisely from the cultivation of the intellect, and so refuse even to consider *arguments* for or against religion.

Nevertheless, despite a considerable degree of pessimism concerning the place of rational argument in most people's evaluation of religion, for or against, and despite my unhappiness with our present social and cultural conditions, I have to say that religion, at least as usually conceived, does not appear to me to be a force for good in the world today. This is in the first place because, as I have argued in Chs 2 - 5, the characteristic assumptions of religion do not appear to be rationally defensible. Religious experience is neither widespread enough nor testable enough to form the basis for any rational belief, while those aspects of human activity which seem to some to require explanation in terms of a God are quite capable of naturalistic explanations. Arguments from cosmological and technological considerations are at most subjectively plausible, while the way religions attempt to account for evil and suffering actually raise more problems than they solve. However, it is not just because certain defences of religion fail that religious belief is rationally unconvincing. A striking and surprisingly little stressed aspect of the whole problem is the way God fails to manifest himself in the world. As Hume has suggested, albeit somewhat equivocally (*Dialogues Concerning Natural Religion* §3), we can envisage extraordinary or miraculous events, such as voices in the sky speaking great sense of a religious and spiritual sort to all men in a variety of languages, which would be highly improbable except as manifestations of a God. Whatever Hume's own position on this, if such a thing happened, or, even more if things of this sort happened with some frequency, it might well be highly irrational not to believe that they emanated from a transcendent intelligence. It is surely a burning question why, if there is a God, there are not such events, and why the miracles believers do claim either are buried in a murky and problematic past, or are cures which are not unequivocally miraculous exceptions to natural regularities. So religious belief is not only weakly defended; perhaps more significant is the absence of particular events which would make it credible.

In answer to this last point, defenders of orthodox theism will often say that God does not wish to compel belief, and that he wants men to believe in him freely for cognitive freedom is the only kind of freedom men can have in relation to God (cf. Hick, 1966, p. 316). Now there is some confusion at this point. We are told by Christians that God wants men to make a free response to him (though we are never told why exactly God should want this except as a boost to his self-esteem). But, despite Hick, making a free response to God surely does not, in Christian terms, entail a leap of faith. Neither Satan nor Adam had to struggle to believe in God, yet both were able to reject God, and to turn their wills from him. Milton's *Paradise Lost* demonstrates admirably that recognition of the existence of a supreme, even divine, power is not the same thing as loving or respecting that power. Not only does a free response to God not require 'epistemic distance' from God on our part. One wonders further why God, who has given us our reason and our intelligence, finds it a good thing that we should, in the case of this one belief alone, assent to something for which we do not have convincing evidence (for this is what talk of epistemic distance amounts to here). Wouldn't a good God paradoxically regard agnosticism in these circumstances as more admirable than a leap of faith?

Orthodox Christians do believe in miracles, which is why they cannot simply sidestep the question as to why there are not more convincing miracles witnessing to the existence of God. But there are other traditions of religious thought which can quite consistently claim that as God (or Brahman or whatever) is not to be regarded as separate from the world, we should not expect particular divine interventions in the course of events; on this view, the course of events as a whole is an expression of the divine essence or a divine emanation, and there could be no sense in which some particular event was more divine than any other. If this approach does not fall foul of the argument to the absence of direct divine manifestation, it does, of course, have its own problems. It is, as we have seen, difficult to see the world as a process of divine self-expression or divine self-discovery. We cannot readily see material processes as conscious or as contributing to a divine consciousness, while conscious processes of men and animals can hardly also be ingredients in a divine super-consciousness. More fundamental than these difficulties, however, is that involved in the conception of the divinity which underlies such thinking: the divinity as pure being, the ground of all else, and itself without form or essence.

The notion of pure being is one we have found wanting in intelligibility on a number of occasions, as being indistinguishable from a pure nothing. Rather than rehearsing this problem once more, I want now to consider the central role this notion plays in so much religious thought. The idea is that whatever the divinity is, it is something more basic than any particular individual being could be, and self-subsistent in a way no particular individual could be. It is basic and self-subsistent not only in an empirical sense. By this I mean that it is not like the eternal and unchanging simple atoms of Epicurean thought. These are in an empirical sense basic (there is nothing more basic in the universe) and self-subsistent (nothing brings them about). But they are not logically basic. We can still ask why they are as they are, why there are so many of them and neither more nor less, why atoms rather than forces are the primary stuff of the universe, and so on. It is just because they have particular, describable identifiable properties that these and many other questions arise about them, and just for that reason that the religious object which grounds all else and satisfies the principle of sufficient reason can have no determinate properties. Having determinate properties is inconsistent with being logically the ground of all else. This is presumably why religious thinkers from both Eastern and Western traditions have insisted that the divine is not *a* being among beings, but in doing this, they have surely reduced the object of their worship to vanishing point. For if the ground of being is not a being, it is nothing at all, unless it is the whole process of existence. But there is no reason to think of the whole process of existence as being any more than what might emerge in empirical science, and certainly not as something conscious or as having any of the attributes of a being we might worship.

In living religious traditions, there are two quite different ways of conceiving God. On the one hand, God is seen as the ground out of which all else emerges mysteriously and to which we all return, denying our separateness from the ground; on the other hand, God is an individual person creating other individuals, who preserve their independence from their creator. Although the ground out of which all else emerges is not quite the same as the pure being itself of the metaphysicians and theologians, it is clearly close in spirit to the conception of God as pure being. It is equally clear that the two conceptions of God are not mutually consistent. We cannot both be scattered elements of the divinity disporting itself throughout the universe, and the creatures of a divine person who creates a world separate and distinct from himself. You cannot see the world in terms both of the Hindu myths of the cosmic egg dividing and sub-dividing, and in terms of the Judaeo-Christian Genesis story of God creating the world out of nothing in seven days (not out of himself, notice).

However, on closer inspection, it is not so clear that particular religions as a whole fall exclusively on one side of the divide. This is reflected, for example, in the fact that in Judaism and Christianity, where creation at first sight seems dominant, we have constant incursions of Cabbalistic and Gnostic or neo-Platonic tendencies, in which the world is conceived as a divine emanation, and God as something non-personal. In Hinduism, to take an example of a tradition which may seem more weighted to the emanation side, the Sankaran view is balanced by the dualism of Ramanuja, as we have already seen. One cannot help wondering whether Aquinas is not once again trying to have the best of all worlds in asserting, on the one hand, that God is being-itself, and an operative cause of all that happens, while, on the other, insisting on the radical separation of God from the world, and the lack of any effect on him of the behaviour of his creatures. Whether Aquinas can be accused of actual inconsistency here is of less importance than seeing why in religion seeing God as pure being and the ground of being needs to be balanced by a view of him as an independent person, and vice versa.

If God is seen as a supernatural person, all sorts of questions can

241

be asked about why he is as he is, and worship of him becomes like idolizing a very powerful human being. So there is (as we have seen in Aquinas) a strong urge in traditional monotheism to seek to transcend the personal and problematic aspects of God as creator by invoking a doctrine of God as pure being. The view that the world is an emanation of the divine essence, although, as remarked, not strictly the same as saying that God is pure being easily and quickly moves to such a position, once it is realized that it would be undesirable simply to identify God with natural processes, these being neither self-explanatory nor worthy of worship in them-selves. God, then, is pure being shattering open into material creation, which will eventually return to its state of original purity. But this purely empty characterization of the divinity is not only logically unsatisfactory, in that it refers to nothing at all. It is also religiously unsatisfactory, as one can hardly worship so empty a notion as pure being. Moreover, pure being emanating into created fragments hardly gives even the form of an account of why things are as they are. It is not for nothing that, in Hindu cosmology, as we saw in the previous chapter, Brahman is transformed into Brahma, a creator God, while Platonic and Gnostic schools characteristically postulate a demiurge breaking out of the primeval oneness to create the material world. (I am deeply indebted in these paragraphs to Peter Munz's paper 'The Two Faces of God'.)

So there is in religious thought a constant oscillation between seeing God in terms of pure being beyond all particular determin-ations, and hence beyond questioning as to why God is like he is, or acts as he does, and seeing God (or some part of God) in terms of a creator with personal attributes and desires. While one can appreciate the reasons for this tension – a creator not being pure enough to satisfy the religious quest for a complete end to questioning, pure being being too pure to explain anything about existence at all – it seems to point to a deep inconsistency at the heart of religion. For the religious, God has to be a something, but no thing can fulfil the tasks it is set by the religious urge; so God has to be a nothing too.

The two faces of God, then, point to a deep inconsistency in the religious quest for an explanation which is, at the same time, substantive and final. The two demands cannot be satisfied together, and the drive to satisfy both explains the shifting in religion between the emptiness of pure being and the question-raising concept of a personal creator. Moreover, God's two faces, as expressed in traditional religious thought, do point to a weakness common to both Eastern and Western religion, that is, their incorrigible geocentricity and anthropocentricity. For, whether we are told that the world is created by God, or he is in some way emerged from the divine being, what is meant by 'the world' is, in all the main religious traditions, very much this earth, and the human beings on it are central to the whole picture. Thus, as we have seen, in Hinduism the self-consciousness of man raises men above even the gods, while in the major monotheisms – Judaism, Christianity and Islam – God enters into a unique relationship with some segment of the human race. If the cosmos is a process, we are asked to see this earth and the creatures on it as in some peculiar way the apogee of the universe, that to which the whole is tending, while creation religions tend to view the human race as that for which the rest of the universe exists.

No doubt many believers would try to dissociate their religious faith from the pre-Copernican cosmologies of their sacred texts; while this is certainly possible in respect of such matters as time-scale, evolutionary order, planetary organization and so on, it is not clear that, with the abandonment of the ancient cosmologies, it is not simply childish to see the earth and its inhabitants as the centre and crown of the universe. This idea is very much of a piece with pre-scientific thinking. Like seeing the universe as something designed, seeing inhabitants of this comparatively insignificant planet as the omega-point of so vast, numberless and apparently chance-ridden a phenomenon as the universe, is something which can be done only in spite of the empirical facts. One can understand why men naturally think of themselves as the focal point of existence. We each tend to regard our own individual self-consciousness as the point around which all else revolves, so it is only natural to regard humanity in general as the centre of the universe. Moreover, in so far as we necessarily see the world in terms of our concepts and through our faculties, it is natural enough to think that the universe mirrors man and man the universe. Religions have, of course, given expression and backing to the natural enough instinct to see man as the measure and centre of all things (and not only religions: Heidegger speaks of mankind as the shepherd of being), but one wonders not only at the intrinsic unlikelihood of any such thing, but also at the presumptuousness of the belief that it might be so. It seems to be simply a symptom of the incorrigible anthropocentricity of religion. But, while the belief that this earth is the centre of the universe now so clearly lacks any cosmological support, it must be problematic how far traditional religious belief, which places mankind so firmly at the centre of the cosmological picture, can be maintained in the absence of any underpinning world-view, and while certain aspects of religious thought can be demythologized in the light of advances in empirical knowledge, without destroying the whole fabric, it is unclear how far a religion that thinks of God creating the universe for mankind or one that sees the world process as climaxing in human self-consciousness can sit comfortably with current astronomical and cosmological theory.

Religious thought is always a product of a particular time, and, as such, is embedded in the thinking of that time. This leads to my second and more fundamental reason for thinking that religion (at least in any traditional form) cannot be a force for good at the present. We have examined a number of specific criticisms and objections to religious views, some of them based on developments in empirical knowledge. This leads to the thought that much of the recent history of religion has been a history of skirmishes with scientific thought. None of these had been totally conclusive either way. It cannot be said that Galileo or Darwin or their successors have definitely shown the tenets of Christianity, say, to be false, or that there is not some truth, expressed in mythological form in the Book of Genesis. On the other hand, it cannot be denied that some scientific theories put some strain on the credibility of some religious ideas, teleology, say, or religious interpretations of the world process. But the particular and specific divergences between religious thought and scientific theory are not where the main contrast between religion and science lies. The main contrast is in the respective attitudes to criticism – even Kuhn, as we have seen, regards criticizability as an important aspect of scientific theories – and this in turn explains why religions give the impression of constantly fighting a rearguard action against intellectual advances from other fields.

The critical attitude, which is a feature of genuinely rational activity, is one which has been exceedingly rare in the history of the world; it is one that not only submits its theories and projects to criticism and abandons or revises them under criticism, it also actively seeks out criticism in order to weed out weaknesses in our thinking as soon as possible and to forestall the possibly calamitous effects of letting those weaknesses be revealed in practice. Seeing human thought in an evolutionary context, we can say, following Popper, that human beings are unlike other living beings in the struggle for survival in that we can formulate our attempts to deal with the environment in theories rather than having to rely solely on our genetic make-up and random changes in it. We are then in a position to allow our theories to die in our stead, when we are confronted with a hostile environment. The rational, critical attitude is a way of exploiting this possibility to its best advantage, for by consciously attempting to probe and weed out the weaknesses in our thinking, we can take evasive action before the environment does it for us, with dire and even lethal effects on us. As Popper has also stressed, it is only those traditions of thought influenced by the example of classical Greece which have regarded criticism as desirable and the main means of intellectual progress. It is, perhaps, most of all in the history of science since the sixteenth century that we have seen anything like an application of the critical method in this sense. On this evolutionary view of knowledge, it is no coincidence that the main and only clear-cut example of the growth of knowledge in human history has been in Western scientific thought since the sixteenth century. Whatever the ideologies of individual scientists over that period, what has clearly happened has been successive attempts to replace modes of thought that have become untenable with new theories, which are then themselves tested against the environment.

The situation in religion has been entirely different. Here we see attempts, often desperate attempts on the part of whole communities, to protect and defend theories that have come under attack. The reason for this cannot simply be that the religious community is identified by adherence to a particular set of beliefs, because at any given time the scientific community, too, may be defined in terms of adherence to a particular set of theories. But the striking thing is that while *physics* may continue without any contemporary Newtonians, each religion can continue only as long as there are people prepared to assert a specific set of dogmas. There is a sense in which physics is quite indeterminate as to its content, while there is no such thing as religion as such, there are only specific religions. And the reason for this is surely the point examined at the start of this chapter, namely the centrality to each religion (and hence to religion itself) of a tradition which is regarded by the believer as being imposed on him, and not in any way dependent on his creative ingenuity. No theologian within an existing religious tradition has ever regarded himself as finding or suggesting something new. They always regard themselves as uncovering the true meaning of the ancient text or tradition. They are always backward-looking, and, I am suggesting, necessarily so. For religion derives its strength and essence from its claim to present a superhuman authoritative wisdom given to us in some way. Even inventors of new religions invariably regard or present themselves as recipients of some message, rather than as creators of it, and again, necessarily so, for the presenter of a new religion could hardly hope to achieve the authority needed to form a new cult, if it was clear that the message came 'only' from him, a 'mere' human being, and hence corrigible and fallible.

The religious message, whether it is in the form of ancient books or a new revelation, is then necessarily regarded as sacred and unalterable. Development of doctrine and accommodation with changing thought patterns must always, on the pain of irreligiousness, take place within the set verbal framework of the authoritative texts. This respect and reverence for specific and unchangeable verbal formulations is quite foreign both to science and to the critical attitude as a whole. There, if a theory or set of policies comes under critical fire, they are revised or even replaced with better ones. Preservation of formulae at all costs is regarded as tantamount to intellectual dishonesty.

It is because of the totally different attitude taken to theories in the critical-rational tradition of Western science from that taken by religious people to their sacred texts and revelations that there is something disingenuous in seeking to justify religious cosmo-logical beliefs by appealing to their similarity to contemporary scientific theory. Thus, for example, it may be true that both Hindu thought and modern cosmology think of a pulsating universe, but this does nothing to establish the credentials of Hinduism as a proto-science, for the Hindu picture is not presented as a speculative theory, to be criticized and tested empirically. In so far as empirical testability is an essential aspect of a scientific explanation, religious cosmological myths cannot be seen as scientific explanations. If they are explanations at all, they are in no sense scientific hypotheses, because they are treated in quite a different way, and serve the quite different function of providing a framework or background for some set of religious practices.

The critical-rationalist attitude is one which is fundamentally naturalistic, seeing men and human thought as chance products of evolutionary development. From this point of view, the most that can be expected, for either us or our theories, is survival for a time. The critical approach to our theories does not expect any of them to be true, but hopes to diminish the effects of their falsity by discovering their weak points as soon as possible. The religious approach to its beliefs, on the other hand, depends on preserving at least the appearance of their absolute and unchanging truth. This is why there will always be problems in reconciling the religious texts of one age, embedded as they inevitably will be in the empirical assumptions and thought-patterns of that age, with what is intellectually acceptable in another age. Religious fundamentalism is clearly no answer, but there is a sense in which it takes the problem more seriously than those more sophisticated believers who attempt the impossible task of reading ancient texts in such a way as to square with their contemporary *Weltanschauung*, of squaring the God of first-century Palestine, for example, with the mammon of twentieth-century science.

I said earlier that the phenomenon of intellectual believers having to make accommodations with the secular thought of their time was no new phenomenon, but it does not seem to me to be less scandalous for that. This is not only because of the way that they then separate themselves in mind from their simpler-minded brethren, but more because of the way it implies that you can justifiably and rationally hang on to certain words or phrases or even books, come what may. Nothing seems to me more harmful for us all in the long term than the idea that the key words and ideas by which one lives one's life could be immunized in so devious a way from all criticism. It would be like a present-day physicist attempting, by conventionalist strategies, to make what we now know of the world square with formulations of Aristotelian physics. The upshot will inevitably be a self-deceiving and ultimately dishonest reinterpretation of the words of the sacred texts, so that one contrives a verbal and outward acceptance of what, in one's heart of hearts, one regards as archaic and indefensible. Moreover, totally at odds with the critical approach, such internal reinterpretation of words suggests a magical attitude to some bits of language, as worth hanging on to in and for themselves apart from any actual meaning they might have. Fundamentalism, on the other hand, amounts to a simple rejection of criticism and results in just that type of inflexibility which precludes a solution to so many of the problems that afflict us today, that are often actually the outcome of an uncritical and unflinching adherence to outworn political and religious dogmas.

Both the fundamentalist and the reinterpretative attitudes to religious texts are symptomatic of the totemic and fetishistic aspects of the human psyche, whose effect is always to react initially to any new problem with unreason and out of fear. Men too easily seek to evade their responsibilities for their own decisions, and there is a constant desire to attempt to ground their lives in something deeper, as we have seen. Indeed, the idea that religion ought to provide a meaning of this sort, for the whole community, but fails to do so in present circumstances, may itself contribute significantly to the present-day sense that lives are meaningless and a sort of hopeless acquiescence by individuals of their manipulation by the forces of business and politics. We live in a situation in which social and economic conditions all over the world have destroyed both from within and without the organically-knit societies of the past and rendered unavailable the type of meaning that the genuinely common cultures of such societies gave to their members. But the response to this cannot be to attempt, factitiously, to restore that type of meaning by invoking the old symbols whose substance is now broken, or to invent new ones, for any such invention would be spurious unless, *per impossible*, it was based in a genuinely shared life and experience. What is needed now is for individuals to learn to find within their own lives and resources the substance that is missing from society as a whole, and above all, for individuals to realize that this is what is needed.

Religion, with its authoritarian, anti-critical stance, stands in stark opposition to the idea that individuals can achieve meaning from their own resources. Its hidden (or not so hidden) message is that the secret of life is to be found elsewhere, in someone else's text, dogma or institution. Religious authorities in effect agree with the manipulators – the managers, propagandists, demagogues and advertisers – in thinking that human life on its own, in the absence of a transcendent message or ancient wisdom, is simply there to be manipulated. Yet religious beliefs and texts not only fail to withstand criticism from within or without; their essence is that they are to be treated as uncriticizable beyond very narrow limits. And religious authorities themselves return into manipulators, attempting to suppress individual creativity in efforts to mould people's lives according to pre-determined patterns, with all the bitterness, frustration and intellectual gerrymandering that that entails.

My thesis in this chapter has been that religion is essentially dogmatic, fetishistic and authoritarian; that this aspect of religion is what religion derives its strength from. Even where, as in the case of the old world religions, sophisticated believers strive to reinterpret the old texts, they still betray the same fetishistic attitude to those texts as their simpler-minded brethren. They do not replace or revise the texts, as they should. And this, I am suggesting, is of the nature of the case. For what is a religion without its message or its texts?

It will, of course, be argued that religion does not have to be as authoritarian and uncritical as I am suggesting, and that something much more like a critical approach is possible to the subject matter of the other world. I can readily concede the second point, having already proposed something along these lines myself in Ch. 2. But religions are not a speculative enquiry into the other world; if they are anything at all, they are frameworks for life in this world, enclosed by dogmatic assertions about this and the other world. These dogmatic assertions do not, in the forms we have examined them, survive criticism, certainly not so as to allow people rationally to base so much on them, and, to return to a point made in Ch. 1, they cannot simply be reduced to the practical behaviour associated with them, though one can see why the perplexed, who see a value in religious life, might be tempted to take this line.

My negative appraisal of religion has been almost entirely based on the pretensions of religions to provide a dogmatic framework of explanation of the world and human life. I have attempted to show how the central tenets of such frameworks – doctrines of God and being – cannot withstand criticisms, and that the search for the type of explanation desired is inherently doomed to frustration. With the withering away of religious dogmas also wither the explanations and life frameworks from which believers derive much of the consolation religion brings. However, there has been one great religious teacher in the world who had the courage and insight to see that the desire for a religious explanation of life – for an explanation at once substantive and complete – was itself a weakness in our make-up, which should be overcome. In the *Sabbasava-suttra*, the Buddha speaks of considering questions such as whence we came and where we will go, whether there is a self or no-self, and so on as being

> enmeshed in views, a jungle of views, a wilderness of views;
> scuffling in views, the agitation of views, the fetter of views,

adding that a man who does not liberate himself from the fetter of views does not liberate himself from suffering. In the refusal to enter into metaphysical speculation and the search for untestable explanations, Buddha and some (though by no means all) forms of Buddhism seem to me to be significantly different from the acritical dogmatisms of all other religions. The idea of religion without dogma and without theoretical teaching is as bold a revolution as any in the history of human thought, and as necessary now as it was in the time of the Buddha himself, for the need for men to come to terms with reality, seeing it as it is and their cravings and desires as simply one element in the whole – in short to adopt a religious attitude to the world – is no less now than it ever was. The Buddha's genius was to abstract the religious attitude from religious dogma at a time when religious dogmas were still easily tenable, but now that they are tenable only with the greatest difficulty, the Buddha can serve as an example to all those who seek from their own resources to find themselves in the midst of things, and who, despite all the horrors of life and death strive for an acceptance of themselves and the world as they are:

> He who has realized the Truth, Nirvana, is the happiest being in the world. He is free from all 'complexes' and obsessions, the worries and troubles that torment others. His mental health is perfect. He does not repent the past, nor does he brood over the future. He lives fully in the present. Therefore he appreciates and enjoys things in the purest sense without self-projections. He is joyful, exultant, enjoying the pure life, his faculties pleased, free from anxiety, serene and peaceful. As he is free from selfish

desire, hatred, ignorance, conceit, pride, and all such 'defilements', he is pure and gentle, full of universal love, compassion, kindness, sympathy, understanding and tolerance. His service to others is of the purest, for he has no thought of self. He gains nothing, accumulates nothing, not even anything spiritual, because he is free from the illusion of Self, and the 'thirst' for becoming. (Walpola Rahula, *What the Buddha Taught*, p. 43)

The beauty of the Buddha's spirituality is precisely that it is a spirituality without faith, without words, without explanation, and without religion.

Suggestions for
Further Reading

Not all the works on philosophy of religion I have been influenced by and benefited from are mentioned in the text, and these brief suggestions for further reading include some important works I have not so far mentioned.

General introductions to the subject at a basic level include John Hick's *Philosophy of Religion* (Prentice Hall, Englewood Cliffs, New Jersey, 1973) and Ninian Smart's *Philosophers and Religious Truth* (SCM Press, London, 1964). More advanced philosophically and more up-to-date is Brian Davies's *An Introduction to the Philosophy of Religion* (Oxford University Press, Oxford, 1982). Basil Mitchell's collection *The Philosophy of Religion* (Oxford University Press, London, 1971) is a useful collection of articles, and contains an extensive bibliography. *New Essays in Philosophical Theology* (edited by A. Flew and A. MacIntyre, SCM Press, London, 1955) is a collection of articles which has had considerable influence on the philosophy of religion. Walter Kaufmann's *Critique of Religion and Philosophy* (Faber & Faber, London, 1959) is an impassioned and learned polemic, useful not least for its comparison between the morality of Christianity and that of other world religions.

No-one studying the philosophy of religion should neglect such classic texts as Hume's *Dialogues Concerning Natural Religion* and Newman's *A Grammar of Assent*.

Important modern studies in the philosophy of religion include those by Antony Flew (*God and Philosophy*, Hutchinson, 1966, and *The Presumption of Atheism*, Elek/Pemberton, London, 1976), P.T. Geach (*God and the Soul*, Routledge & Kegan Paul, London, 1969), Kai Nielsen (*Scepticism*, Macmillan, London, 1973, and the relevant sections of *Reason and Practice*, Harper & Row, New York, 1971), Terence Penelhum, (*Problems of Religious Knowledge*, Macmillan, London, 1971), Alvin Plantinga (*God and Other Minds*, Cornell University Press, Ithaca, New York, 1967, *The Nature of Necessity*, Clarendon Press, Oxford, 1974, and *God, Freedom and Evil*, George Allen & Unwin, London, 1975) and Richard Swinburne's trilogy *The Coherence of Theism*, *The Existence of God* and *Faith and Reason* (Clarendon Press, Oxford, 1977, 1979 and 1981). Most recently, and highly recommended is the late J.L. Mackie's *The Miracle of Theism* (Clarendon Press, Oxford, 1982).

On the specific topics discussed in this book, there is a general survey of Wittgenstein's attitudes to religious belief in W.D. Hudson's *Wittgenstein and Religious Belief* (Macmillan, London, 1975). D.Z. Phillips's books include *Faith and Philosophical Enquiry* (Routledge & Kegan Paul, London, 1970), *Religion Without Explanation* (Blackwell, Oxford, 1976) and *The Concept of Prayer* (Blackwell, Oxford, 1981). An interesting study on the relationship between ritual and belief is John Skorupski's *Symbol and Theory* (Cambridge University Press, Cambridge, 1976).

On religious experience, William James's *Varieties of Religious Experience* remains a basic starting point. Also worth consulting are T.R. Miles's *Religious Experience* (Macmillan, 1972) and the relevant parts of A.J. Ayer's *The Central Questions of Philosophy* (Penguin Books, Harmondsworth, 1976), H.D. Lewis's *Our Experience of God* (George Allen & Unwin, London, 1959) and C.B Martin's *Religious Belief* (Cornell University Press, Ithaca, New York, 1959). On the connection between explanation and empirical acceptability, see James W. Cornman's *Skepticism, Justification and Explanation* (Reidl, Dordrecht, 1980).

On Aquinas, see F. Copleston's *Aquinas* (Penguin Books, Harmondsworth, 1955), A. Kenny's *The Five Ways* (Routledge & Kegan Paul, London, 1969) and D. Burrell's *Aquinas, God and Action* (Routledge & Kegan Paul, London, 1979). On analogy, see Humphrey Palmer's *Analogy* (Macmillan, London, 1973). The most important work of neo-Thomist natural theology is Bernard Lonergan's *Insight* (Longman, London, 1957). Hans Küng's main contribution to the philosophy of religion is his vast *Does God Exist?* (Collins, London, 1980), which, despite its philosophical crudity, contains a massive amount of information about the positions various modern thinkers of various types have taken to belief in God.

On the *tu quoque* defence of religion, and on problems of rationality generally, W.W. Bartley's *Retreat to Commitment* (Knopf, New York, 1962) is highly recommended. Also on standards of rationality in religion and science, see I.G. Barbour's *Myths, Models and Paradigms* (SCM Press, London 1974). On rationality in science, see W. Newton-Smith's *The Rationality of Science* (Routledge & Kegan Paul, London, 1981). On rationality in science and ethics, see Hilary Putnam's *Reason, Truth and History* (Cambridge University Press, Cambridge 1981).

On the cosmological and teleological arguments, apart from the treatments of them in the studies already mentioned, reference may be made to Hugo Meynell's *The Intelligible Universe* (Macmillan, London, 1982). On the ontological argument, Jonathan Barnes's *The Ontological Argument* (Macmillan, London, 1972) is recommended. Useful collections on the argument are those edited by J. Hick and A. McGill (*The Many Faced Argument*, Macmillan, London, 1968) and A. Plantinga (*The Ontological Argument*, Macmillan, London, 1968).

On process thought, there is *Process Theology: an Introductory Exposition* by John B. Cobb and David Ray Griffin (Christian Journals, Belfast, 1976). Hartshorne's own works include *A Natural Theology for Our Time* (Open Court, La Salle, Illinois, 1967) and *The Logic of Perfection* (Open Court, La Salle, Illinois, 1962). Nelson Pike's *God and Timelessness*

Further Reading

(Routledge & Kegan Paul, London, 1970) is a useful study.

On the problem of evil Pike's *God and Evil* (Prentice Hall, Englewood Cliffs, New Jersey, 1964) is a good collection of basic articles and readings. John Hick's *Evil and the God of Love* (Macmillan, London, 1977) is an important study.

On the comparison between various religions and various conceptions of God, Ninian Smart's work should be mentioned. See, for example, his *Reasons and Faiths* (Routledge & Kegan Paul, London, 1958), *The Phenomenon of Religion* (Macmillan, London, 1973) and his articles on the various world religions in *The Encyclopedia of Philosophy* (edited by Paul Edwards, Macmillan Publishing Company, New York, 1967). Also worth consulting is H.P. Owen's *Concepts of Deity* (Macmillan, London, 1971). R.C. Zaehner's *At Sundry Times* (Faber & Faber, London, 1958) is well worth reading. On Hindu thought, I found Pratima Bowes's *The Hindu Religious Tradition* (Routledge & Kegan Paul, London, 1978) clear and coherent.

References

Anselm, St *Opera Omnia*, Thomas Nelson, Edinburgh, 1945-51.

Aquinas, St Thomas *De Malo*.

Aquinas, St Thomas *Summa contra Gentiles*.

Aquinas, St Thomas *Summa Theologiae*.

Aquinas, St Thomas *De Veritate*.

Attenborough, D. (1979) *Life on Earth*, Collins/BBC, London.

Augustine of Hippo, St *Confessions*.

Ayer, A.J. (1976) *The Central Questions of Philosophy*, Penguin Books, Harmondsworth.

Baillie, J. (1949) *Our Knowledge of God*, Oxford University Press, London.

Barbour, I.G. (1974) *Myths, Models and Paradigms*, SCM Press, London.

Barnes, J. (1972) *The Ontological Argument*, Macmillan, London.

Bartley, W.W. (1962) *The Retreat to Commitment*, Knopf, New York.

Bartley, W.W. (1976) 'The Philosophy of Karl Popper; Pt. 1: Biology – Evolutionary Epistemology', *Philosophia 6*, pp. 463-94.

Bartley, W.W. (1982) 'Logical Strength & Demarcation' in Gunnar Andersson, ed., *Rationality in Science and Politics*, Reidel, Dordrecht.

Bowes, P. (1978) *The Hindu Religious Tradition*, Routledge & Kegan Paul, London.

Brown, S. (1973), *Religious Belief*, Open University Press, Milton Keynes.

Burrell, D. (1979) *Aquinas, God and Action*, Routledge & Kegan Paul, London.

Chellas, B. (1980) *Modal Logic, An Introduction*, Cambridge University Press, Cambridge.

Copleston, F. (1955) *Aquinas*, Penguin Books, Harmondsworth.

Damascene, St John *De Fide Orthodoxa*.

Darwin, C. (1974 edn) *Autobiography*, Oxford University Press, London.

Davidson, D (1980) *Essays on Actions and Events*, Clarendon Press, Oxford.

Davies, B. (1982) *An Introduction to the Philosophy of Religion*, Oxford University Press, Oxford.

Dawkins, R. (1978) *The Selfish Gene*, Granada Publishing, London.

Descartes, R. *Meditations*.

Dionysius (Pseudo–Dionysius) *Concerning Mystical Theology*.
Of the Divine Names.

Donceel, J. (1973) 'A Case in Reason for God's Existence?' in *God*,

255

Knowable and Unknowable, ed R.J. Roth, Fordham University Press, New York, pp. 159-86.

Dummett, M. (1973) *Frege, Philosophy of Language*, Duckworth, London.

Edwards, P. (1958) 'The Cosmological Argument' in *The Rationalist Annual, 1959*, C.A. Watts, London.

Frazer, J. (1922) *The Golden Bough*, quoted from abridged ed, Macmillan, London, 1957.

Geach, P. (1969) *God and the Soul*, Routledge & Kegan Paul, London.

Goodman, N. (1978) *Ways of Worldmaking*, Harvester Press, Hassocks.

Harman, G. (1965) 'The Inference to the Best Explanation', *Philosophical Review*, 74, pp. 88-95.

Hartshorne, C. (1953) *Reality as a Social Process*, Free Press, Chicago, Illinois.

Hartshorne, C. (1962) *The Logic of Perfection*, Open Court, La Salle, Illinois.

Hartshorne, C. (1968) 'What did Anselm Discover?', in Hick and McGill, pp. 321-33.

Hick, J. (1966) *Evil and the God of Love*, Macmillan, London.

Hick, J. (1968) 'A Critique of the "Second Argument"' in Hick and McGill, pp. 341-56.

Hick, J. and McGill, A (1968), *The Many Faced Argument*, Macmillan, London.

Hubbeling, H.G. (1981) 'Process Philosophy and Modern Reconstructions of the Ontological and Cosmological Argument', paper presented at '*God: The Contemporary Discussion*' conference, 1981.

Hughes, G.E. and Cresswell, M.J. (1972) *An Introduction to Modal Logic*, Methuen, London.

Hume, D. (1779) *Dialogue Concerning Natural Religion*.

Isaye, G. (1953) 'La finalité de l'intelligence et l'objection kantienne', *Revue Philosophique de Louvain*, 51, pp. 42-100.

James, W. (1902) *Varieties of Religious Experience*, quoted from Fontana ed, London, 1972.

James, W. (1912) *Essays on Radical Empiricism*, quoted from Harvard University Press ed, 1976.

Kant, I. (1787) *The Critique of Pure Reason*, transl. N. Kemp Smith, Macmillan, London.

Kenny, A. (1969) *The Five Ways*, Routledge & Kegan Paul, London.

Kneale, W. and Kneale, M. (1962) *The Development of Logic*, Clarendon Press, Oxford.

Kolakowski, L. (1982) *Religion*, Fontana, London.

Kripke, S. (1980) *Naming and Necessity*, Basil Blackwell, Oxford.

Kuhn, T.S. (1962) *The Structure of Scientific Revolutions*, Chicago University Press, Chicago, Illinois.

Küng, H. (1980) *Does God Exist?*, Collins, London.

Lehrer, K. (1974) *Knowledge*, Clarendon Press, Oxford.

Lonergan, B. (1957) *Insight*, Longmans, London.

Lossky, V. (1957) *The Mystical Theology of the Eastern Church*, James Clark & Co., Cambridge.

References

McCloskey, H.J. (1960) 'God and Evil', *Philosophical Quarterly, 10*, pp. 97-114.

MacIntyre, A. (1981) *After Virtue*, Duckworth, London.

Mackie, J.L. (1955) 'Evil and Omnipotence', *Mind, 64*, pp. 200-12.

Mackie, J.L. (1977) *Ethics*, Penguin Books, Harmondsworth.

Mackie, J.L. (1982) *The Miracle of Theism*, Clarendon Press, Oxford.

Malcolm, N. (1960) 'Anselm's Ontological Arguments', *Philosophical Review, 69*, pp. 41-62.

Maréchal, J. (1927-49) *Le point de départ de la métaphysique*, Edition universelle, Brussels (5 vols).

Martin, C.B. (1959) *Religious Belief*, Cornell University Press, Ithaca, New York.

Meynell, H. (1972) 'The Euthyphro Dilemma', *Supplementary Proceedings of The Aristotelian Society, 46*, pp. 223-34.

Monod, J. (1971) *Chance and Necessity*, Collins, London.

Munz, P. (1980) Our Knowledge of the Growth of Knowledge (mimeographed).

Munz, P. (1981) 'The Two Faces of God', paper presented at *God: The Contemporary Discussion* conference, 1981.

Newman, J.H. (1870), *A Grammar of Assent*, quoted from the Image Books, New York ed, 1952.

Newton-Smith, W. (1981) *The Rationality of Science*, Routledge & Kegan Paul, London.

Nietzsche, F. (1872) *The Birth of Tragedy*.

Nietzsche, F. (1882) *The Gay Science*.

Nietzsche, F. (1887) *On the Genealogy of Morals*.

Nietzsche, F. (1888) *The Twilight of the Idols* (quoted as from Penguin Books, Harmondsworth ed, 1968).

Nietzsche, F. (post) *The Will to Power*.

O'Hear, A. (1980) *Karl Popper*, Routledge & Kegan Paul, London.

O'Hear, A. (1981) *Education, Society & Human Nature*, Routledge & Kegan Paul, London.

Otto, W. (1954) *The Homeric Gods*, Thames & Hudson, London (1979 ed).

Paley, W. (1802) *Natural Theology*, quoted from Gould and Lincoln, Boston ed. 1851.

Parfit, D. (1971) 'Personal Identity', *Philosophical Review, 80*, pp. 1-27.

Phillips, D.Z. (1970) 'Religious Belief and Language Games', *Ratio, 12*, pp. 26-46.

Plantinga, A. (1965a) 'Symposium: the other minds problem. Ziff's other minds', *Journal of Philosophy, 62*, pp. 587-9.

Plantinga, A. (1965b) 'The Free Will Defence', in M. Black (ed.), *Philosophy in America*, George Allen & Unwin, London, pp. 204-20.

Plantinga, A. (1967) *God and Other Minds*, Cornell University Press, Ithaca, New York.

Plantinga, A. (1974) *The Nature of Necessity*, Clarendon Press, Oxford.

Plantinga, (1975) *God, Freedom and Evil*, George Allen & Unwin, London.

Plato *Sophist, Phaedo, Phaedrus, Euthyphro, Republic, Timaeus*.

Plotinus *Enneads*.

References

Popper, K.R. (1957), *The Poverty of Historicism*, Routledge & Kegan Paul, London.

Popper, K.R. (1966) *The Open Society and Its Enemies*, Routledge & Kegan Paul, London (5th ed).

Popper, K.R. (1974) 'Replies to My Critics', in P.A. Schilpp (ed.), *The Philosophy of Karl Popper*, Open Court, La Salle, Illinois.

Popper, K.R. (1979) *Objective Knowledge*, Clarendon Press, Oxford.

Putnam, H. (1975) 'Other Minds' in *Mind, Language and Reality: Philosophical Papers, Vol II*, Cambridge University Press, pp. 342-61.

Putnam, H. (1981) *Reason, Truth and History*, Cambridge University Press, Cambridge.

Quine, W.V. (1953) 'Two Dogmas of Empiricism' in *From a Logical Point of View*, Harper Torchbooks, New York, pp. 20-46.

Rahner, K. (1968) *Spirit in the World* (transl. W. Dych), Herder and Herder, New York.

Rahner, K. (1969) *Hearers of the Word* (transl. W. Dych), Herder and Herder, New York.

Rahula, W. (1967) *What the Buddha Taught*, Gordon Fraser, Bedford.

Ramsey, I.T. (1964) *Models and Mystery*, Oxford University Press, London.

Rilke, R.M. *Selected Works, Vol. II, Poetry* (transl. J.B. Leishman), The Hogarth Press, London.

Salmon, W. (1978) 'Religion and Science: A New Look at Hume's Dialogues, *Philosophical Studies, 33*, pp. 143-76.

Salmon, W. (1981) 'Rational Prediction', *British Journal for the Philosophy of Science, 32*, pp. 115-25.

Scruton, R. (1980) *The Meaning of Conservatism*, Penguin Books, Harmondsworth.

Scruton, R. (1981) *From Descartes to Wittgenstein*, Routledge & Kegan Paul, London.

Smart, N. (1961) 'Omnipotence, Evil and Supermen', *Philosophy, 36*, pp. 188-95.

Smart, N. (1971) *The Religious Experience of Mankind*, Fontana, London.

Stegmüller, W. (1969) *Metaphysik, Skepsis, Wissenschaft*, Berlin.

Stern, J.P. (1978) *Nietzsche*, Fontana, London.

Strawson, P.F. (1966) *The Bounds of Sense*, Methuen, London.

Swinburne, R. (1977) *The Coherence of Theism*, Clarendon Press, Oxford.

Swinburne, R. (1979) *The Existence of God*, Clarendon Press, Oxford.

Taylor, R. (1963) *Metaphysics*, Prentice Hall, Englewood Cliffs, New Jersey.

Tennant, F.R. (1928) *Philosophical Theology*, vol. I, Cambridge University Press, Cambridge.

Tolstoy, L. (1882) *A Confession* quoted in the World's Classics Version, Oxford University Press, London, 1940.

Whitehead, A.N. (1951) 'Immortality' in P.A. Schilpp (ed.), *The Philosophy of Alfred North Whitehead*, Tudor Publishing Co., New York, pp. 682-700.

Wittgenstein, L. (1958) *Philosophical Investigations* (second ed), Basil

Blackwell, Oxford.

Wittgenstein, L. (1967) *'Bemerkungen über Frazer's Golden Bough'*, *Synthese*, *17*, pp. 233-53. (All the quotations from these remarks, except for the last, are taken from the translation that appears in *The Human World*, No. 3, May, 1971, pp. 18-41, and references refer to that translation.)

Wittgenstein, L. (1969) *On Certainty*, Basil Blackwell, Oxford.

Wittgenstein, L. (1972) *Lectures and Conversations on Aesthetics, Psychology and Religious Belief*, University of California Press, Berkeley and Los Angeles.

Wittgenstein, L. (1978) *Remarks on the Foundations of Mathematics* (3rd ed), Basil Blackwell, Oxford.

Wittgenstein, L. (1980) *Culture and Value*, Basil Blackwell, Oxford.

Index

Index

Lonergan, B., 57, 59-62, 64, 67, 253
Lossky, V., 146

McCloskey, H.J., 203
McGill, A., 253
MacIntyre, A., 78, 82-6, 235, 252
Mackie, J.L., 80-1, 118-19, 133, 180-1, 212-20, 252
Madhyamika, 232
magic, 8-11, 21-2, 247
Malcolm, N., 12, 150-1, 162-4, 167-70, 173, 176-7, 182
Maréchal, J., 57
Martin, C.B., 44, 253
maxima, intrinsic, 150, 152
maximal excellence, 177-82
maximal greatness, 151, 177-82, 184
maya, 4, 227-8
meaning, theories of, 6-8, 17-24
Medici, Lorenzo de, 86
Meynell, H., 72-3, 253
Michelson, A., 11
Midas, King, 152
Miles, T.R., 253
Mill, J.S., 236
Milton, J., 239
Mimamsa, 225
minds, other, 100-5, 178
miracle, 25-7, 52-3, 239
Mitchell, B., 252
Mohammed, 47
moksa, 229
Molina, L. de, 217
Moltmann, J., 186
Monod, J., 130
monotheism, 52, 229, 234, 242-3
Moon, S.M., 17
morality, 56, 71-88
Munz, P., 51, 98, 242
Muslim, 17
mystery, 16-17, 72, 104, 194
mysticism, 26, 28-9, 43, 49, 52-3, 144-5, 147, 193, 200

nature, 9-10, 32, 48, 52-3, 89-93, 107, 116, 124, 129, 131-2, 135, 140-1, 185, 200, 223, 227, 242
necessity (of God), 66, 89, 109, 120-2, 144-85, 199-200
necessity, logical, 108, 120, 122, 144, 147, 153, 156, 158, 163-77, 180-2, 199, 201
Nemi, 8-11
Neo-Platonism, 145-6, 241-2
Nero, 85
Newman, J.H., 16-17, 252
Newtonian, 245
Newton-Smith, W., 99, 253
Nielsen, K., 252
Nietzsche, F., 68, 76-9, 85-6, 152, 203
Nirvana, 46, 75, 231-2, 250
numbers, 173

objects, abstract, 173
objects, physical, 15, 27, 30-7, 43, 48-9, 55, 100, 103-4, 132, 134, 138
Olympia, 85, 150
omnipotence, 100, 112, 117, 132-3, 154, 177-80, 183, 202, 206, 213, 215-16
omnipresence, 161
omniscience, 68-9, 112, 177-80, 183, 189-90, 215-17
ontological arguments, 66, 143-85, 253
order (in the world), 106, 122-43
Otto, W., 47
Owen, H.P., 254

pain, 7, 16, 20, 78, 100-5, 151, 195, 198, 202, 212-13, 217, 229, 233, 233-4
Paley, W., 123-4, 127-8, 131
Palmer, H., 253
Panathenaia, 3
panpsychism, 196, 240
paradigm, scientific, 97-8, 100
paradise, 221-2
Paramatman, 227
Parfit, D., 223
Parmenides, 116, 173
Paul, St, 50

264

Peirce, C.S., 117, 191
Penelhum, T., 252
perception, extra-sensory, 28
perception, sensory, 26-40, 135,
    141, 231
perfection (of God), 144, 149-53,
    160-7, 177, 184, 186, 191-200
Phillips, D.Z., 18, 253
physics, 11, 20, 35, 37-8, 40, 43, 50,
    82, 84, 104, 107, 114, 138-9,
    245, 247
Pike, N., 253-4
Plantinga, A., 100-5, 123, 150, 152,
    155-8, 177-8, 200, 215-18, 252-3
Plato, 71, 145
Plotinus, 145-6
Popper, K.R., 19, 32, 34, 62, 91-2,
    94-6, 111, 115, 129-30, 245
Prakriti, 226
prayer, 18
predestination, 14
Priam, 86, 203
Priestly, J., 11
process theology, 89, 185-200, 217-
    19, 222, 229, 233-4, 253
projects, human, 81-2, 84-5
prudence, 74-5, 81
psychic phenomena, 28, 48, 50, 53
Ptolemy, 35
Putnam, H., 36-7, 39, 83, 99, 103,
    105, 184, 253
Pythagoras' theorem, 38-9

Quine, W.V., 38

Rahner, K., 57-9
Ramanuja, 228-9, 241
Ramsey, I.T., 97
rationalism, 94-7, 244-7
redemption, 5, 14, 130, 191, 211,
    229
Regulus, 77
reincarnation, 222-5
resurrection, 26
revelation, 72-3, 83, 228, 236, 246
Rilke, R.M., 204, 206
rites, ritual, 3, 8-12, 15, 18, 83

S4, 167, 201
S5, 166-8, 181, 201
Salmon, W., 91, 123, 139
Samkhya, 232
Sankara, 227-9, 241
Satan, 73, 239
Schelling, F.W., 185
science, natural, 1, 6-7, 9-10, 20-2,
    35, 43, 45, 47, 50, 60, 62, 64-5,
    68, 70, 89-100, 104, 106, 110,
    112-16, 132, 135, 140, 200, 241,
    243-7
scientia media, 216-17
Scruton, R., 64, 236
selection, natural, 124-31
self, 49, 223-5, 227-8, 231-2, 251
Shakespeare, W., 138-9
Silenus, 152
similarity, perception of, 29-30
simplicity (of God), 61, 146, 161,
    173, 176, 194
simplicity (of hypotheses), 99, 104,
    112-19
sin, 4, 13, 202-3, 218-19
Skorupski, J., 253
Smart, N., 27, 205, 252, 254
Socrates, 71
Stegmüller, W., 94-6
Stern, J.P., 79, 87
Strauss, R., 151
Strawson, P.F., 25
suffering, 13-15, 74, 81, 86-7, 97,
    193, 195, 197-9, 202-34, 238
sufficient reason, principle of, 106-
    9, 119-22, 144
superstition, 13, 18
Swinburne, R., 108-19, 122-3, 130-
    43, 173, 186-7, 200, 252

Taylor, R., 119-22, 170
teleological argument, versions of,
    100, 102, 111, 122-43, 173, 200,
    208, 238, 253
Tennant, F.R., 89-93, 97
Teresa of Avila, St, 43, 46, 50
testability (of hypotheses), 32-5,
    44-6, 48-50, 52-4, 70, 99, 110,
    129-30, 246

Index

theology, 15, 54, 58, 64, 214, 241, 246
theology, natural, 64
thermodynamics, second law of, 107, 137-8, 172
Thorpe, W.H., 128
Tillich, P., 147
time (in God), 113, 186-91, 217
Tolstoy, L., 2, 5-6, 17
tradition, religious, 4-5, 235-6, 238, 246
Trinity, 16
truth, 8-9, 17, 21-3, 28, 43, 57, 67-70, 81-2, 85, 95-6, 115, 250
truth-conditions (of sentences), 7, 21, 69, 156, 184

uniformity of nature, 9, 89-91

Vaishnavism, 225,228
value, 75, 77-8, 80, 191, 221, 227, 235
verificationism, 23

Virgin Birth, 2
virtue, 82-4, 203, 235
Visuddhimagga, 44, 46
vocation, 236

Wagner, R., 223
war, holy, 76
Wesley, J., 3
Whitehead, A.N., 185, 191
Whyte, L.L., 128
wisdom, religious, 235, 246, 249
Wittgenstein, L., 2, 6-20, 90, 113, 197, 214, 253
worlds, possible, 117, 164-70, 173, 177-82, 216-17
worship, 64, 72, 143, 163, 170, 193, 198-200, 240-2

Yogacara, 232

Zaehner, R.C., 254
Zen, 66, 144